Biochemical
Individuality

Biochemical

Individuality

THE BASIS FOR THE GENETOTROPHIC CONCEPT

Roger J. Williams, Ph.D.

Consultant and Co-Founder, Clayton Foundation Biochemical Institute
The University of Texas at Austin

With a New Introduction by Jeffrey S. Bland, Ph.D.

KEATS PUBLISHING ✠ NEW CANAAN, CONNECTICUT

BIOCHEMICAL INDIVIDUALITY
© 1956 Roger J. Williams
Copyright renewed 1984 Roger J. Williams
© 1998 The University of Texas at Austin
By gift of Mrs. Roger J. Williams
All rights reserved.

No part of this book may be reproduced in any form without the written consent of the publisher.

ISBN: 0-87983-893-0

Library of Congress Cataloging-in-Publication Data

Williams, Roger John, 1893–
  Biochemical individuality : the basis for the genetotrophic concept / Roger J. Williams : with a new introduction by Jeffrey Bland.—2nd ed.
    p. cm.
  Previously published: 1956.
  Includes bibliographical references and index.
  ISBN 0-87983-893-0
    1. Biochemical variation.   2. Human genetics—Variation.   3. Nutrition—Genetic aspects.   I. Title.
  QH345.W49   1998
  612'.015—dc21   98-5055CIP

Publication History
John Wiley & Sons, Inc., hardcover (1956) and softcover (1963)
The University of Texas Press, softcover 1969 (seven printings; out of print 1988)
Translations published in Russian (1960), Italian (1964) and Polish languages (1969)

Printed in the United States of America

Keats Publishing, Inc.
27 Pine Street (Box 876)
New Canaan, Connecticut 06840-0876
Full catalog and ordering information: www.keats.com

Contents

Introduction to 1998 Edition

What are the characteristics of a "classic book"? Is it the timelessness of the message? The insight which spurred the development of a field? The contribution to a new way of thinking that significantly improved the state of society? Or the ability to see the "obvious" in a way that had never been seen before and so well communicated?

The book *Biochemical Individuality*, authored by the late world-renowned biochemist Roger Williams, Ph.D., first published in 1956, fulfills all of these characteristics. It is a book that should be on the bookshelf of all students and practitioners of modern molecular medicine. It is with great admiration and respect that I have the privilege of writing the introduction to the republication of this timeless work.

Molecular medicine was a term used by two-time Nobel laureate in chemistry and peace Linus Pauling, Ph.D., in his landmark article on the mechanism of production of sickle cell anemia published in 1949.[1] It defined a new perspective on the origin of disease based upon the recognition that specific mutations of the genes can create an altered "molecular environment" and therefore the modified physiological function associated with specific diseases.

Dr. Williams contributed to the evolution of the understanding of the molecular origin of disease with the development of the concept of biochemical individuality. He described anatomical and physiolog-

ical variations among people and how they related to their individual
responses to the environment. He was the first to gain recognition
for the term "biochemical individuality" and how this related to
differing nutritional needs for optimal function among different people. He pointed out that even identical twins could be different in
their needs for optimal function based upon the fact that they developed in different environments *in utero*. Although identical twins
share the same genes, their differing nutrition and developmental environments can result in different expression of the genes as they
grow older.

In the 1980s the field of biochemical individuality became fashion-
able within science as a consequence of the progress made in understanding the molecular biology of the gene. The Human Genome
project represented a major international commitment of scientists to
understand the genetic code of life by sequencing the human chromo-
somes. As this story has unfolded from laboratories around the
world, its implications have been revolutionary in terms of how medicine views genes and their function. The genetic structure is no
longer seen as "rigid" as previously considered. Rather, as Bishop
and Waldholz pointed out in their book *Genome*, "aberrant genes
do not, in and of themselves, cause disease. By and large their impact
on an individual's health is minimal until the person is plunged into
a harmful environment. . . . The list of common diseases which has
its roots in this genetic soil is growing almost daily. . . . How many
human ills will be added to the list is unknown, although some con-
tend that almost every disorder compromising a full and healthy four
score and ten years of life can be traced in one way or another to
this genetic variability" (Simon and Schuster, New York, 1990).

The first major breakthrough that resulted in this revolutionary
change in thinking about the origin of disease was the recognition
that we are much more different biochemically than was previously
acknowledged.[2] Dr. Williams in *Biochemical Individuality* pioneered
this revolution in thinking forty years ago. Genetic polymorphism is
the term which has emerged in the past decade to describe this variation in function surrounding a specific genetic trait.

The second major breakthrough in thinking made by Dr. Williams
is the recognition that nutritional status can influence the expression
of genetic characteristics.[3] Once again Dr. Williams foresaw this

important concept in *Biochemical Individuality* and set in motion research and discoveries over the past four decades that have transformed medicine. It is now well recognized that our genotype gets transformed into our phenotype as a consequence of nutritional, lifestyle and environmental factors which are important in determining our health patterns.

In 1976 Dr. Williams and his colleague Donald R. Davis, Ph.D., co-authored a paper entitled "Potentially useful criteria for judging nutritional adequacy" in which they provided observations about how nutritional status can influence the functional expression of the genes. They pointed out that phenotypic characteristics such as voluntary consumption of food, sleeping time after anesthesia, weight gains after surgery, healing time after surgery, hair growth after clipping, voluntary sugar consumption and recovery time after poisoning could all be influenced by nutritional influence on gene expression.[4]

The concept of biochemical individuality has become part of most contemporary clinical and experimental medical and nutritional research. People are now known to fit into personally unique biochemical profiles based upon their own genetic structure, nutrition and environment.[5] There is no such thing as a truly "normal" individual—meaning average. We are all biochemically unique and need to be dealt with as such. The Recommended Dietary Allowances (RDAs) which were developed by the Food and Nutrition Board of the National Research Council to establish the nutritional needs of "practically all healthy people" were not based upon the more recent information concerning the range of biochemical individuality among individuals. The RDAs that describe "normal" nutritional needs have questionable relevancy to the concept of optimal nutrition based upon individual needs. The contributions of Dr. Williams have opened the door for personally tailored nutritional and medical interventions that take biochemical individuality into account.

Some of the world's foremost nutrition and medical researchers are now actively involved in developing a better understanding of the field which Dr. Williams pioneered. Rucker and Tinker from the University of California at Davis, Department of Nutrition, have described the role of nutrition in gene expression and its relationship to biochemical individuality as "a fertile field for the application of molecular biology."[6] It is now well known that significant biochemical diversity occurs in such physiological functions as the ability of the individual to detoxify both exogenous and endogenous substances, the control of blood cholesterol, the metabolism of the potentially harmful amino acid homocysteine, and the response of certain cancer genes to the diet and environment. These are all examples of how nutritional status can influence disease patterns based upon biochemical individuality.

Dr. Williams coined the term "genetotrophic disease" to describe diseases which resulted from genetically determined nutritional or metabolic needs not being met by the individual and which resulted in poor gene expression. Motulsky has recently argued that many of the common degenerative diseases are the result of the imbalance of nutritional intake with genetically determined needs for good health.[7]

The genetic concept with which most nutrition and medical researchers grew up intellectually before the contribution of Dr. Williams was that of Gregor Mendel. His concept of dominant and recessive genetic characteristics gave us the belief that our characteristics are "locked in stone" when the sperm meets the egg. Dr. Williams opened the eyes of the research communities that the expression of genes and therefore phenotypic function was modifiable through altered diet and nutritional status. He pointed out that human biochemical variation in function was much greater than nutrition and medicine recognized prior to his publications.[8] Simopoulos has stated that "of all the recent scientific advances contributing to our understanding of the role of nutrition in disease prevention and the variability in human nutrient needs, the recognition of genetic variation as a contributing factor must rank among the highest."[9]

Dr. Williams made this complicated story easy to understand and compelling to health scientists and the general public alike. His clarity of thought and language helped open up this field which had been dominated by Mendelian thinking for nearly one hundred years before the publication of *Biochemical Individuality*. In one of his lectures at which I was in attendance he responded to an inquiry as to why the RDAs were not sufficient to define a person's nutritional needs with the simple insight, "Nutrition is for real people. Statistical humans are of little interest."

It is very timely that *Biochemical Individuality* is being reprinted over forty years after its initial publication, and that it is even more timely today than at the time of its original publication. By all definitions *Biochemical Individuality* fulfills the definition of "a classic" and should have an honored place among the principal reference books of anyone interested in health and nutrition.

—Jeffrey S. Bland, Ph.D.
HealthComm International, Inc.
Gig Harbor, WA

REFERENCES

1. Pauling L, Itano HA. Sickle cell anemia: a molecular disease. *Science* 1949; 110:543–548.
2. Motulsky AG. The 1985 Nobel Prize in physiology and medicine. *Science* 1986; 231:126–127.
3. Holtzman NA. Genetic variation in nutritional requirements and susceptibility to disease: policy implications. *Am J Clin Nutrition* 1988; 48:1510–1516.
4. Davis DR, Williams RJ. Potentially useful criteria for judging nutritional adequacy. *Am J Clin Nutrition* 1976; 29:710–715.
5. Robertson EA, Young DS. Biochemical individuality and the recognition of personal profiles with a computer. *Clin Chemistry* 1980; 26:30–36.
6. Rucker R, Tinker D. The role of nutrition in gene expression: A fertile field for the application of molecular biology. *J Nutr* 1986; 116:177–189.
7. Motulsky A. Nutrition and genetic susceptibility to common diseases. *Am J Clin Nutrition* 1992; 55:1244S–1245S.
8. Motulsky A. Human genetic variation and nutrition. *Am J Clin Nutrition* 1987; 45:1108–1113.
9. Simopoulos AP. Genetic variation and nutrition. *Nutrition Today* 1995; 30:157–167.

Foreword

Traditionally the role of the biochemist has often been to remind the clinician of biochemical laws as well as discover them, to accent the uniformities as well as find them. Dr. Williams' refreshing message in this book accentuates the meaning and significance of the exceptional, the peculiar, the individuality of the individual. In this book he champions biochemical variety. As a biochemist, expert in metabolism, by what he calls the genetotrophic approach, he provides us with a way of reconciling the unusual and so-called abnormal bodily chemical processes with the "normal." This he does by being mindful of the almost infinite variety of interplaying genetic factors. Hereditary factors have been shown in morphology and in disease susceptibility. Dr. Williams carries a comparable set of interpretations into the observations of the body's myriad metabolic processes.

It behooves students of human biology to examine with as much imagination as rigor the kinds of thinking we apply to our observations of living tissue. Especially in clinical work we need to be chary of assuming uniformly sufficient single causation or cause for events. We need to remember not merely the environment, but also the individual make-up of what the environment surrounds. For every organism brings its own environment from the past—its heredity.

And, if a biochemist elects to insist on these things, what voice could be more fresh and strong? The new insights which are developed in this book should be explored by every student of medicine.

ALAN GREGG, M.D.

Preface

The writing of this book is based upon the need in human biology and medicine for more attention to variability and individuality at the physiological and biochemical levels. The potentialities arising from intensive study in this area are believed to be truly phenomenal because of the widespread existence of critical individual needs which can often be cared for if they are recognized.

Although ancients and moderns alike have called attention to variability and individuality as factors particularly related to disease susceptibility and moderns have recognized that variability is indispensable to evolution, comparatively little research time and effort have been devoted to definitive study in physiology and biochemistry as to precisely how so-called normal individuals differ from each other. Such study necessarily involves repeated observations on the same individuals, in contrast to a series of single observations on representative populations. No attempt to bring together the available biochemical material on normal variation has been previously made so far as I know.

Because of the diverse types of recorded observations which are pertinent to the subject and the fact that many of the observations have been made by those who have had little or no interest in individuality as such, it has not been possible to collect the material for this book in a highly systematic manner. If, for example, one looks up the word "variability" in various indices, virtually nothing is found. Because of the diverse nature of the data it has not been possible to cover at all adequately the various topics on which some information may be available, and incompleteness must be taken for granted. My regret is that the thought, opinions, and data of many individuals, particularly physicians, who may be genuinely interested in the subject, have not been cited. This is partly because an interest in variations and individuality has often been considered a hobby and has not led to serious publications. This field of interest has not gained the respectability that it deserves.

My own particular interest in this subject probably stems from the laboratory observation, over twenty years ago, that, although creatine was described by Beilstein as a bitter biting substance, it was found to be absolutely tasteless to many. About the same time, I noted that some otherwise normal individuals were unable to detect skunk odor. I began to be convinced more than ten years ago that *differences* between human beings (as well as their similarities) needed to be brought to light, because they are crucially important factors which must be taken into account if many human problems are to be solved. The ideas which grew out of this concept were set forth in two books, *The Human Frontier* and *Free and Unequal*. When my interest in this area first developed, I regarded it as considerably divergent from my chosen field of research interest—biochemistry. However, as time has gone on and research results have accumulated, it has become clearer to me that individuality and applied biochemistry are inextricably intertwined. I no longer regard my interest in individuality as a departure from biochemistry.

Individuality in nutritional needs is the basis for the genetotrophic approach and for the belief that nutrition applied with due concern for individual genetic variations, which may be large, offers the solution to many baffling health problems. This certainly is close to the heart of applied biochemistry.

The point of view which has developed as a result of this study has important implications not only for biology and medicine, but also for anthropology, psychology, child development, education, and even religion, business, law, and politics. These implications are, of course, outside the scope of this volume.

Although I am convinced of the substantial truth of the general thesis of this book, I have endeavored to avoid dogmatism or the expression of my ideas with any degree of finality. Much of the evidence presented is far from being as satisfactory as it would have been had the investigations cited been interested in the problem of individuality. Within a relatively few years, it is my hope that much better evidence will be forthcoming which will be the basis for the acceptance and probable modification of the point of view set forth in this volume. It is inevitable that there will be some mistakes and some questions of interpretations which can reasonably be raised. Serious students can be trusted, however, not to discard the basic thesis because they have doubts about a few items.

For the errors of omission and commission I take full responsibility, but I do wish to express my gratitude to my colleagues who have shown forbearance and to those who have given material assistance. The list of those who have contributed ideas, furnished material or citations, or have given substantial moral support includes the following:

Errett C. Albritton

Barry J. Anson

Ernest Beerstecher, Jr.

Helen K. Berry

Otto A. Bessey

Ludwig W. Blau

Oscar Bodansky

William Duane Brown

Helen B. Burch

Leland C. Clark

Konrad Dobriner

Harry J. Deuel, Jr.

L. C. Dunn

Vincent duVigneaud

Charles H. Eades, Jr.

Martin G. Ettlinger

Arthur L. Fox

Daniel H. Funkenstein

John W. Gowen

Alan Gregg

T. F. Gallagher

Arild E. Hansen

Harry Helson

Joel H. Hildebrand

Hudson Hoagland

Julia Outhouse Holmes

T. Duckett Jones

Ancel Keys

C. Glen King

Kenneth Hurley

Elwood H. LaBrosse

William K. Livingston

Pauline Beery Mack

Roy B. Mefferd

Herschel K. Mitchell

John P. Nafe

Richard B. Pelton

Gregory Pincus

Oscar Riddle

Lorene L. Rogers

William C. Rose

Frank W. Sayre

Robert W. Shideler

Howard T. Simpson

Robert P. Wagner

Alfred H. Washburn

Robert R. Williams

Lemuel D. Wright

This list does not include a number of students who have contributed citations in connection with their course work and to whom I am most grateful.

To Mrs. Katherine Neal and Mrs. Martha Ann Zivley I am much indebted for clerical and editing help.

ROGER J. WILLIAMS
Austin Texas

To Benjamin Clayton
whose support—moral and material—
has been invaluable

I
Biochemical Variation:
Its Significance in Biology and Medicine

Since the days of Darwin, it has been generally recognized by biologists that variability in organisms is a *sine qua non* of evolution. Variability has been subjected to extensive mathematical study and is a basic concept with which the vast field of statistics is concerned. Biologists have not been unappreciative of the fact that intra-species variability may be great. Julian Huxley[1] has pointed out that the variability in the human species is of much greater magnitude than that in animals, because men have much greater migratory propensities and are more neglectful of large differences in color and appearance when choosing mates. Among his illustrations of divergence he says that the "difference between the mind of, say, a distinguished general or engineer of extrovert type and an introvert genius in mathematics or religious mysticism is no less than that between an insect and a vertebrate."

Hippocrates spoke of man as "that infinitely variable organism without which human disease is impossible," and Gray[2] has suggested that Hippocrates' ideas translated into modern terms may be stated: "it takes two to make a case of illness; he who gets sick and the bug that bites him." Galen, the Greek physician, about 600 years after Hippocrates, voiced the same general thought when speaking of disease; he said, "No cause can be efficient without an aptitude of the body." Coming to more modern times, Sir William Osler quoted with approval the statement of the older physician, Parry of

I

Bath, to the effect that it is "more important to know what sort of patient has a disease, than to know what sort of disease a patient has." One of the most modern exponents of the same idea was George Draper, who founded the Constitutional Clinic of the College of Physicians and Surgeons, Columbia University, in 1916, and who with his collaborators published a book, *Human Constitution in Clinical Medicine,* in 1944.[3]

The subject of *variation* with which we are predominantly concerned is, therefore, an old one, and it might be supposed that there would be little new to say. It is our opinion, however, based upon the data presented in this volume, that variability is vastly more important in the biological sciences and in medicine than it is currently assumed to be. And, because of what a study of variability in nutritional needs can do for medicine, such study deserves ten times more direct attention in terms of research time and effort than it is now receiving. The reader must be left to judge for himself whether these opinions are based upon a reasonable interpretation of the facts.

A commonly accepted point of view in the field of biology and related disciplines—physiology, biochemistry, psychology—and in the applied fields of medicine, psychiatry, and social relations appears to be that humanity can be divided into two groups: (1) the vast majority possess attributes which are within the normal range; (2) a small minority possess attributes far enough out of line so that they should be considered deviates. This point of view is more often tacitly assumed than expressed and is illustrated by the fact that when an obstetrician can inform a mother that her newborn child is "normal in every way," everyone is happy; but if the infant must be pronounced abnormal, everyone concerned is distressed.

The most commonly accepted line of demarcation between normal and abnormal in biological work is the 95 per cent level.[4, 5] That is, all values lying outside those possessed by 95 per cent of the population may be regarded as deviant values, and any individual who possesses such deviant values may be regarded as a deviate.

If we consider the possibility that among the numerous measurable attributes that human beings possess there may be many which are not mathematically correlated, we are confronted with an idea which is opposed to the basic dichotomy of normal and abnormal mentioned above. If 0.95 of the population is normal with respect to one measurable item, only 0.902 (0.95^2) would be normal with respect to two measurable items and 0.60 (0.95^{10}) and 0.0059 (0.95^{100}), respectively, would be normal with regard to 10 and 100 uncorrelated items.

The existence in every human being of a vast array of attributes which are potentially measurable (whether by present methods or not), and probably often uncorrelated mathematically, makes quite tenable the hypothesis that *practically every human being is a deviate in some respects*. Some deviations are, of course, more marked and some more important than others. If this hypothesis is valid, newborn children cannot validly be considered as belonging in either one of two groups, normal and abnormal. Substantially all of them are in a sense "abnormal." In the majority, the "abnormalities" may be well enough concealed so that they are not revealed by clinical examination, though they may easily have an important bearing upon the susceptibility of the individual child to disease later in life.

Though this hypothesis may appear perfectly plausible, it has not been tested by experiment so far as we have been able to ascertain. Individual human beings have never been measured in enough different ways in which norms are established so that the data are conclusive.

The question of the validity of this hypothesis is not an academic one. As will be made clear in the later pages of this volume, there is a strong probability that the postulated deviations existing in almost everyone are closely related to the fact that practically every individual born into this world sooner or later gets into distinctive health difficulties of one kind or another. And the number of kinds of such difficulties, like the number of possible deviations, is legion.

To make this discussion more concrete, let us consider briefly some studies on groups of "normal" young men made in our laboratories which tend to support the hypothesis outlined above.[6] In one study five samples (sometimes six) of blood were drawn from each of eleven individuals at weekly intervals under basal conditions; by the use of conventional clinical methods, the samples were carefully analyzed for sugar, lactic acid, urea, creatinine, uric acid, inorganic phosphorus, amylase, lipase, acid phosphatase, alkaline phosphatase, and acetylcholinesterase. In another related investigation a similar group of nine normal young men (eight of whom were individuals included in the other study) was studied by analyzing repeated samples of blood plasma, blood cells, urine, and saliva, for calcium, magnesium, sodium, and potassium and by repeated tests on the same individuals of their taste thresholds for the chlorides of calcium, magnesium, sodium, and potassium.

Although for certain items applicable to certain individuals the quantitative values obtained appeared to be a random assortment of values within the "normal" range, this randomness was not universal. One individual, for example, showed consistently a low blood sugar; every one of six determinations yielded values below a commonly accepted normal range. Another individual had high blood uric acid; every value was above the accepted range. A third individual exhibited serum amylase values below the accepted "normal" range. A fourth individual exhibited high alkaline phosphatase values; every one was above the accepted normal range. A fifth individual exhibited high acetylcholinesterase values, every one of which was well above the accepted normal range.

Not only did individuals exhibit high or low blood values, but other distinctive characteristics also appeared in the individual data. One individual, for example, showed a 2-fold spread in his blood creatinine values, with general lack of agreement between values. In contrast, the majority of the individuals showed high consistency with respect to blood creatinine values; one individual yielded *identical* values in six determinations. One individual showed relatively high blood values for sugar, creatinine, urea, uric acid, and lactic acid and no low values for any of the items studied. Another individual showed relatively low blood values for acetylcholinesterase, sugar, phosphorus, lipase, and acid phosphatase but a relatively high value for urea.

Among the distinctive differences observed in the mineral analysis study were: (1) nearly a 6-fold difference between two individuals (no overlapping in values) in urinary calcium excretion, (2) nearly a 3-fold variation in plasma magnesium, (3) over a 30 per cent difference (no overlapping of values) in the sodium content of blood cells, (4) a 4-fold variation (with no overlapping values in 21 to 25 samples, respectively) in salivary sodium, (5) a 5-fold variation in salivary magnesium with no overlapping values in 7 to 15 samples, (6) taste threshold values that often differed consistently from individual to individual over a 20-fold range.

It was noted that not only were certain blood values above or below the "normal" range for specific individuals but also that, regardless of the positions in the ranges, each individual exhibited a distinctive pattern. Abundant evidence was obtained from these two studies alone to suggest the importance of studying biochemical individuality and its relationship to susceptibility to a host of diseases. The distinctiveness of these studies lies in the fact that repeated samples from the same well individuals, collected under basal conditions, were analyzed for many different constituents. This procedure is not often followed.

The whole problem of human health and welfare is vastly different if the population, instead of being composed mostly of individuals with normal attributes, is made up of individuals all of whom possess unusual attributes—individuals who deviate from the normal range in several of the numerous possible particulars.

To make the pertinence of our hypothesis even clearer, let us consider the import of this idea in connection with a hypothetical situation. Let us assume the existence of a population of ten men (Group I) all of whom have about average height, about the same average foot size, about the average amount of hair on their heads, about the average tendency to put on body fat, about the average tendency to consume alcoholic liquors, about average sex urge, about the average type of lenses in their eyes (neither farsighted nor nearsighted), about average emotional reactions, about average digestive tracts, and about average teeth.

Contrast this group with another hypothetical population of ten men (Group II). The men in this second group may yield similar average values and be average or near average in many respects. One, however, is six feet six inches tall, one has long and very narrow feet, one is highly rotund and finds it very difficult to reduce, one is completely bald, one is an alcoholic, one has an extreme sex urge, one is nearsighted, one is subject to fits of anger and depression, one suffers from digestive upsets, and one has very bad teeth.

In the population represented by Group I the problem of finding a hotel bed long enough to sleep in doesn't exist; the problem of finding shoes that fit is negligible; dental problems are not serious; the problem of mental health may be absent; the problems of obesity, baldness, alcoholism, sex aberrations, nearsightedness, farsightedness, and indigestion are all practically nonexistent. Within Group II, however, *all* of these problems exist in acute form.

Both of these two imaginary populations of ten are possibly illustrative caricatures as compared with any real population, but we wish to call attention to the fact that Group II (each member of which is a deviate) may be much more like a real population than is Group I, consisting of individuals none of whom possess any marked deviations. It seems highly probable, or at least well worth considering as a possibility, that a host of human problems, medical and nonmedical, exist because real populations resemble Group II more than they do Group I. If we consider populations to be like Group I, we dodge (and fail to solve) this host of problems. If Group II approaches, in principle, a typical population, the inescapable problems cannot be solved until we become conversant with the nature, magnitude, and distribution of the underlying deviations.

Biochemical individuality thus becomes basic to the solution of those problems in which *biochemical* deviations come into play. How numerous these problems are and how pertinent the deviations are will be more evident as the various areas of biochemistry are considered.

Certainly, one of the drives which has impelled many workers in the biological and related sciences to neglect, comparatively, the deviations which we consider as possibly crucially important is the desire to make generalizations. Without generalizations and laws science cannot exist. From the standpoint of developing a science of biology, it seems extremely desirable to formulate valid generalizations that will encompass all humanity, all mammals, or all members of any biological group. Actually, in the human-centered sciences directly related to medicine, there appears to be a strong tendency to focus attention on "normal man," a being about whom generalizations can be made. Almost any treatise which one may find dealing with the subjects of physiology, biochemistry, pharmacology, or physiological psychology is concerned almost wholly with normal man and his reactions. The subject of the significance of variation is most often neglected entirely, and it would appear not to be regarded as important.

We are of the opinion, however, that the hypothesis—every one a deviate—is potentially important enough for the understanding of susceptibility to disease that extensive data not now available need to be collected to test its validity and to open the way to more effective therapy and prophylaxis. The open door which presents itself when every individual is considered to be a potential deviate with respect to his nutritional needs will be discussed in Chapter XI, after the basis for this individuality in nutritional needs has been adequately explored.

The development of the area of biochemical individuality is made urgent by the foregoing considerations. It is made possible because of the introduction of new techniques and tools. Many of the facts related to biochemical individuality which are presented in later chapters of this book could not have been brought to light if it were not for some of the newer tools: chromatography, isotopic techniques, and physical methods of analysis and separation. The collection of data in the area of individuality is in its infancy, and newer techniques will make possible the collection of vastly more pertinent and satisfactory information than is available at present. Many of the data which are now available have been collected by investigators who appear to have no particular interest in variation as such or concern with its possible significance.

REFERENCES

1. Julian S. Huxley, *Man Stands Alone*, Harper & Bros., New York, N.Y. and London, England, 1941, p. 8.
2. George W. Gray, *The Advancing Front of Medicine*, Whittlesey House, New York, N.Y. and London, England, 1941, p. 24.
3. George Draper, *Human Constitution in Clinical Medicine*, Paul B. Hoeber, Inc., New York, N.Y., 1944.
4. Errett C. Albritton, ed., *Standard Values in Blood*, W. B. Saunders Co., Philadelphia, Pa. and London, England, 1952, p. 1.
5. Errett C. Albritton, ed., *Standard Values in Nutrition and Metabolism*, W. B. Saunders Co., Philadelphia, Pa. and London, England, 1954.
6. Roger J. Williams, William Duane Brown, and Robert W. Shideler, *Proc. Natl. Acad. Sci. U.S.*, 41, 615–620 (1955).

II

Genetic Basis of Biochemical
Individuality

All geneticists are agreed that what is inherited by organisms from their forebears is a range of capacities to respond to a range of environments. The characteristics that an organism possesses are fundamentally the outcome of the interaction of heredity and environment. If we state that characteristics are inherited, we make a false implication that environment had nothing to do with their production. This is never the case.

There are numerous characteristics, however, including many morphological features, in which under ordinary circumstances heredity plays the important role. The essential determinants for the duplication of the morphology of an oak tree, a rabbit, or an elephant are resident in the respective fertilized egg cells from which these organisms spring. Environment, as ordinarily encountered by these developing organisms, makes development possible and may, to a degree, modify the course of development, but the basic morphology is determined by the carriers of inheritance.

Not only are morphological species-differences transmitted through inheritance, but morphological characteristics which are peculiar to an individual organism are transmitted to its offspring in a similar manner. It is well known, for example, that because of their postulated identical inheritance, the facial features of identical twins are often indistinguishable. It may be presumed that the morphological features of all the internal organs, which also show a high degree of variance (p. 19), are likewise inherited in the same sense. There is substantial evidence on this point to be cited later.

Although it is theoretically possible for environments to be altered artificially or otherwise so that morphological features will be substantially changed, the color of one's eyes, the relative size of one's feet, the curliness of one's hair, the patterns of one's fingerprints, and a host of other morphological features are primarily, under ordinary living conditions, the result of inheritance. Once the egg is fertilized, the living conditions in a healthy uterus established, and good food furnished the mother, many morphological features are substantially determined. Even here, however, we must not forget the interplay of environment, because nutritional lacks or the effects of foreign chemicals may cause the production of even gross abnormalities in growing embryos.

It has also long been recognized that gross metabolic differences between organisms of different species are genetically determined. In birds the principal end product of nitrogen metabolism is uric acid; in mammals it is urea. In most dogs the end product of purine metabolism is allantoin (in Dalmatians uric acid constitutes an important part); in humans, uric acid is the corresponding principal end product. Inheritance is the determining factor here, as is true also for the differences with respect to ascorbic acid synthesis in rats, guinea pigs, and humans. Rats inherit the ability to synthesize ascorbic acid; neither guinea pigs nor humans inherit mechanisms for doing this, and hence these species are dependent on a dietary source of this vitamin.

As the subject of biochemical genetics has developed, it has become clear that inheritance and mutations govern not only the *gross* metabolic differences between different species but also intraspecies differences of a lesser magnitude.

Much of the earlier development in this area came about through the study of induced mutations in *Neurospora,* but the general principles clearly are applicable to organisms high in the biological kingdom. There is, on the part of those familiar with the field, not the slightest doubt that inheritance and the concurrent mutations govern the minute details of intricate chemical processes which take place in any organism. The finding in *Neurospora* of the ornithine cycle, for example, is one of many observations which tie together the whole biological kingdom and make more certain the universal application of the principles of biochemical genetics. Obviously the availability of suitable substrates (ultimately derived from food) is a factor which enters into determining exactly what chemical reactions take place in any organism, but there can be no serious doubt that the potentiality for producing every enzyme and enzyme system in our bodies arises from inheritance.

We are not concerned here with many of the details of genetic machinery.* In higher organisms especially, the mechanisms are extremely intricate. Our discussion is by no means dependent upon the acceptance of any simple 1-gene-1-enzyme relationship, but it does rest upon the widely substantiated principle that the potentiality possessed by organisms for carrying out any and every chemical reaction arises from inheritance and intervening mutations. There is no other way in which such potentialities can arise.

An important feature in the mechanism of inheritance from the stand-point of our discussion lies in the existence of what have been inelegantly called "leaky genes" or less picturesquely "partial genetic blocks." Observation of a phenomenon of this sort was first made by Mitchell and Houlahan[1] in 1946 and was an outgrowth of the earlier pioneer studies on the genetics of *Neurospora* by Beadle and Tatum.[2]

Beadle and Tatum had found that irradiation of *Neurospora* spores produced mutants which were incapable of carrying out certain well-defined chemical reactions, and it was at first supposed that as a result of the *destruction* of a specific gene, the potentiality for producing a particular enzyme was completely lost. The "wild type" of *Neurospora* could propagate satisfactorily when biotin was the only vitamin-like substance supplied in the culture medium. Of the many mutant strains produced, however, one needed, in addition to biotin, the vitamin riboflavin. Without a supply of riboflavin in the culture medium this so-called "riboflavinless mutant" would not grow. Since riboflavin is a part of an enzyme system always found in *Neurospora*, it is an obligatory cell constituent and either has to be produced by the cells themselves (as in the wild type) or supplied exogenously in

---

*For pertinent material on this subject the reader should consult R. P. Wagner and H. K. Mitchell, *Genetics and Metabolism*, John Wiley & Sons, Inc., New York, 1955, and other detailed treatises on the subject of genetics.

the culture medium. The "riboflavinless mutant" presumably was completely lacking in some enzyme which was necessary for the endogenous synthesis of riboflavin.

The highly important finding of Mitchell and Houlahan proved, however, that this presumption was false, since the "riboflavinless mutant" was found to retain, but in a modified condition, its inherent ability to produce riboflavin. By growing the organism at a lower temperature (25° or below), they found that it was able to produce riboflavin with sufficient rapidity to make possible good growth. Since this observation was initially made in 1946, "leaky genes" or "partial genetic blocks" have repeatedly been observed. In fact, it has come to be the opinion of many workers in the field of biochemical genetics that partial genetic blocks are the rule rather than the exception. Whenever mutant organisms appear not to be able to carry out a specific reaction which is carried out by the original strain, the inability is only relative, not absolute. The potentiality for carrying out the reaction is most often impaired (possibly severely so) but is not wholly lost.

The important principle to be derived from numerous studies related to partial genetic blocks is that organisms not only can inherit the potentialities for carrying out chemical reactions efficiently but that they can also inherit impaired potentialities which will allow the reactions to take place at reduced rates (less efficiently) under prevailing conditions. There are presumably all degrees of "leakiness" in genes, and the enzyme systems within one's body may each vary through wide ranges in the effectiveness with which they individually operate.

It is well recognized that the number of genes involved in human inheritance is very large indeed, and that the assortments of genes possessed by different members of the human family are widely different. Because of the complexity of inheritance, children of the same parents may have very different gene assortments, though their assortments are statistically more alike than the assortments of unrelated individuals. There are isolated inbred human populations in which the gene distributions are more alike than they are in a heterogeneous human population, but even within such inbred groups the gene distributions are highly diverse. When, in addition to recognizing differences in gene distribution, we accept the principle of partial genetic blocks (from which there appears to be no escape), we have abundant basis for recognizing a high degree of variation and individuality. In this connection Wagner and Mitchell state: "Although mutation is a sudden event, it can produce almost any degree of effect from those barely detectable by known means to those too extreme for a cell to survive."[3]

No two human beings possess the same genes. Even in "identical" twins, although the genes are theoretially identical initially, they occur in such large numbers and the possibility of somatic mutations is sufficient (minor mutations may be very common) that the metabolism in fully developed "identical" twins is likely not to be identical in every respect. Maternal influence can also operate so as to make "identical" twins not quite identical. The question of the nonidenticalness of "identical" twins is an important one to which a conclusive answer must await further investigation. This investigation is particularly desirable in the light of such striking examples as that cited by Warkany, Guest, and Cochrane[4] in which one identical twin at the age of 8 became a diabetic and the other began to develop obesity.

What may be expected to result from the diversity of human genes and their different degrees of "leakiness"? As we have indicated earlier, morphological features are often determined by inheritance. *How* different gene assortments give rise to different bodily features is not well understood, but the fact that they do is incontrovertible. The intricate nature of the mechanisms is illustrated by the fact that several genes are involved in determining the pattern of one's fingerprints alone.

On the morphological side we should expect that the size and shape of every internal organ as well as that of the external bodily features would be determined to a highly significant degree by inheritance (p. 19). The influence of heredity should be present in the determination of the morphology of every cell and every cluster of cells in the whole body.

So far as metabolism is concerned, we should expect that the potentiality for every chemical reaction which takes place in human bodies would vary in efficiency from individual to individual. It is well established that genes determine the character of these reactions, and we know that our genes are very diverse.

On the basis of the broad principles of biochemical genetics we should expect not only that the chemical reactions of the body as a whole would vary from individual to individual, but also that the chemical reactions taking place in any specific organ or tissue would vary in efficiency from individual to individual. The production of each digestive enzyme should vary in effectiveness from individual to individual; the phosphorylating enzymes, which are essential to absorption (as well as to a multitude of other processes), should be expected to vary in effectiveness from individual to individual. Not only may such variations exist, but also the phosphorylating enzyme in the intestinal wall might be "strong" in individual 1 and "weak" in individual 2, whereas a similar enzyme might be "strong" in the kidney of individual 2 and "weak" in the kidney of individual 1. On the basis of such diversities as these, the ways and the extent to which members of the human population can vary from one another are limitless. When an individual fertilized egg has a genetic make-up so much at variance that its environment is inadequate, the individual egg fails to develop. And the fact that the egg develops into a full-grown fetus does not insure its ability to cope with the extra-uterine environment which it encounters at birth. Genetic variance may still be enough to mark the organism for early death, unless a special environment is provided.

We must not overlook, even in this discussion, the fact that genes and the enzymes which in a sense they beget cannot produce chemical metabolites from nothing. The raw materials for the numerous and intricate chemical operations must be provided. This is where nutrition comes in and where there is a necessary interplay between the genetic factors and the environmental ones. Genetics determines the detailed potentialities of organisms to carry on their intricate chemical operations, provided the necessary raw materials, ultimately derived from food, are supplied. Without these raw materials, nothing develops or lives. A very important feature of this volume is the elucidation in Chapter XI of the genetotrophic concept, which is concerned with how genetic "weaknesses," which probably are inherent in most normal individuals, may be overcome by special nutritional treatment when the nature of these specific weaknesses is delineated.

It seems desirable at this point to call attention to what, for the want of a better designation, we will call the *principle of genetic gradients.* What we have in mind is a suggestive principle which is probably widely applicable, though not necessarily universally so. Its tentative acceptance will clarify many observations which are highly pertinent to our subject matter. It should also stimulate many new observations and the recording in an orderly manner of many other observations which have been recorded heretofore only in a casual manner.

The principle may be crudely stated as follows: Whenever an extreme genetic character appears in an individual organism, it should be taken as an indication (unless there is proof to the contrary) that less extreme and graduated genetic characters of the same sort exist in other individual organisms. This principle can best be made clear by a few examples. If one should find in a standard environment an individual rat which had adrenal glands one-fifth the average size, this principle would lead one to suspect that this was merely an extreme case and that other rats should exist having adrenal glands of various sizes intermediate between this minimal (?) size and the maximum size, whatever it is, in the environment under consideration. If an individual child is found to have, because of genetic reasons, an extremely low content of arginase in the blood, it would be assumed that probably other children would be found to have graded amounts intermediate between the observed low value and the maximum. If some individuals, for genetic reasons, have extremely low thyroid activity and others extremely high, the principle of genetic gradients would suggest that graded intermediate activities should exist in any sample population. If one individual is found to excrete, because of genetic reasons, a large amount of urinary cystine and another is found to excrete no detectable amount, it may be presumed that intermediate graded amounts are excreted by other individuals. If some individuals (for genetic reasons) are severely or even fatally poisoned by garlic, it would be presumed on the basis of this principle that other people might be found for whom garlic is more or less deleterious, depending on the extent to which they possess the affected metabolic characteristic.

The principle of genetic gradients will be most valuable if it is accepted only tentatively and is used as a basis for stimulating new observations and interpreting old ones. We will observe in the course of our later discussions many cases in which it appears to hold and other uninvestigated cases where the question of whether it holds is highly important and needs to be settled. It is possible that as more information in the field becomes available, the principle will be found to be restricted somewhat as to its applicability.

The principle of genetic gradients and other considerations raise serious questions about the traditional use of culled out and inbred experimental animals for all types of physiological experiments. If one is using rats (or other test organisms) as the basis for a quantitative test for riboflavin, for example, then one wants to use animals which are as uniform as possible for the test. Any effective means for obtaining uniform animals is justified. If one were studying the fundamental question of how riboflavin functions in mammals generally, then the use of a uniform strain of animals would greatly simplify the study. If, however, one is studying the riboflavin requirements of rats as representative mammals, then one might get a wholly erroneous picture by using a highly inbred strain. This strain might happen to have relatively very high or very low requirements. The uniformity within the strain which might be observed would be entirely misleading with respect to rats as representative omnivorous mammals.

From the standpoint of our main thesis, it would seem indefensible to eliminate from a colony of animals, as far as possible, all deviants and animals showing abnormal characteristics and then use the resulting group to throw light directly on *human* problems, when the human population which is the ultimate concern is made up of individuals who probably possess deviant and abnormal characteristics galore. A saving factor in this situation is the inability to obtain, even by the closest inbreeding, experimental animals with identical genetic characteristics. Such animals, if available, might be very useful for certain basic scientific purposes but would be thoroughly worthless for many studies looking to the solution of human problems.

It seems to the author that ideas resting upon the importance of genetics are inherently difficult to sell. One reason has already been discussed briefly in the preceding chapter. When we recognize the facts of genetics and biological variability, we find generalization difficult and the whole biological world more complex. We would like to think that things are simpler than they actually are.

Human pride enters also and makes more difficult the acceptance of the genetic facts which are applicable to human beings. If an individual develops into a great athlete, mathematician, musician, or philosopher, he would like to feel that he has gained his stature by virtue of his own efforts. Whatever must be charged to native endowment may be regarded as on the debit side of the ledger so far as his self-esteem is concerned.

Another unfortunate idea has gained a foothold, namely, that insofar as inheritance is concerned in any disease or difficulty, nothing can be done to ameliorate the situation because one cannot change one's ancestors. Acceptance of this idea means a rejection of the importance of the interplay of environment and inheritance. It is by no means impossible to deal with diseases which have a hereditary basis. We do so every time we use insulin or thyroid tablets, correct nearsightedness or farsightedness with spectacles, or have dental work done; and it is ridiculous to suppose that knowing about the hereditary basis of diseases will not help us cope with them. The genetotrophic approach which will be discussed in later chapters emphasizes the vast potentialities of nutrition (an environmental factor) in overcoming unusual nutritional demands of genetically determined origin.

Contrary to the idea which often prevails, the recognition of the genetic basis for numerous human difficulties may do quite the opposite from injecting gloom into the outlook. Only by understanding the genetic basis can we hope to be able to modify the environment appropriately so that the difficulty may be overcome. Every bit of insight which we develop with respect to the genetic basis will contribute to our effectiveness in modifying the environment more expertly.

It may seem out of place in a book of this sort to mention another difficulty which lies in the way of accepting in a straightforward manner the basic facts of inheritance and its importance in connection with the many problems related to it. This difficulty appears to lie in the philosophical or religious abhorrence of the idea of determinism or fatalism. The author shares this distaste, but he is convinced that acceptance of the importance of heredity does not lead to a belief in fatalism any more than accepting the importance of environment does.

A fatalist *may* emphasize the role of heredity. He may conceivably take the extreme position that all that we become and all that we do as human beings is foreordained in the fertilized egg from which we develop and that environmental influences are relatively ineffective in forming our lives.

A fatalist may, however, take the opposite position and hold that fertilized eggs are initially all about the same and that it is environment which molds our individual lives. Each of us, according to this view, is surrounded from the first by a distinctive environment, and this explains why we are all different. Environmental influences, by definition, come from the outside. Beginning from the moment of fertilization, they impinge on the developing organism from without (the fatalist may say), and the individual developing organism has absolutely no choice as to whether or not it will receive the stimuli or how it will react to them. How the individual reacts to these stimuli during prenatal or postnatal life (the fatalist may say) can be explained completely on the mechanistic basis of tropisms and conditioned reflexes. The individual has no ability to choose his own environment—it molds him. "Moving to a new environment" is an illusion of freedom (he may say); the moving itself is a result of tropisms and reflexes.

There are those who are inclined to adopt a mechanistic view of life, including human life, and to place complete trust in human reasoning. They come out with the dictum that only two factors count at all, heredity and environment. They are then driven to determinism inevitably, whether they assign 99 per cent importance to heredity and 1 per cent to environment, or 99 per cent to environment and 1 per cent to heredity, or whether they assign different percentages to each, or refuse to separate the two factors by insisting that they always work together. The acceptance of a fatalistic point of view has *nothing whatever* to do with the relative importance of heredity and environment. One may be an out and out fatalist on the one hand, or extremely adverse to fatalism on the other, and at the same time hold any possible shade of opinion with respect to the relative importance of the genetic and the environmental aspects of life.

We therefore make a plea for an unprejudiced facing of the facts of heredity. We urge that such facts be accepted with as great readiness as any others. This plea seems necessary in view of the attitude which we have repeatedly noted, namely, that of willingness to arrive at "environmentalistic" conclusions on the basis of slender evidence while rejecting points of view which would emphasize the role of heredity, even though the weight of the evidence, viewed without prejudice, appears overwhelming. Curiously, even some geneticists have tended, in the author's opinion, to underplay the importance of genetic influences in their desire not to be thought one-sided or extreme. Thus, for example, they say—and rightly—that eye colors (in humans, for example) are not inherited; it is the *chemical mechanism* for producing certain eye colors in certain environmental circumstances that is inherited, a mechanism which cannot work without the interplay of nutrition and other environmental influences. Although this is quite true and the statement is the result of clear thinking, such a statement can, to the partially informed, give a false impression, namely, that environmental influences, *as ordinarily encountered,* are about on a par with hereditary influences so far as determining eye color is concerned. This is not the case. Whether the mother eats spinach, smokes, exercises little or much, lives in a cold or hot climate, is interested or uninterested in having a child are so far as we know completely without effect.

What we have been saying should not suggest to the reader the desirability of accepting uncritically evidence for the importance of genetics. We advocate instead that all phases of the subject be looked at with the same critical attitude, and that the evidence to be found in the field of genetics be given fair consideration and not be rejected a priori on the basis of false philosophical implications.

REFERENCES

1. Herschel K. Mitchell and Mary B. Houlahan, *Am. J. Botany,* 33, 31–35 (1946).
2. G. W. Beadle and E. L. Tatum, *Proc. Natl. Acad. Sci. U.S.,* 27, 499–506 (1941).
3. Robert P. Wagner and Herschel K. Mitchell, *Genetics and Metabolism,* John Wiley & Sons, Inc., New York, N.Y., 1955.
4. Josef Warkany, George M. Guest, and William A. Cochrane, *Am. J. Diseases Children,* 89, 689–695 (1955).

III

Anatomical Variations—Significance

Anatomy and biochemistry are always intimately related even though the two disciplines may be regarded as quite dissimilar. The chemical composition of the body as a whole is relatively meaningless; what is far more meaningful is the chemical composition of the different organs, tissues, and cells—the *anatomical* structures—which make up the body. The metabolism of the body taken as a whole is also relatively meaningless to the serious student of biochemistry since it lumps together the metabolisms of different organs, tissues, and cells. Biochemistry is vitally concerned with the chemical transformations which are taking place in specific organs, tissues, and cells and, hence, cannot be studied apart from the anatomical basis of the organism concerned. Anatomical variations are thus basic and closely related to biochemical variations.

Before citing illustrative material from the field of human anatomy, let us consider a nearly 30-year-old study—about the only one of its kind—involving the comparative anatomical study of a large number of laboratory animals of the same species. Wade H. Brown and co-workers of the Rockefeller Institute[1] collected data with respect to the organ weights in 645 normal male adult rabbits from stock used for experimental purposes. This study is particularly pertinent because, since the animals were not genetically homogeneous, the results can be taken as indicative of what would be revealed if a random sample of a human population were studied in a similar manner.

The results as they stand are rather astounding to one who has been brought up to think of normal animals of one species as being approximately uniform. The ranges in the weights of different organs expressed in terms of grams per kilo of net body weight of animal are given in Table 1. Ranges of 5- to 10-fold are commonplace.

Table 1.
Range in Relative Organ Weights of Rabbits

Organ	Grams per Kilo of Net Body Weight		High/Low
	Minimum	Maximum	
Gastrointestinal mass	70.4	452.0	6
Heart	1.95	4.42	2
Liver	23.2	117.0	5
Kidneys	3.45	17.28	5
Spleen	0.035	2.93	80
Thymus	0.248	3.315	13
Testicles	0.47	4.93	10
Brain	3.33	8.16	2.5
Thyroid	0.048	1.23	25
Parathyroid	0.001	0.022	22
Hypophysis	0.007	0.035	5
Suprarenals	0.080	0.572	7
Pineal	0.002	0.025	12
Popliteal lymph nodes	0.05	0.382	8
Axillary lymph nodes	0.019	0.24	13
Deep cervical lymph nodes	0.02	0.295	15
Mesenteric lymph nodes	0.67	6.91	10

From Wade H. Brown, Louise Pearce, and Chester M. Van Allen, *J. Exp. Med.*, 43, 734–738 (1926).

The fact that this study was actually carried out independently on two groups of animals (numbering 350 and 295, respectively) and that very similar results were obtained with each of the two groups should be convincing evidence of the tremendous anatomical variability which exists in normal rabbits—and presumably in other animals (and humans) which have not been investigated from this point of view.

A more recent extensive genetic study carried out by Riddle[2] indicates clearly that similar wide variability of organ weights exists between different *strains* of doves and pigeons. Although the number of organs and tissues studied was not as great as in the study on rabbits, it is clearly demonstrated that intestinal length, thyroid size, pituitary size (incomplete data), liver size, age at maturity, testis weight, egg weight, and heart weight are all under genetic control and differ with different strains of pigeons and doves. From this and other indirect evidence it may be presumed that organ weights in mammals (which, of course, are often subject to some fluctuation with time) are inherited as are other anatomical features.

The details and ramifications of the subject of human anatomy are so great that all we could hope to do in a single chapter would be to give illustrative material taken from various broad areas of the subject. These examples, along with what we might infer from the animal data already given, should be indicative of the character and range among individuals of anatomical variations which may exist in human bodily structures. To one whose primary interest is outside the subject of anatomy, it seems that human anatomists have been aware of variations for many generations but that for pedagogical reasons they have concentrated on the "norm" and have shown little or no concern for the possible significance of the ever-present variations. Some anatomists have in recent years recorded more fully the factual material related to variation, and we shall refer to their work.

Digestive Tract

What happens in the body to consumed food is a matter of primary concern to biochemists. We shall therefore indicate some of the variable anatomical features which bear on this problem.

We shall pass over variations in dentition with only a mention because of the intricate problems encompassed by the large field of dental science. This is an area in which variations are great and highly significant from the standpoint of food utilization.

Adequate information regarding the variation in the size of the

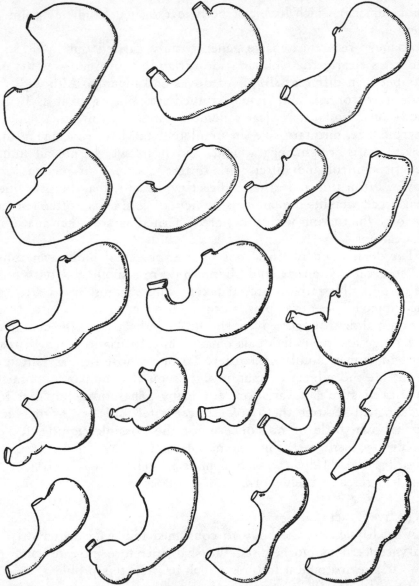

Figure 1.   Stomach, variations in form. From laboratory specimens. The author is deeply indebted to Dr. Barry J. Anson of Northwestern University, who has kindly allowed him to reproduce illustrative material from his valuable *Atlas of Human Anatomy* (W. B. Saunders Co., Philadelphia, Pa., 1951). This illustration is on page 287.

esophagus appears not to be available, but it seems that cross-sectional areas might vary at least 4-fold and that this might be an important matter from the standpoint of swallowing. If one's esophagus is large, swallowing is easier, other things being equal, and the bolting of food is encouraged. A person with a small esophagus, on the other hand, may find the bolting of food impossible. It is a fact that some individuals can swallow with ease large capsules or stomach tubes in a doctor's office or hospital while others have great difficulty. This inability is sometimes ascribed to differences in nervous reactions or to the uncooperativeness of the patients; it appears that the obvious bearing of the anatomical variations may not have been adequately considered. It is common to speak of the *habit* of eating rapidly or slowly. It seems highly doubtful, however, that this behavior is purely habit; anatomical differences may be basic.

Human stomachs vary greatly in size and shape as is seen from Figure 1 which pictures various normal specimens.[3] It is evident that some stomachs hold six or eight times as much as others. It is no wonder from this standpoint that our eating "habits" are not all alike. Coupled with the gross differences in stomach sizes and shapes are the well-known wide differences in the emptying time of stomachs as well as other differences which will be mentioned in later discussions (pp. 65–67). Clearly, from the anatomical standpoint it is normal for the stomach to have any one of a great variety of shapes and sizes.

The position of the stomach in the body is also widely variable (Fig. 2). With the tip of the breastbone (sternum) used as a point of reference, the bottom of the stomach may be anywhere from about 1 to about 9 in. below this position. It is not abnormal to have the bottom of the stomach within an inch or two of the level of the base of the sternum, because about 25 per cent of people have their stomachs in this position; neither is it abnormal to have it about 7 in. lower, because more than 10 per cent have their stomachs in this position.

The most important digestive juice in the body comes from the pancreas gland and empties into the intestine a few inches beyond the pyloric end of the stomach. The bile, which is important both in digestion and absorption, empties into the duodenum at about the

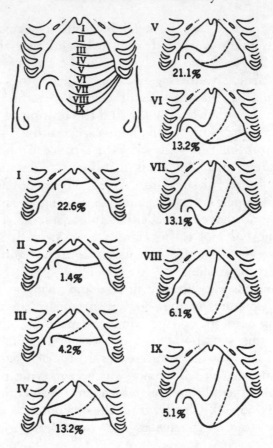

Figure 2. Stomach. From Barry J. Anson, *Atlas of Human Anatomy*, p. 286.

same position. However, there is no set uniform relationship between these two ducts. A diagrammatic representation of the ways these two ducts enter the duodenum and the percentages of the population said to exhibit each is shown in Figure 3.[4] Mixing of the two secretions before entrance into the duodenum can take place in arrangement *D* and possibly in arrangement *C*, especially if a gallstone is lodged in the common duct. It is clear that a gallstone might have quite different effects in different individuals, depending upon their respective anatomies in this region. From this standpoint, arrangement *A* might be considered superior to the others, but certainly the others are not abnormal, nor is there any one "normal" arrangement.

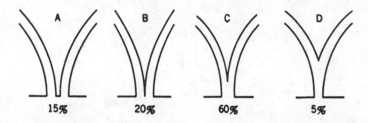

Figure 3. Entrance of bile duct and pancreatic duct into the duodenum (diagrammatic). From William A. Sodeman, *Pathologic Physiology* (W. B. Saunders Co., Philadelphia, Pa., 1950), p. 346.

In an earlier study[5] it was found that in 33 per cent of the cases the pancreatic and bile ducts have separate openings. This and other similar variations probably occur in different percentages among populations with different racial origins. Some evidence on this point has been found in connection with the variations in the junctions of the hepatic and cystic ducts.

The pathways followed by the intestines are highly diverse, as is indicated, for example, by the variable positions of the transverse colon (Fig. 4). It will be noted that its position in some individuals is almost at the level of the sternum, but in others it is 10 to 12 in. lower. No particular position can be considered normal because about 30 per cent of the population is near one extreme or the other. In the other 70 per cent, various intermediate positions apply.

More important possibly from the standpoint of function is the diversity of the anatomy of the pelvic colon itself. Figure 5 shows the various types of anatomical structures and the percentage occurrence of each. These percentages should be taken as indicative rather than accurate since they are based upon examination of only 210 specimens. If these percentages were accurate for the whole population of the United States, each of the least common forms (represented at the bottom of Figure 5) would exist in about 600,000 persons. It seems obvious that with this array of different types of pelvic colons (as well as transverse colons), people should differ tremendously (as they do) with respect to their problems of elimination. It is interesting to note in this connection that healthy newborn ba-

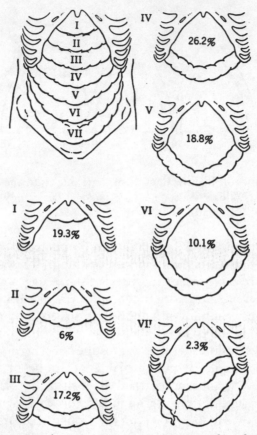

Figure 4. Transverse colon. From Barry J. Anson, *Atlas of Human Anatomy*, p. 286.

bies show tremendous variability with respect to the stools they pass. In a group of 800 *healthy* infants[6] less than a week old, it was found that there were some who passed as many as 12 to 14 stools in the course of 24 hours; on the other hand, 16 of the babies (2 per cent) had no stools at all during the day of observation. These differences are no doubt related in part to anatomical differences in the intestines, as well as to other anatomical, physiological, and neurological differences.

The liver is an organ of more than average interest to biochemists; its functions are intimately related to digestion, absorption, and metabolism. It varies in shape like other internal organs (Fig. 6), and

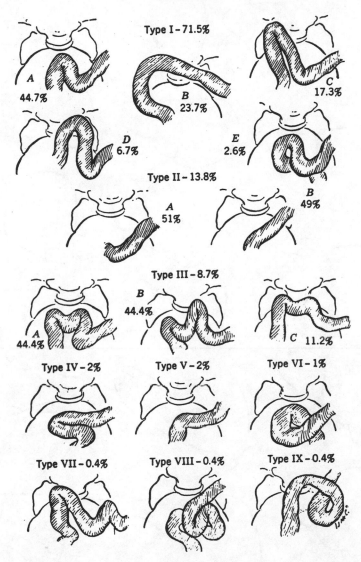

Figure 5. Pelvic colon. Variation in form and position. Diagrammatic. Major types (I to IX) are illustrated, together with varieties (*A* to *C*, etc.) within the more inclusive categories. The percentage occurrence of each type and subtype is recorded, as determined from an examination of 210 specimens. From Barry J. Anson, *Atlas of Human Anatomy*, p. 349.

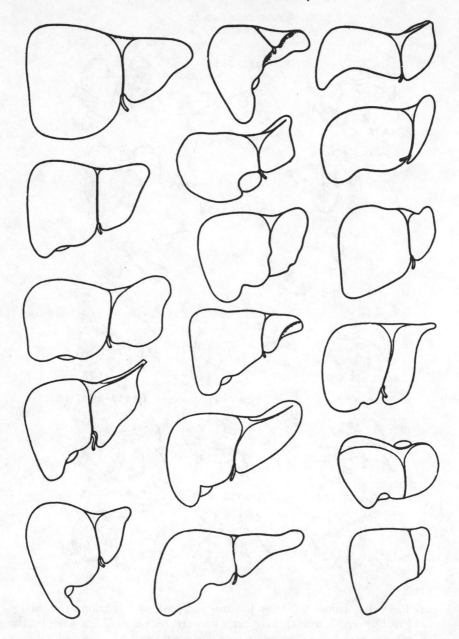

Figure 6. Liver, variations in form. Laboratory specimens. Anterior views. From Barry J. Anson, *Atlas of Human Anatomy*, p. 288.

the size variations (mass) are about 4-fold and correspond to the 5-fold liver mass variations noted in rabbits (p. 20). The position of the liver, like that of the stomach, is not the same in different individuals (Fig. 7). In some (about 4 per cent), it lies almost entirely behind the ribs on the right side. In about 10 per cent of the population, however, it is almost wholly below the level of the front ribs—about 6 in. lower and farther toward the left. Since different livers are shaped quite differently, it is difficult to compare their positions with accuracy.

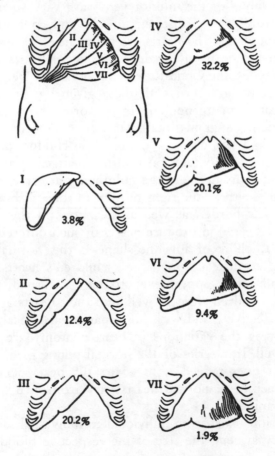

Figure 7. Liver. From Barry J. Anson, *Atlas of Human Anatomy*, p. 286.

Heart—Circulatory System—Blood

The circulatory system is, of course, basic to the transport of food, oxygen, carbon dioxide, and the end products of metabolism and, hence, is of fundamental biochemical interest.

Elementary students are taught to think of the heart as a pump built according to a single straightforward pattern; any variations from the pattern which might exist would be trifling, except, of course, in "abnormal" cases. That such is far from the case is shown by the twelve variations in the right atrium of the heart (Fig. 8). The forms of the valves of the inferior vena cava vary so much and the detailed structures are so different in size and contour as to make one almost doubt that the hearts are from the same species.

Maresh,[7] in his study of the development of hearts during childhood sponsored by the Child Research Council of Denver, has made findings perfectly in accord with these given by Anson. From the study of repeated roentgenograms of 71 normal boys and 57 normal girls (3,205 roentgenograms total), Maresh concluded: "Variations in cardiac shape and size are very common in childhood. The 'typical average heart' seldom obtains on routine roentgenograms. Variations in the size and prominence of the pulmonary artery contours, in the curvature and length of the right border, in the width and curvature of the lower left border, as well as variations in the angulation of the long axis all serve to produce hearts of such different shapes that it is difficult to think of any one shape as the 'normal.'" He goes on to emphasize that, although these children's hearts were highly distinctive and might appear even to be "abnormal" by accepted standards, the children were all well, and their hearts appeared to be functioning effectively and with no impairment of health.

Accompanying the variations in heart anatomy are variations in function as well. In a series of 182 normal young men[8] it was found that the heart rates ranged from 45 to 105 beats per minute. The pumping capacities of normal hearts vary from 3.16 to 10.81 liters of blood per minute.[9]

Wide variations exist from individual to individual with respect to the circulatory system, the size of the respective blood vessels, and their distribution patterns. One might suppose that the main arteries arising out of the aorta, which comes directly from the heart, would always branch in about the same way and follow the same general

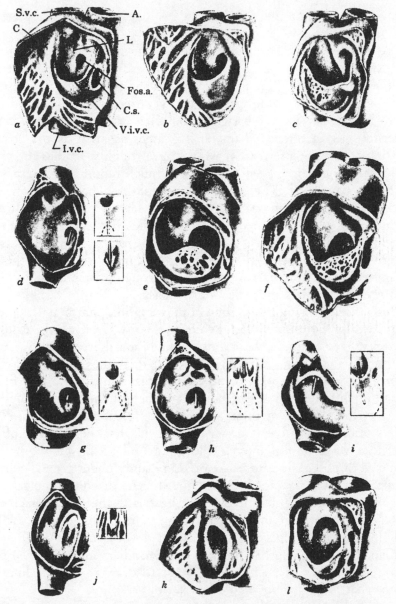

Figure 8. *a* to *l*, Right atrium of the heart. Variations in form of the valve of the inferior vena cava and of the interatrial foramen. Insets: portions of interatrial wall, from the right atrium (foramen probed). From Barry J. Anson, *Atlas of Human Anatomy*, p. 215.

pattern. This is not the case as can be seen from the six patterns depicted in Figure 9.

The number of arteries coming directly out of the aortic arch varies from two to four. In patterns *E* and *F,* there are four branches each, but they are not the same four arteries in the two cases. It is also to be observed that the same specific artery varies in size from individual to individual. Thus the right subclavian artery (A. subcl. d.) in pattern *F* has an outside diameter 1.7 times as great as the corresponding artery in pattern *C.* It would have roughly 3 times the cross section and therefore at least 3 times as much blood-carrying power as that in pattern *C.* The aorta, after these branches come off, has twice the cross section in pattern *F* as it has in pattern *D.* If, for example, the aorta (which ultimately supplies the lower extremities) is relatively small after the branches come off of the arch (as in pattern *D*), no enlargement farther down can make up for the retarding effect of this narrow opening through which the blood to the lower extremities must necessarily pass.

The variation in modes of branching not only starts at the aortic arch but also continues throughout the body. In Grant's *Atlas of Anatomy,*[10] for example, variations in the brachial arteries (arm), cystic arteries, and hepatic arteries are depicted. Bodies, therefore, must differ greatly with respect to the relative (as well as absolute) blood supply of different parts, organs, and tissues of the body, including the heart itself. Some of these and other differences are discussed by Hollinshead.[11] It has been shown by Schull[12] that the patterns of the superficial veins of the anterior thorax are inherited, and it may be presumed that all such features are predominantly under genetic control.

Our discussion has not included the dozens of congenital anomalies (abnormalities) which involve the heart and the great vessels and which have been regarded as pathological. It is suggestive that, although many individuals who are afflicted with such anomalies die in infancy or early youth, some live to beyond seventy and then may die of some other disease. It is difficult to draw the borderline between what is anomalous and what is not.

The implications of the commonly occurring differences in the circulatory systems of different individuals may be far-reaching. The circulating blood accomplishes purposes which are essentially biochemical. Oxygen and easily burned fuel are carried to the tissues,

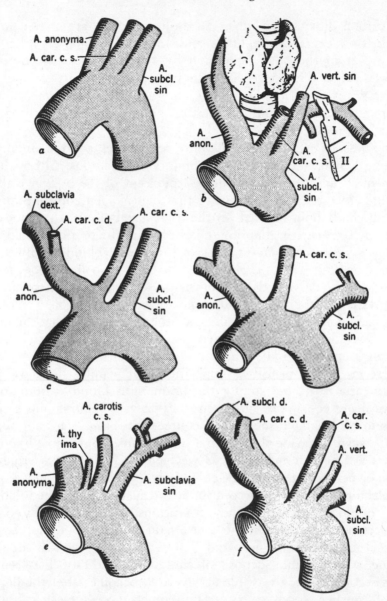

Figure 9. Branches of the aortic arch. Variation in the pattern of origin. *a* and *b*, Common pattern; *c* and *d*, left common carotid artery from the innominate (long and short stem); *e*, separate origin of a thyreoidea ima artery; *f*, independent origin of a left vertebral. From Barry J. Anson, *Atlas of Human Anatomy*, p. 197.

and carbon dioxide and other metabolic products are carried to the elimination centers, the lungs and kidneys. The metabolism of every part of the body is limited by the quality of the blood it receives. If the brain receives an insufficient supply of oxygen, essential nutrients, and hormones, the regulating mechanisms cease to operate properly, and the vital processes such as breathing and heart beat may cease.

The brain is extremely sensitive to lack of fuel, and the amount of burning which takes place in the brain is tremendous. Although the brain of an adult makes up about 2 per cent of the body weight, it accounts for about 25 per cent of the total oxygen consumption. In a small child about one-half of the total metabolism of the body, as gaged by oxygen consumption, takes place in the brain. Fainting and dizziness are often manifestations of inadequate blood supply to the brain. Impaired brain metabolism may be due to impaired enzyme systems in the nervous tissue, but the presence of an effective circulatory system to the brain would tend in the direction of overcoming enzymatic deficiencies. In senile dementia it is thought that the blood vessels have become so "corroded" with deposits of cholesterol, etc., that an adequate blood supply does not get to the brain.

It seems a very plausible supposition that people who have large carotid arteries (these supply the brain with blood) would, other things being equal, have little tendency toward fainting and in later years toward senile dementia. Of course, other things are not always equal, as will be made clear in later discussions. This simple hypothesis has not been tested so far as we have been able to ascertain. In senile dementia and borderline conditions, peculiarities in metabolism or selection of foods may contribute to cause an intensified "corrosion" of blood vessels, and these conditions may not prevail in others who are not afflicted. On the other hand, if two blood vessels with internal diameters of 4 mm. and 3 mm. are "corroded" in the same manner with a 1 mm. deposit of cholesterol, the ratio between the cross sections, which was initially 16 to 9, becomes after the deposit 4 to 1. Smaller blood vessels are thus much more subject to impairment in this way than are large blood vessels. Knowing the facts about the relationships between blood-vessel size, fainting, and senile dementia, therefore, might make possible ameliorative measures. Perhaps people with relatively small carotid arteries should follow very special precautions in their eating, so as to keep the blood vessels as free from internal deposits as possible. People with large carotid arteries might not have to be concerned with this problem.

These data constitute convincing evidence that anatomical and related functional differences in the heart and the blood vessels are sufficiently large to have a profound influence on the metabolism of each and every tissue and, hence, on the health and well-being of all the individuals concerned. Concentration on "the normal human being" causes us to miss seeing these relationships and may make unlikely the application of remedial measures which would be effective in individual cases.

Blood itself, from the standpoint of anatomy, shows wide variations in its make-up. We are now speaking of course, in terms of microscopic anatomy, since macroscopically blood has no structure.

In a group of 15 healthy normal babies, the red cell counts at one week of age varied from 4.46 to 7.29 millions per cu. mm.[13] At the same time reticulocytes (immature red cells) varied in these same infants from 0.1 to 4.5 per cent. It appears that not only do babies differ substantially at birth in this regard but that they also follow different patterns of change and, hence, may at different stages of development show quite different red cell counts as well as reticulocyte counts. For adults the normal red cell counts are said to vary from 4.6 to 6.2 million.

Newborn healthy infants vary in their total leukocyte counts from 9,000 to 30,000 per cu. mm., in neutrophils from 6,000 to 26,000, in eosinophils from 20 to 850, in basophils from 0 to 640, in lymphocytes from 2,000 to 11,000, and in monocytes from 400 to 3,100. In healthy adults the total leucocytes vary from 3,500 to 14,800, which may be distributed within the following ranges:

	Per Cent
Segmented neutrophils	38–70
Band neutrophils	0– 6
Eosinophils	0–15
Basophils	0– 2
Lymphocytes	18–49
Monocytes	2–14.5

Table 2.
Types of Cells in Bone Marrow

	Range Per Cent	High/Low
Proerythroblasts	0.2 – 4.0	20
Early normoblasts	1.5 – 5.8	4
Intermediate normoblasts	5.0 –26.4	5
Late normoblasts	1.6 –21.5	13
Myeloblasts	0.3 – 3.1	10
Progranulocytes	0.5 – 4.5	9
Myelocytes	0.9 –20.3	23
Metamyelocytes	5.6 –22.0	4
Band cells	6.1 –36.0	6
Segmented cells	8.7 –27.0	3
Lymphocytes	2.7 –24.0	9
Monocytes	0.7 – 2.8	4
Megakaryocytes	0.03– 0.4	13
Plasmacytes	0.1 – 1.5	15
Reticulum cells	0.03– 1.6	53
Unclassified cells	0.02– 3.3	165
Disintegrated cells	1.1 –20.8	19

From Errett C. Albritton, ed., *Standard Values in Blood*, W. B. Saunders Company, Philadelphia, Pa., and London, Eng., 1952, p. 72.

The venous blood platelet count in healthy adult males varies from 150,000 to 690,000 per cu. mm.[14]

Adequate data on individuals, taken over periods of time, are not available; but it seems evident that, even though there may be substantial intra-individual fluctuations, the histological blood picture differs from individual to individual and follows a different pattern of change for each individual. Some types of cells are relatively abundant in the blood of certain individuals but are practically absent from the blood of others. Individuals who suffer from allergies are thought to have, under comparable environmental conditions, high eosinophil counts in their blood. Individual differences in blood histology are found in experimental animals which are kept under the same carefully controlled environmental conditions.

The bone marrow is intimately concerned with blood formation. When obtained by sternal puncture, it contains many different types of cells and the ranges of each are wide. Table 2 illustrates this fact. There is on the average a 22-fold range in values; the median range is 13-fold. Again, as in the case of the blood, adequate information with respect to repeated samples from the same individuals is not available. However, in view of the other information which we have on blood composition, etc. (Chap. IV), we may infer with considerable safety that the histological differences in samples of bone marrow represent to a considerable degree differences between individuals. This does not mean necessarily that a given individual maintains the same histological pattern indefinitely; each may exhibit a characteristic pattern of change with age, which in turn may be influenced by various environmental factors.

Respiratory Tract

Respiration is fundamentally a biochemical process, and variations in the respiratory apparatus are of interest in that they bear upon our central theme, biochemical individuality.

That large anatomical variations in the lungs and the respiratory tract exist is perhaps most clearly demonstrated by a study of the functional activity in different healthy individuals. In a study of 209 healthy young men[8] it was found that the average tidal air (the amount of air passing into and out of the lungs in an ordinary breath) varied from 350 to 1299 cc., nearly a 4-fold range, and the ventilation in liters per minute varied from 3.5 to 14.4 liters per minute. The respiratory rate varied over 5-fold, from 4.0 to 20.9 respirations per minute. While these are physiological rather than anatomical data, it seems safe (especially in view of the available anatomical data with respect to other organs) to conclude that they reflect substantial anatomical differences in the organs of respiration.

One anatomical study which is interesting from this standpoint is that of Maresh,[15] which has to do with paranasal sinuses. In Figure 10 are shown two contrasting patterns taken from roentgenograms of a small group of *typical* children. These tracings from successive x-ray pictures of the same two children taken at different ages show how the sinuses varied with age. It is evident from the material presented in the original publication that it is not unusual for the combined paranasal and frontal sinuses in one normal child to have twenty or more times the volume of the corresponding sinuses in another normal child. The implications of these differences are obvious, especially when it is realized that these structures cannot vary in this way without there also being other simultaneous variations as, for example, variations in the nasal and throat passages.

Because of preoccupation with the problem of what is normal, differences of this sort have received little attention. It is interesting that Turgenev, the Russian novelist, has taken a "dig" at science because of this fact—"a man's capable of understanding anything—how the ether vibrates and what's going on in the sun—but how any other man can blow his nose differently from him, that he's incapable of understanding." Certainly where variations are as large as these,

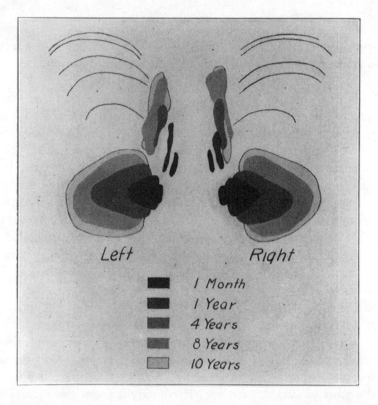

Figure 10a. Composite drawing showing size and growth of the sinuses in R. Q. (actual size of the tracings from the roentgenograms at each age represented).

thinking in terms of the average leads to error. For anatomical as well as other reasons, every individual has the right (and the necessity) to breathe, sneeze, and blow his nose, as befits the make-up of his respiratory apparatus. So far as paranasal sinuses are concerned, it is normal for them to be large, small, or intermediate in size, and to have any of a number of shapes.

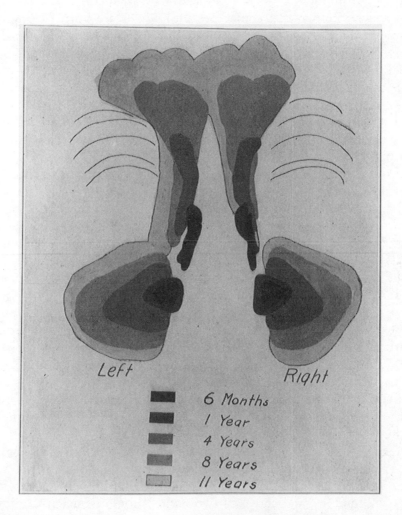

Figure 10b. Composite drawing showing size and growth of the sinuses in W. S. (actual size of the tracings from the roentgenograms at each age represented).

Musculature

Variations in musculature are not as interesting from the standpoint of biochemistry as those involving other structures, but there are some available facts regarding variation in this area which are of considerable general interest. Because they emphasize the general importance of individuality, they support the specific theme of this book—the importance of biochemical individuality.

It is well known that sometimes individuals are born lacking certain abdominal muscles. This is regarded, of course, as abnormal. It is not so well appreciated, however, that in the normal populations there may be a high degree of variation. Anson,[3] for example, shows how the pectoralis minor muscle varies in an unselected population. In 42 per cent it overlaps the 2nd, 3rd, 4th, and 5th ribs; in 28.5 per cent it misses the 2nd rib; in 15 per cent it misses the 5th rib; and in 5 per cent it misses both the 2nd and 5th ribs. There is no one normal pattern.

From the standpoint of general interest the variations in the musculature of human hands are worthy of attention, especially so since it is often supposed that *the human hand* is a standard piece of equipment which all normal people possess. The writer has seen a magnificently produced motion picture using a highly involved model, which showed just how every intricate movement of "the hand" is made. There was no hint, however, that hands do not all work in the same way.

In Anson's *Atlas*[3] are depicted in two full pages the variations in the extensor muscle of the index finger. One set of these patterns is reproduced in Figure 11. It will be noted that accessory muscles to the middle finger, to the ring finger, and other accessory muscles of several forms are present in some patterns and absent in others. The result is that there are depicted eleven different patterns, each distinctive. In the same source book there are presented eight different patterns of the extensor tendons on the back of the hand. If the patterns of the nerves were depicted as the patterns of facial nerves are (p. 46), we would doubtless find many variations in this area, too. *The hand* is far from an assembly-line product. Even if the muscles, tendons, and nerves of two hands should be macroscopically alike, these still may differ in mircoscopic anatomy as well as bio-

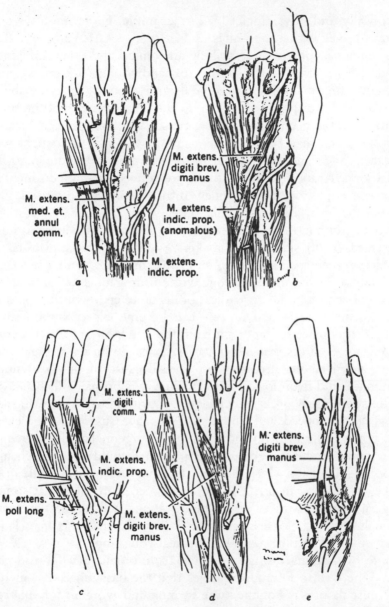

Figure 11. Extensor muscle of the index finger. Variations. *a*, Accessory muscle to the ring finger. *b* to *e*, Accessory manual muscle of several forms. From Barry J. Anson, *Atlas of Human Anatomy*, p. 160.

chemically and physiologically. For example, nerve impulses do not always travel at the same rates.

The implications of these striking anatomical and other differences in hands are obvious, as they relate to handwriting (signatures), manual dexterity, finger dexterity, tweezer dexterity, ability to type, ability to play the violin or piano, ability to do the intricate work of the surgeon, or to make the manipulations of a masseur, a card trickster, or a magician. Children may be given the same copy books and taught writing in exactly the same manner, but in the end each will write distinctively because their hands, including the nerve connections, are distinctive and different. For some, it is extremely difficult to learn to write legibly at all, yet they may be very able in other ways.

To the author it appears that on the basis of the information just presented, *highly* skilled watchmakers, typists, violinists, pianists, scientific experimenters, mechanics, surgeons, masseurs, and magicians are probably born *and* made. No one without the requisite hands, anatomically and neurologically, regardless of his other endowments could really excel in these fields, and no one can become expert without training and practice. It seems important from the standpoint of the conservation of human resources that individuals who have unusual manual endowments be given the necessary training. Because of our inattention to anatomical and neurological individuality, it is probable that many who are extraordinarily well equipped for activities such as are mentioned above go unnoticed and untrained. We have suspected, for example, that the training of a potentially superb surgeon has not infrequently been nipped in the bud because the individual could not learn chemistry, a special subject for which he needs to have very little aptitude in order to be outstanding in his field. To us, it seems probable that some day surgical practice with all of its ramifications will utilize the help (for difficult stitching, for example) of skilled artisans who may lack the capacity for absorbing a general medical education.

Since we are digressing somewhat from biochemical consideration, it may be well to remind ourselves that the basic anatomy, including the musculature, is not the same in men and women; for this reason a woman cannot throw a ball as a man can, nor can women run in competition with men. However, as swimmers women show up very well, in contrast to their lack of ability to throw well or run fast. Within the sexes, however, there are variations in anatomy so that some women are able to throw a ball very much as a man does; in fact, they are able to outthrow some men whose anatomy in this respect partakes of feminine characteristics and who consequently "throw like a woman."

Developing excellent performers in specialized athletic activities comes about through selection and training, and the selection is fully as important as the training. Competent track coaches become expert in appraising a particular individual's possibilities as a distance runner, a sprinter, a high jumper, a broad jumper, for example, and they train the individual for the activity to which he seems best suited. The kind of anatomy and physiology which is best suited to distance running is not best suited to sprinting. The same holds in other sports; different positions on the baseball team or football team require different types of anatomical and physiological make-up. Of course, coaches can make mistakes, and some individuals, by determination, can make up for deficiencies. Some individuals are remarkably versatile, though they always are more able in some ways than others because of their distinctive anatomical and physiological make-up.

Very interesting observations have been made on young children showing how at birth their anatomical distinctiveness begins to show itself.[16] In 28 males at birth, the percentages of the fat, muscle, and bone layers in the calf of the leg were 20, 50, and 30, respectively, as determined by X-ray pictures; whereas, for thirty females at birth, the corresponding figures were 23, 56, and 21. In a large percentage of cases, these measurements are so distinctive that it is possible to tell the sex of the child from them. In some cases there would be doubt. Such observations are in line with many other observations regarding endocrine differences (Chap. VI) and what we know about the genesis of sex glands and how they influence development.

In Table 3 are given the widths of the shadow of the subcutaneous tissues and skin on both sides of the leg bone in girls and boys 6 to 10 years of age.[17] According to these data, there is a substantial percentage difference between the average values for boys and for girls. However, when the values for individual children are scrutinized, it becomes apparent that some boys tend toward the feminine and some girls tend toward the masculine so that there is actually some overlapping of values.

That each child exhibits a distinctive pattern is shown by the data[18] in Table 4 with regard to two girls (B.N. and C.S.) of the same age. Although their gross measurements are about the same, the thicknesses of fat, muscle, and bone layers are marked by differences.

Table 3.
Width of the Subcutaneous Tissues and Skin
(On both sides of leg bone in girls and boys)

	Boys		Girls	
Age	Number	Width, cm.	Number	Width, cm.
6	59	1.06	58	1.35
7	73	1.04	63	1.32
8	64	1.06	52	1.35
9	45	1.06	37	1.33
10	25	1.11	24	1.38

From Harold C. Stuart and Penelope H. Dwinell, *Child Development,* **13,** 205 (1942).

Table 4.
Measurements of Two Girls

	B.N.	C.S.
At 7½ years		
Weight, lb.: oz.	45:8	48:1
Height, cm.	123.7	124.3
Calf diameter, mm.	79.0	77.5
Calf circumference, mm.	244	242
Tibia, mm.	251	252
Percentage for relative breadth of tissue:		
Fat layer	13	20
Muscle layer	41	25
Bone layer	28	33
At 8½ years		
Percentage for relative breadth of tissue:		
Fat layer	11	18
Muscle layer	39	29
Bone layer	29	35

From Earle L. Reynolds, *Child Development,* **15,** 201–202 (1944).

Neuroanatomy

Comparatively little definitive data are available with respect to neuroanatomical variations. Some idea of the extent of the variation may be gained, however, from a consideration of Figure 12 in which are depicted eight patterns of the facial nerve. It may be observed that, as among other anatomical features, there is no single pattern (or even two or three patterns) and that there are no set or normal positions for anastomoses.

Other nerve structures are also subject to variation. The position in the vertebral column at which the spinal cord terminates varies over three full vertebrae, and no *standard* terminal position exists. The positions at which various nerves enter the spinal cord likewise vary from individual to individual. About 15 per cent of the population do not have a "direct pyramidal" nerve tract in the spinal cord. Most human beings have 31 pairs of spinal nerves corresponding to 30 vertebrae; some, however, have 32 and some 33 pairs, corresponding to 31 and 32 vertebrae, respectively. Most people have two splanchnic nerves (sympathetic nerves to the digestive system), but occasional individuals have three. In some individuals the sciatic nerve is so embedded that it is always fully protected; in others, the pathway of the nerve is such that injury is very likely to occur.

In a recent study[19] of recurrent laryngeal nerves based on the dissection of 100 cadavers, it was found that of the 200 nerves 57 per cent entered the larynx without having branched at any point, whereas 43 per cent were divided trunk nerves with from two to as many as six branches. Furthermore, in 35 per cent of the cadavers, both recurrent laryngeal nerves were single-trunk nerves; in 24 per cent, both were divided-trunk nerves; and in 41 per cent, one nerve had a divided trunk and the other did not. No consistency of patterns between the right and left sides was found.

It is commonly supposed that neuroanatomical variations such as we have been considering have little or no functional significance. However, the Schneider Index, a measure of "neuro-circulatory efficiency" or "anatomic efficiency," was found to vary in 75 adolescent girls and boys from 0 to 14, when 18 is the highest possible score. The efficiency scores were so distributed that about equal numbers were in three groups: 0 to 6, 7 to 10, and 11 to 14, respectively.[20]

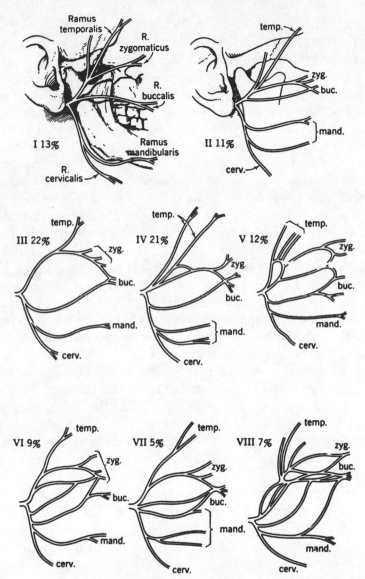

Figure 12. The facial nerve. Major types of facial nerve branching and anastomosis, with percentage occurrence (in 100 facial halves). I, Major divisions (temporal and facial) independent; II, anastomosis between rami of the temporal division; III, connection between adjacent rami from the major divisions; IV, anastomoses representing a composite of those in II and III; V, proximal anastomosis within the temporal component, and distal interconnection between

Evidently, the supposed unimportance of seemingly minor anatomical variations can also be seriously questioned on the basis of
the general principles which we have sought to establish. For example, people with three splanchnic nerves may "get along," but so
little attention has been paid to such variations and their significance
that the question as to whether individuals with this peculiarity are
more subject to motion sickness or gastric ulcers (other things being
equal) has apparently never been considered.

The fact that people differ in their nerve patterns and the distribution of the nerve endings, as well as in their circulation patterns, has
a great deal to do with their sensitivity to cold and heat, to touch
(including ticklishness), and to pain arising in various areas. Some
individuals are born who are unable to feel pain; these are regarded
as "abnormal." But if the principle of "genetic gradients" holds, then
we should expect that such individuals represent merely an extreme,
and that other individuals will be found whose sensitivity to pain
ranges from nearly none up to the highest limit. Lack of attention
to individual anatomical differences with respect to the nervous system has left us in ignorance with respect to how anatomical differences and susceptibilities to pain are related. It has often been
observed by physicians that of two people suffering from substantially the same injury, one may be disabled with pain while the other
is practically free from it. In Figure 12 there is a considerable area
in pattern III which is devoid of large nerves; the corresponding area
in pattern VIII has a number of nerves which anastomose, and it is
likely that an injury at this particular region would have entirely
different effects for the two individuals. Such differences as these,
coupled with the differences with respect to numbers of nerve endings and the relative efficiency of nerves, could explain many differences in the responses to injury.

Few studies are available concerning the structural variations in

---

the latter and the cervical component; VI, two anastomotic rami sent from the
buccal division of the cervical to the zygomatic part of the temporal; VII,
transverse ramus, from the trunk of the nerve, contributing to the buccal ramus
formed by anastomosis between the two major divisions; VIII, richly plexiform
communications, especially within the temporal portion of the nerve. From
Barry J. Anson, *Atlas of Human Anatomy*, p. 37.

human brain tissue, considering the possible importance of their relation to behavior. The relative lack of attention to this field is indicated by the statement of one medical anatomist, "Virtually nothing is known about disharmonies of development in the central nervous system except for very gross deficiencies."[21]

Lashley has published an important review article about the structural variation in the nervous system.[22] The article deals principally with studies on animal brains, though the center of interest is on human beings. In summary, Lashley says:

> The status of the study of variation and inheritance of structure in the central nervous system may be summarized as follows. The brain is *extremely variable* in every character that has been subjected to measurement. Its diversities of structure within the species are of the same general character as are the differences between related species or even between orders of animals. Some of the structural variations have been shown to correlate with functional disturbances. From what is known of the variations in other systems, it may be concluded that the variants which produce pathological symptoms are not discontinuous characters but are the extremes of a normal distribution. Lesser deviations in the same direction, resulting in behavior which is not classed as pathological, are to be expected.
>
> Some of the more conspicuous structural differences have been shown to be hereditary. The heredity of the smaller variants has not been studied and we can only argue their probable genetic determination by analogy with variations in more readily observed structures. . . . Discussions of heredity and environment have tended to regard the nervous system, if it is considered at all, as a vaguely remote organ, essentially similar in all individuals and largely moulded by experience. Even the limited evidence at hand, however, shows that *individuals start life with brains differing enormously in structure;* unlike in number, size, and arrangement of neurons as well as in grosser features. The variations in cells and tracts must have functional significance. It is not conceivable that the inferior frontal convolutions of two brains would function in the same way or with equal effectiveness when one contains only half as many cells as the other; that two parietal association areas should be identical in function when the cells of one are mostly minute granules and of the other large pyramids; that the presence of Betz cells in the prefrontal region is without influence on behavior. Such differences are the rule in the limited material that we

have studied. . . . Except for total weight, the normal range of variation has not been determined for any of the hundreds of measurable elements and structures in the brain. Genetic studies of the nervous system have included no more than a dozen family groups. Our own studies of variability are based on only seven hemispheres. Such investigations are extremely laborious but they are not impossible. They require only endless counting and measurement on well prepared specimens. The correlation of variations with behavior presents much greater difficulties. Yet I believe that the results of such studies will repay the labor. Until they have been made generalizations concerning the relative significance of constitution and experience will rest upon an insecure basis. *(Italics supplied)*

Endocrine Glands

We will merely call attention here to the tremendous inter-individual human variability which exists in the anatomy of the endocrine glands. This variability is foreshadowed by the data already given with respect to rabbits and pigeons (pp. 20–21). Since a separate chapter is devoted to these glands and their functioning, specific anatomical information with respect to the specific glands will be presented there. It is possible that these anatomical variations are more important from the standpoint of health and well-being than any we have so far discussed.

Summary

In summarizing the material on anatomical variations, it may be pointed out that the observed variations encompass all structures, brain, nerves, muscles, tendons, bones, blood, organ weights, endocrine-gland weights, etc. Data are presented which show that these structures often vary tremendously from one individual to another and that their structural differences in general are under genetic control.

REFERENCES

1. Wade H. Brown, Louise Pearce, and Chester M. Van Allen, *J. Expt. Med.*, 43, 733–741 (1926).
2. Oscar Riddle, *Endocrines and Constitution in Doves and Pigeons*, Carnegie Institution of Washington, Washington, D.C., 1947.

3. Barry J. Anson, *Atlas of Human Anatomy,* W. B. Saunders Co., Philadelphia, Pa. and London, England, 1951.
4. William A. Sodeman, *Pathologic Physiology,* W. B. Saunders Co., Philadelphia, Pa. and London, England, 1950.
   (See also F. Büchner, *Allemeine Pathologie,* Urban & Schwarzenberg, München-Berlin, 1950.)
5. Esko Näätänen *Z. Anat. Entwicklungsgeschischte,* 111, 348–355 (1942).
6. W. L. Nyhan, *Pediatrics,* 10, 414 (1952).
7. Marion M. Maresh, *Pediatrics,* 2, 382–404 (1948).
8. Clark W. Health, *et al., What People Are,* Harvard University Press, Cambridge, Mass., 1945.
9. G. C. Ring, *et al., J. Applied Physiol.,* 5, 99–110 (1952).
10. J. C. B. Grant, *An Atlas of Anatomy,* Williams and Wilkins Co., Baltimore, Md., 3rd ed., 1951.
11. W. Henry Hollinshead, *Postgraduate Medicine,* 16, 86–96 (1954).
12. William Jackson Schull, *Abstracts of Doctoral Dissertations,* No. 60, The Ohio State University Press, Columbus, Ohio, 1950.
13. Alfred H. Washburn, *Am. J. Diseases Children,* 62, 530–544 (1941).
14. Errett C. Albritton, ed., *Standard Values in Blood,* W. B. Saunders Co., Philadelphia, Pa. and London, England, 1952.
15. Marion M. Maresh, *Am. J. Diseases Children,* 60, 55–78 (1940).
16. Earle L. Reynolds and Patricia Grote, *Anat. Record,* 102, 45–53 (1948).
17. Harold C. Stuart and Penelope H. Dwinell, *Child Development,* 13, 195–213 (1942).
18. Earle L. Reynolds, *Child Development,* 15, 181–205 (1944).
19. William H. Rustad, *J. Clin. Endocrinol. Metabolism,* 14, 87–96 (1954).
20. Theodora M. Abel, *J. Psychology,* 6, 377–383 (1938).
21. Donald Duncan, Personal Communication.
22. K. S. Lashley, *Psychological Reviews,* 54, 333–334 (1947).

IV

Individuality in Composition

In the present chapter we shall attempt to review and discuss the published literature pertaining to three questions: Are there direct analytical chemical data which show that every individual body has a distinctive chemical composition? How great are the inter-individual differences with respect to specific items? Are these differences significant?

At the outset we must apologize for the paucity of studies which have been directed specifically toward answering these questions. A large part of the data which we have assembled on this subject was collected initially with disregard of these particular problems. In some cases the best we can do is point out and discuss material which seems at least to have some bearing. We shall only mention here the highly pertinent studies carried out in our laboratories and published in abbreviated form, which are referred to earlier (pp. 3–4). These studies, speaking most conservatively, strongly suggest the importance of this type of investigation, but more detailed discussion must await their completion and final publication.

On the basis of the high degree of individuality of excretion patterns demonstrated in our laboratories[1] as well as the genetic considerations set forth in Chapter II, it appears probable that individuality in composition exists. The brain, blood, bones, muscles, and glands are probably distinctive for each individual not only in anatomy but also in chemical composition. This does not mean, of course, that chemical compositions are fixed throughout life or that they are uninfluenced by nutrition. From our excretion pattern studies, however, it may be inferred that even if nutrition were identical for a human population, distinctive patterns of composition (and of aging) would probably exist for each individual.

Direct definitive data supporting or opposing this probability are meager because in the past there has been a general lack of interest in the question. It has usually been assumed that compositional differences which lie within the "normal range" are relatively meaningless.

It is obvious that one should not expect to find in the literature extensive information regarding the composition of the brains, livers, or even muscles of healthy human individuals—especially so since repeated samples would have to be taken for analysis in order to determine conclusively the importance of inter-individual differences. The best that could be hoped for would be extensive "horizontal" studies relative to the composition of blood, secretions, etc., of individual human specimens and, perhaps, more comprehensive data including tissue composition with respect to animals. However, satisfactory studies of this sort have seldom, if ever, been made. More often than not, such horizontal studies as have been made have not been published in complete enough form to give the kind of information needed to answer the questions which we are considering.

To a large extent we will have to rely for our information about these vital organs on data pertaining to blood, secretions, and tissues which can be obtained from well individuals without too great inconvenience. Data with respect to animals, if available, would be pertinent; but, because of lack of interest in the potential importance of the study of individual differences, there is little material which is directly applicable to our questions. Incidentally, the use of highly inbred strains of animals in laboratory research has resulted in partially wiping out some of the differences which would be most interesting from the standpoint of our study.

Body Water

Before passing to a consideration of the results of blood analyses, etc., we may mention body water content, a determination which can be made on the whole bodies of well individuals. By a deuterium oxide dilution[2] method, the percentage of water in 18 "normal" males and 11 "normal" females has been found to vary through rather wide limits: 45.6 to 70.2 per cent. The average for the males was 61.8 per cent and for the females 51.9 per cent, a substantial difference according to sex. The "intracellular water," as determined by volume of distribution of antipyrine,[3] in 11 male subjects was found to vary from 34.7 to 48.0 per cent of the body weight.

Since it is well known that individuals vary in the total fat content of their bodies and since fatty tissue contains less water than other tissues, some variation in water content is to be expected on this basis alone. It should not be concluded, however, that fat content is the only factor contributing to variation in body water.

Blood Groupings—Proteins

Extensive investigation of blood groupings has established that the number of immunological types of blood is legion and that, from this standpoint, the bloods from different individuals are not the same. For practical purposes, incident to an occasional transfusion, bloods can be placed in relatively few categories; and in a sense blood is relatively nonspecific and interchangeable between individuals. A careful analysis on a purely scientific basis, however, reveals that bloods are not merely "positive" or "negative" with respect to the numerous and sometimes seemingly unimportant specific immune substances, but that among the "positive" there are *gradations of concentration*. When these facts are taken into consideration, it is apparent that every sample of blood is distinctive immunologically. Since the subject of blood groups has received a great deal of attention and is covered in a number of treatises and reviews,[4,5,6,7] it is not necessary to go into a detailed discussion here. Studies completed within the past few years suggest that blood groups may be significant in a sense not heretofore evidenced. The first finding was that Type A blood is more common in patients suffering from cancer of the stomach.[8] Secondly, Type O blood was found to be associated with peptic ulcer; after studying the records of twelve hospitals in England including 3011 patients with peptic ulcer, the authors state: "The results have proved remarkably clear-cut: blood group O is strikingly high and the other three groups correspondingly low in patients suffering from peptic ulcer."[9]

Other studies have seemed to implicate blood groupings (including Rh factors in one case) in toxemia of pregnancy, bronchopneumonia, fertility, abortions, oat cell lung tumors, and squamous cell carcinomas of the lung.[10,11]

A number of studies not involving immunological tests have indicated that there is substantial variation in the plasma proteins of different normal individuals. For example, Hill and Trevorrow[12] studied 547 well persons, many at different seasons, and found wide inter-individual variations in the albumin, globulin, and fibrinogen contents of their blood. The albumin data were thoroughly studied statistically, and it was concluded that "the true biological variation is much the larger component of the standard deviation." The range in fibrinogen content was especially large, about 5-fold.

More recent electrophoretic studies[13,14,15] have all yielded evidence which clearly demonstrates that the plasma protein patterns as determined in this manner are distinctive for each individual.

Inorganic Blood Constituents

In Table 5 are given some of the ranges in concentration of blood electrolytes and minor elements which have been observed in normal blood.[16,17] It is a striking fact that for eight of the above items there is at least a 3-fold range, and for seven others the range is about 2-fold. Since repeated samples were not usually taken from the same individuals, it cannot be stated that these data depict real and significant inter-individual differences with respect to the concentrations of the various minerals in blood. We shall discuss more fully the meaning of the tabulated values for blood in a separate section.

Among animals, there are substantial species and even strain differences so far as the sodium and potassium contents of the blood corpuscles are concerned. Kerr,[18] in a study conducted in Syria, found among the animals tested three groups of sheep (strains or races) which differed greatly from each other with respect to the amounts of potassium and sodium in their blood corpuscles (Table 6). The phosphate concentrations in the three groups were about the same. The animals in Group II average nearly four times as much potassium and less than one-fifth as much sodium as do those in Group I; the animals in Group III, on the other hand, have almost the same

Table 5.
Some Ranges in the Inorganic Composition of
Normal Human Blood[a]

Element	Source	Range		
		meq./1000 ml.		
Sodium	Whole blood	72	–	91
	Serum	132	–	144
	Corpuscles	8.7	–	28.6
Potassium	Whole blood	39	–	62
	Serum	3.6	–	4.8
	Corpuscles	89	–	101
Calcium	Plasma	4.3	–	5.2
	Corpuscles	0.6	–	1.4
Magnesium	Plasma	1.4	–	2.4
Chloride	Whole blood	71	–	87
Phosphate	Plasma	2.2	–	4.2
Sulfate	Plasma	1.0	–	1.5
		mg./100 ml.		
Phosphorus	Corpuscles	0.91	–	3.3
		μg./100 ml.		
Bromine	Serum	0.7	–	1.0
Copper	Corpuscles	49	–	101
	Plasma	68	–	143[b]
Fluorine	Corpuscles	11	–	44
	Plasma	10	–	45
Iodine	Whole blood	3	–	13
Iron	Plasma	32	–	177
Manganese	Whole blood	0	–	25
Silicon	Whole blood	33	–	63
Zinc	Whole blood	488	–	1272
	Corpuscles	911	–	1969
	Plasma	0	–	613

[a] Unless otherwise indicated, data are from Errett C. Albritton, ed., *Standard Values in Blood*, W. B. Saunders Company, Philadelphia, Pa. and London, England, 1952, pp. 103, 117–119.
[b] From M. E. Lahey, C. J. Gubler, G. E. Cartwright, and M. M. Wintrobe, *J. Clin. Invest.*, **32**, 322–323 (1953).

Table 6.
Sodium and Potassium Contents of Sheep Corpuscles

Group	Potassium, m./100 gm. corpuscles		Sodium, mg./100 gm. corpuscles	
	Range	Average	Range	Average
I	38– 95	72	64–226	192
II	194–337	251	16– 69	36
III	223–231	227	102–110	106

From Stanley S. Kerr, *J. Biol. Chem.*, **117**, 233 (1937).

amount of potassium as those in Group II, but about three times as much sodium.

If differences of this magnitude exist within a species of sheep, certainly important differences may also exist among the human population—and they may be indicative of substantial differences in mineral metabolism. The more than 3-fold variation in the sodium in human corpuscles is in line with this idea.

The case of iodine, in which various samples of blood exhibit more than a 4-fold range in content, is worthy of especial note since highly pertinent data with respect to the more specific measurement, the "serum protein-bound iodine," are available. From one study[19] of a group of 402 men 18 to 56 years of age, the spread in the protein-bound iodine was calculated for 99 per cent of the (normal) population to be 3.32 to 9.82 µg. per 100 ml. The actual spread in the 402 men appeared to be 2.5 to 11.5 µg. per cent. In another study[20] in which the "normal range" was concluded to be about the same as in the paper cited above, the actual range, including patients with various pathologies, was from 0 to 48.2 µg per cent. One individual, not classed as hypothyroid, exhibited a value as low as 0.6 µg. per cent. In a third study[21] the range found in 47 plasma samples was from 1.1 to 28 µg. per cent. It is highly significant from the standpoint of our discussion that in these studies and others[22] the protein-bound iodine values are found to be relatively constant for any given healthy subject over a considerable period of time. In this case we have strong evidence of individuality and a wide spread in values.

The case of copper is also worthy of special note because several investigations have indicated that while inter-individual variations in plasma copper may be about 2.4-fold, the intra-individual variations (particularly in males) from day to day and week to week are relatively small.[23] Little attention has been paid to the specific problem of inter-individual differences in this connection.

Miscellaneous Organic Constituents of the Blood

Various organic constituents of blood have been found in normal individuals in the ranges of concentration shown in Table 7.[16,24-32] There are many items in the list for which there is a 3- or 4-fold variation, and about a dozen for which the variation is of the order of 10-fold or more. These data strongly suggest that marked inter-individual differences exist, but they do not offer proof except where repeated samples have been analyzed from the same individuals.

The glucose values are worthy of attention because of the large number of determinations that have been made in many laboratories. There is evidence of substantial intra-individual variation in glucose values which is in part responsible for the range of the observed values.[33,34] In spite of this normal variance in values in the same individual, however, there is evidence that inter-individual differences exist among well people. Some, on repeated tests, tend to have low values, some intermediate, and some high.

The acetylcholine values show an unusually wide spread. Although no specific study has apparently been made to ascertain the magnitude of intra-individual differences, relative constancy of values in the same individual seems to be taken for granted, and the range of values is reported to be at a higher level for those suffering from bronchial asthma.[28]

The histamine values of normal individuals have been found to vary about 8-fold (1 to 8 μg. per cent), but repeated tests on the same persons indicated that an individual's values do not vary to a marked degree.[29] The histamine content of the blood in leukemias[35,36] varies from 2.1 to 706.2 μg. per cent, and some investigators have been concerned about deciding when an individual is normal. In case a supposedly normal individual shows a highly unusual value, there is a temptation to discard his value and if necessary find something wrong with him which might justify such an exclusion. It is interesting that there are very wide interspecies differences in histamine blood levels.[37,38] The evidence indicates that each individual probably

Table 7.
Some Ranges in Concentrations of Miscellaneous Organic Constituents of Normal Human Blood[a]

Constituent	Source	Range, mg. per cent
Glucose	Whole blood	84—125[b]
		60—160[c]
		(40—160)[c]
Glycogen	Whole blood	1.2—16.2
Ribonucleic acid	Plasma	3.9—5.9
Desoxyribonucleic acid	Plasma	0—1.6
Adenosine triphosphate	Whole blood	31—57
Pyridine nucleotides	Whole blood	2.6—4.6
Lactic acid	Whole blood	0—41.0
Pyruvic acid	Plasma	0.4—2.0
a-ketonic acids	Whole blood	0.0—3.1
Citric acid	Serum	1.6—3.2
Malic acid	Plasma	0.1—0.9
Glucuronic acid	Serum	1.6—3.6[d]
	Whole blood	2.5—8.5[e]
Creatine	Plasma	0.0—0.8
Creatinine	Whole blood	1.0—2.0
Glutamine	Plasma	5.0—12.0
Urea	Whole blood	11—48[c]
Uric acid	Plasma	2.0—5.6
	Corpuscles	0.8—3.0
Acetylcholine	Plasma	0.30—4.8μg[f]
Histamine	Whole blood	0.02—0.08[g]
Ergothioneine	Whole blood	1.9—5.5
Neutral fat	Corpuscles	11—148
	Plasma	24—260
Phospholipid	Plasma	110—220
Total lipid carbon	Plasma	218—1780[h]
Total lipid phosphorus	Plasma	(0.7) 1.8—16.6[h]
Total lipid nitrogen	Plasma	(1.7) 4.0—23.9[h]
Lipid amino nitrogen	Plasma	(0.2) 0.5—8.2[h]
Total cholesterol	Plasma	109—428[h]
	Plasma	116[k]—700[i]
Lecithin	Serum	50—204
Cephalin	Whole blood	31—118
	Plasma	0—29[j]

tends to maintain a characteristic level of histamine in his blood. This does not, of course, mean that the value is static or is uninfluenced by environmental factors.

In the case of the blood lipids the evidence that many of the variations are inter-individual is convincing. Man and Gildea,[39] in studying the variation in blood lipids in normal subjects (in the postabsorptive and well state), collected repeated samples from the same individuals over a period of 3 months to 4 years. The four men and six women studied tended to have characteristic levels. One of the four men had consistently the lowest minimum and lowest maximum values for cholesterol, lipoid phosphorus, and titrated fatty acids. Another of the four had the highest values of the group. One of the six women (M.G.) had the lowest minimum and the lowest maximum among the women in practically every case. Sperry[40] concluded, in his study of the blood cholesterol values, that "the range of variation in a given person over considerable periods of time is far less than the variation among different persons."

Page, et al.,[41] found that "variations of age, from 20 to 90 years, have not been found to have a determinable influence on either the amount or the composition of the plasma lipids." From this work, it is clear

---

[a] Unless otherwise indicated, data are from Errett C. Albritton, *Standard Values in Blood*, W. B. Saunders Company, Philadelphia, Pa., and London, Eng., 1952, pp. 89–92, 101.

[b] Clark W. Heath, *et al.*, *What People Are*, Harvard University Press, Cambridge, Mass., 1946, p. 124.

[c] F. William Sunderman and F. Boerner, *Normal Values in Clinical Medicine*, W. B. Saunders Company, Philadelphia, 1949, pp. 112, 111.

[d] Abraham Saltzman, Wendell T. Caraway, and Irving A. Beck, *Metabolism, Clinical and Experimental*, **3**, 13 (1954).

[e] W. G. Fishman, M. Smith, D. B. Thompson, C. D. Bonner, S. C. Kasdon, and F. Homburger, *J. Clin. Invest.*, **30**, 685 (1951).

[f] Harold H. Scudamore, Louis J. Vorhaus, II, and Robert M. Kark, *J. Lab. Clin. Med.*, **37**, 862 (1951).

[g] E. Haworth and A. D. Macdonald, *J. Hygiene*, **37**, 237–238 (1937).

[h] Irvine H. Page, Esben Kirk, William H. Lewis, Jr., William R. Thompson, and Donald Van Slyke, *J. Biol. Chem.*, **111**, 616–618 (1935).

[i] Maurice T. Fliegelman, Charles F. Wilkinson, Jr., and Eugene A. Hand, *Arch. Dermatol. Syphilol.*, **58**, 414–417 (1953).

[j] V. Posborg Petersen, *Scand. J. Clin. Lab. Invest.*, **2**, 45 (1950).

[k] Schoenheimer-Sperry method.

that, although there is some tendency for the various lipid values to be correlated with each other, this is by no means always the case. Patterns are exhibited, so that an individual may exhibit a high value for one lipid constituent and a relatively low one for another. These, too, are doubtless influenced by environmental factors, particularly nutrition. We shall refer to this study in a later paragraph.

Table 8.
Ranges in Amino Acids in Blood Plasma

	Range, mg./100 ml.
Alanine	2.4 – 7.6
Lysine	2.3 – 5.8
Valine	2.5 – 4.2
Cysteine-cystine	1.8 – 5.0
Glycine	0.8 – 5.4
Proline	1.5 – 5.7
Leucine	1.0 – 5.2
Isoleucine	1.2 – 4.2
Arginine	1.2 – 3.0
Histidine	1.0 – 3.8
Threonine	0.9 – 3.6
Phenylalanine	1.1 – 4.0
Tryptophan	0.9 – 3.0
Serine	0.3 – 2.0
Tyrosine	0.9 – 2.4
Methionine	0.25– 1.0
Glutamine	4.6 –10.6
Glutamic acid	0.0 – 1.3
Aspartic acid	0.0 – 1.2

From Harold A. Harper, Maxine E. Hutchin, and Joe R. Kimmel, *Proc. Soc. Exp. Biol. Med.,* **80**, 770 (1952).

Amino Acids in Blood

In a recent quantitative microbiological study of the amino acids in the plasma of 17 young fasting males,[42] the wide ranges shown in Table 8 were observed. The ranges for ten of these amino acids average about 4-fold or more. Since the above study and similar ones preceding it[43,44] often involved the analysis of a single sample from each individual, one cannot conclude that significant inter-individual differences exist. One might be inclined to regard these observed differences as due to chance intra-individual fluctuations were it not for the fact that we find in urine and saliva[45] incontrovertible and wide inter-individual differences in the concentrations of the individual amino acids. These findings are borne out by earlier studies on single samples.[46] On the basis of available evidence, it seems probable that each individual tends to maintain a distinctive pattern of amino-acid concentrations in the blood.

Vitamins in Blood

In Table 9 are given the ranges in the concentration of various vitamins in human blood.[16,47,48,49] It perhaps seems idle to speculate in advance of experimental determination, but in view of (1) the substantial ranges indicated in Table 9, (2) the genetic origin of enzyme systems and the close association of many vitamins with them, and (3) other blood patterns which clearly are exhibited, it seems probable that significant inter-individual differences exist and that patterns of vitamin concentration in the blood are distinctive for individuals as well as are patterns involving other constituents. It is worthy of note that sex differences have not infrequently been observed. We shall have further light to throw on the problem of blood-vitamin variation in connection with our discussion of individuality in nutrition.

Interpretation of Tabulated Normal Blood Ranges

In Tables 5 to 9 are presented ranges in the concentration of numerous blood constituents. Several facts need to be borne in mind in interpreting these data. First, these do not, as they stand, represent the range of inter-individual differences because intra-individual variations, diurnal, lunar, seasonal, etc., may be included.[50] If repeated tests were made on the same individuals, some fluctuation in each would be expected, and the *average value* for an individual exhibiting a high value might easily be substantially lower than the value recorded from a single observation. Similarly an extremely low single value might be obtained from an individual whose average value was more moderate. This factor would tend to make the inter-individual

Table 9.
Ranges of Concentration of Various Vitamins in Human Blood[a]

Constituent	Source	Range
		100 ml. Blood
Vitamin A (carotene)	Whole blood	20 –300 µg.
Vitamin A (carotenol)	Whole blood	9 – 17 µg.
Thiamine	Whole blood	4 – 11 µg.
		0.6 – 7.2 µg.[b]
Riboflavin	Whole blood	15 – 60 µg.
Nicotinic acid	Whole blood	0.2 – 0.9 mg.
Pantothenic acid	Whole blood	15 – 45 µg.
Folic acid (total)	Plasma	1.5 – 5.0 µg.
Vitamin B_{12}	Serum	0.008– 0.042 µg.[c]
Biotin	Whole blood	0.8 – 1.7 µg.
Choline (free)	Whole blood	1.0 – 4.0 mg.
Ascorbic acid	Whole blood	0.2 – 0.7 mg.
Vitamin D (as D_2)	Plasma	1.7 – 4.1 mg.
Vitamin E	Plasma	0.9 – 1.9 µg.
		0.46 – 2.01 mg.[d]

[a] Unless otherwise indicated, data are from Errett C. Albritton, ed., *Standard Values in Blood,* W. B. Saunders Company, Philadelphia, 1952, pp. 109–111.
[b] Esben Kirk and Margaret Chieffi, *J. Nutrition,* **38**, 356 (1949).
[c] Harold L. Rosenthal and Herbert P. Sarett, *J. Biol. Chem.,* **199**, 437 (1952).
[d] P. N. Joshi and R. G. Desai, *Indian J. Med. Research,* **40**, 285 (1952).

ranges lower than those recorded. Another factor which might work in the same direction (although presumably in a minor way) is that of experimental and instrumental errors. The values as recorded in Tables 5 to 9 are values *as measured,* and, if the measurements are in error, the recorded ranges might be higher than the actual ones for this reason.

However, there are other factors which operate in the opposite direction, namely, to make the actual ranges in a representative population larger than those recorded.

First, the tabulated ranges are often based upon observations of 50, 20, 10, or even 5 or less individuals. Such numbers are wholly inadequate to represent a large population. If inter-individual differences are as wide-spread as we suspect them to be, then the observed ranges would become larger with increasing numbers of individuals: A relatively small 2-fold range based upon 10 individuals might easily become a 5- to 10-fold range if 1000 individuals were included.

The second factor which would tend to make effective ranges larger than those recorded is that these designated ranges for single items often purport to apply to only 95 per cent of the population,[16] and it seems unjustified to disregard, for example, for each item measured, the approximately 8 million people in the United States who would happen to fall near the end of the distribution curve for one item but not for another.

Thirdly, investigators not infrequently tend to throw out data as spurious when the results are too diverse or too far removed from what was expected. Many would feel perfectly justified in throwing out one analysis out of fifty if it appeared out of line with the others, when actually, if our hypothesis is correct, this one value might be a wholly valid and potentially significant one.

A specific example is to be found in the article of Page, et al.,[30] previously cited. In this investigation 67 individuals were chosen for study. They were judged to be normal and by ordinary clinical examinations were healthy. After the data on these individuals were collected, the following observations were made: "Subject 24 showed a total lipid content so far above the range of all the other subjects that it appears consistent with the probable truth to consider that he had a lipemia from some undetected metabolic abnormality. On the other hand Subject 67 showed a total lipid content much below the range of all others. We have accordingly considered these two subjects as probably abnormal with respect to their lipid metabolism and have omitted their data from the calculations and from the graphs."[51] A careful examination of the detailed data, which are fortunately complete for each individual, shows that although Subjects 24 and 67 were responsible for the extremes of the *total* lipid values, there were a number of other individuals who, in a similar manner, contributed extreme values with respect to individual items and one could with equal justification throw out a substantial percentage of the individuals in the group as "abnormals." If our general hypothesis is correct, every one of the 67 individuals would probably have been proved "abnormal" if a large number of diverse and repeated measures had been made on all of them. Unfortunately, the study under consideration did not involve repeated samples or give information as to how much influence change of diet could have.

There is little doubt that sound experimental investigations have been abandoned in some cases when the measurements were too diverse or divergent from those expected to "make sense." The author actually knows of one case in another laboratory in which, in his opinion, this was the case. The findings were not even submitted for publication.

The fourth factor which would tend to make the tabulated ranges small relative to the more realistic useful ranges is based upon a disbelief in any fundamentally adequate biochemical basis for differentiating between "normal" and "abnormal" cases. If the principle of genetic gradients is valid (and it clearly is in some cases), then what are regarded as "abnormal" values are merely relatively extreme cases in a continuum of variable values. It is widely admitted that *perfectly* well individuals are rare if they exist at all. "Normal" in the medical sense means "nothing abnormal found on examination," but does not presuppose that every organ and tissue in the body has been examined. Hence, in a group of "normal" people (in the medical sense) there will always be those with defects, difficulties, and idiosyncrasies—and it would seem more reasonable from the standpoint of advancing public health to consider those ranges which are applicable to the whole population. *Grossly* abnormal cases may demand separate considerations, but they differ only in degree from others whose deviations must be sought out before they can be recognized.

Saliva Composition

Saliva is known to be highly individual in its make-up and behavior. Its manner of collection, however, may greatly influence its composition. It is a common laboratory observation, for example, that even in a relatively small group of individuals some will be found whose saliva exhibits diastatic activity far removed from the average. A recent striking demonstration of the individuality of saliva is found in the observation that in order for an individual to taste phenylthiocarbamide, it must be dissolved in *his own* saliva.[52] Neither water nor the saliva of another individual is effective.

It is also well established that among those people who belong in blood group A, some (usually a relatively large percentage) secrete

A antigen in the saliva while others do not. This is thought to be due to the possession of different types of antigens, some of which appear in the saliva and some do not. Both the blood groups and the ability to secrete an antigen in the saliva are known to be inherited.

Additional evidence that saliva differs in composition from individual to individual and that variations are not due to chance fluctuations has been obtained in our laboratories.[53]

In Table 10 is given a summary of the uric acid and amino acid values obtained from *repeated* samples from 9 individuals of both sexes, all collected in the same manner.

Table 10.
Salivary Amino Acid Secretion Patterns

Substance	Range for Different Individuals, µg./ml.	Per Cent Secreting Detectable Amounts
Uric acid	2.5–150	100
Aspartic acid	0 – 3.3	33
Glutamic acid	0 – 20	89
Serine	0 – 12	44
Glycine	0 – 36	89
Alanine	0 – 29	89
Lysine	0 – 15	44

From Helen K. Berry.

Not only is the amino acid composition of each saliva distinctive, but available data with respect to different electrolytes suggest that inter-individual variation in composition may also be large in these instances (Table 11).[54,55,56] Differences in mode of collection and in the diets of the subjects tend to lessen the meaning of these data.

Gastric Juice Composition

The two most important functional constituents of gastric juice, pepsin and hydrochloric acid, are known to vary substantially in concentration from individual to individual.

In an extensive study involving a total of over 5000 analyses, Ost-

Table 11.
Salivary Electrolytes

	Range	Mean
	meq./liter	
Sodium[a]	16 –78	44
Potassium[a]	8.8–28.6	20.4
Calcium[a]	4.0– 8.3	6.5
	µg. per cent	
Copper[b]	2 –22	
Copper[c]	10 –47.5	
Cobalt[c]	0 –12.5	

[a] From Ralph E. Bernstein, *J. Lab. Clin. Med.*, **40**, 710 (1952).
[b] From S. Munch-Petersen, *Scand. J. Clin. Lab. Invest.*, **2**, 335 (1950).
[c] From S. Driezen, H. A. Spies, Jr., and T. D. Spies, *J. Dental Research*, **31**, 139 (1952).

erberg, *et al.*,[57] found that about 80 per cent of the individuals yielded "normal" values (0 to 449 units) of pepsin in the test meal juice. About 20 per cent were above "normal"—most of them (18 per cent) yielded 500 to 999 units; 1 per cent, 1000 to 1999 units; and 1 percent, over 2000 units. These and other samples were taken from individuals who showed no signs of gastric disease of any kind. Even though the range was extraordinary (0 to 4300), it might have been larger if it had included a sample of the general population among whom are those with gastric difficulties.

Two noteworthy observations regarding the concentration of pepsin in the gastric juice are: (1) There is a tendency for the amount to decrease with age;[57] (2) the concentrations in different samples from the same individual may vary markedly, and, hence, little reliance can be placed on a single observation. Variability appears to be greatest in nervous and temperamental individuals.[58]

The concentration of *hydrochloric* acid found in the gastric juice of an individual depends in part on the method of collection, but there is no doubt as to wide inter-individual differences. In a group of 96 "apparently normal men," Osterberg, *et al.*,[57] found that achlorhydria was found in 5 per cent, 29 per cent, or 47 per cent, respectively, depending on whether the samples of gastric juice used were (1) test meal juice, (2) fasting juice, or (3) histamine juice (first collection). In 63 apparently normal women the corresponding percentages were 3 per cent, 61 per cent, and 43 per cent, respectively.

In another study in which the test meal procedure was used,[59] "true achlorhydria" was found in about 3 per cent of the younger men, but the incidence increased up to 23 per cent for men between 60 and 69 years old. Corresponding values for women were about the same for the younger group, but the incidence was 26 to 28 per cent in women between 60 and 70. Presumably the lack of hydro- chloric acid would show a much higher incidence in older people if the fasting juice or the first collection of histamine juice were analyzed.

In a study from another source[60] well individuals are classified as follows with respect to the concentration of hydrochloric acid in the gastric juice: about 12 per cent, no acidity; 15 per cent, hypoacidity; 50 per cent, normal acidity; and 23 per cent, hyperacidity.

Although single samples from a particular individual may vary in acid content (as do the pepsin values), there is no question that well individuals (viz., those free from gastric disturbances) vary tremen- dously from individual to individual in their output of hydrochloric acid. The output decreases markedly with age, and the aging pattern differs from individual to individual.

In another study[54] it was found that not only does the free acid vary but that minerals vary also. In 50 fasting samples of gastric juice the following electrolyte concentrations were exhibited.

Free acid	0.0–66.0 (mean 32) meq./liter
Sodium	18.7–69.5 (mean 49) meq./liter
Potassium	6.4–16.6 (mean 11.6) meq./liter
Calcium	2.0– 4.8 (mean 3.6) meq./liter

All of the studies on gastric juice fall in line with the idea that there is a continuum of values none of which can be regarded as normal to the exclusion of the others.

Duodenal Juice Composition

By the use of paper chromotography, an investigation[61] of the amino acid composition of the duodenal juice from 10 individuals has revealed that in each case a distinctive and relatively constant amino acid pattern is exhibted. Fifty-six patients[62] with various pathological conditions (in gall bladder and liver) were also studied in the same way with similar results. Evidence was found that certain pathologies were associated with specific characteristics of the patterns.

Milk Composition

Studies related to the possible differences between the chemical composition of milks from individual animals of the same species have been few. It is well known that among farm animals some individual mothers supply milk on which their offspring and foster offspring thrive, while the milk from other mothers is deficient for this purpose. It is commonly supposed that the deficiency is purely that of the quantity of milk, and little evidence is available one way or the other with respect to whether deficiencies of quality may also be involved.

In the case of human mothers it is also recognized that some are able to nurse their babies effectively while others are not. Whether the quality of the milk is partially at fault is pretty much an unanswered question.

It is well known that the protein content of milk from different species varies and is inversely related to the period of development of the young. The content of the B vitamins is likewise much higher in the milks of small, rapidly maturing animals[63] than in human or cow's milk. There can be no serious doubt that the ability to produce milk at all, and also the composition of milk, is controlled to a large extent by genetic factors. On this basis one would expect that milk would vary in composition from individual to individual.

In experiments carried on in the author's laboratory several years ago, the B vitamin content of milks from individual cows and from individual human mothers was determined.[63] So far as this study is concerned, involving as it did only B vitamins, the intra-individual variation (that is, from day to day) appeared to be greater than inter-individual differences. The number of human cases studied was not sufficient to be the basis of any sound conclusion on this point.

A more recent study[64] (however, in single samples) indicated for vitamin A and riboflavin something less than a 2-fold variation (7 to 10 individuals), for thiamine a 4-fold variation (9 individuals), and for vitamin C nearly a 10-fold variation in 10 individuals (0.77 mg. to 6.8 mg.). In another recent report[65] the range (10 individuals) for folic acid in human milk is given as 0.1 to 1.8 mg. per liter (18-fold range) and for vitamin B_{12}, 0.1 to 1.5 µg (15-fold range).

In view of the lack of satisfactory data, the evidence for substantial inter-individual differences in milk composition is limited, and satisfactory conclusions must await further study of both inter-individual and intra-individual differences. The available data suggest that inter-individual differences may be substantial and important in the case of ascorbic acid, folic acid, and vitamin B_{12}.

Bone

The question as to whether there are significant inter-individual differences in normal animals or human beings with respect to the inorganic composition of bone has apparently never been seriously studied.

In a recent study involving the inorganic analysis of human ribs from 10 subjects,[66] it has been found that the calcium content varied from 24.12 to 26.91 per cent, the phosphorus from 10.75 to 12.11 per cent, and the carbonate as carbon dioxide varied from 2.81 to 3.95 per cent. Inter-individual differences of this magnitude would seem to exist since the inorganic composition of bone is probably relatively stable and not subject to short-term fluctuations.

The question of whether the variances are not even wider than this and the compositions (including total ash content) stable enough to be distinctive for each individual is particularly interesting and important from the standpoint of the existence of Osteogenesis imperfecta (brittle bones) in its various forms and related congenital bone "defects."

It has long been known that certain individuals are exceedingly susceptible to bone fractures. In some cases fractures may occur during fetal life, in other cases the difficulty may show up during infancy, and in still others it appears in later life. The severest cases die very early, but those with less severe conditions may live to suffer from scores of broken bones during childhood. This condition is often associated with blue sclerotics and less often with deafness, which may make a late appearance. Individuals having this difficulty have been found to have a deficiency in the retention of calcium, phosphate, and magnesium,[67] but no comparative study has been made, so far as we know, of the composition of the bones of individuals suffering from *Osteogenesis imperfecta* and those of individuals classed as normals.

It would appear, since the condition has long been known to be hereditary, that some defect in the mineral metabolism constitutes the basic difficulty. Since there are widely varying degrees of severity of the disease, the question arises whether there are not many gradations of composition between the bones of severe cases of *Osteogenesis imperfecta* on the one hand and at the other extreme the bones of those individuals who can experience falls from relatively high elevations without having what may be regarded as the "normal" number of fractures.

It seems likely that an extended study of bone composition, as well as related phenomena, on an individual basis might yield highly valuable information relating not only to fractures and their mending but also to numerous features of mineral metabolism. Such studies should by no means exclude "normal" individuals, because individuals who are seemingly normal often have bone difficulties, for example, fractures that are very difficult to heal. It is interesting, as well as complicating to the picture, that some individuals whose bones fracture with great ease also exhibit unusual rapidity of bone healing.

P. B. Mack[68] has made an extensive and very careful study which is related to the problem of variability in bone composition, and she has been kind enough to furnish me with some of the data previous to publication. A wide range of human subjects of various ages, 10,200 in number, were studied by a technique developed by her and her associates for determining skeletal density.[69] These determinations are based upon microdensitometric traces which were made of X rays of a cross section 1 mm. wide of the *os calcis* (heel bone).

In young adults 20 to 39 years of age, for example, the range, calculated in terms of grams of apatite per cubic centimeter of bone, was from 0.30 to 1.72 gm. (av. 0.77 gm.) for males and 0.39 to 1.34 gm. (av. 0.71 gm.) for females. The range for males was 5.7-fold and for females 3.4-fold.[68] This information is definitely contrary to the idea that bone, as it exists in real human specimens of the same age group, is of relatively uniform composition. The density of bone is affected by environmental influences, particularly nutrition, but these data strongly suggest that some individuals are inclined, for genetic reasons associated with their peculiarities in mineral metabolism, to have far more dense bones than others.

It is interesting and possibly significant that the boron content of bones of 33 individuals has been found to vary from 16 to 138 ppm. by weight.[70]

Skin

In an investigation of the water-soluble vitamins in human skin,[71] it was found that 15 individuals showed relatively small ranges (less than 2-fold) for vitamin B_{12}, folic acid, and biotin; about 2-fold ranges in the cases of riboflavin, niacin, and thiamine; about a 4-fold range in the case of ascorbic acid, and more than a 5-fold range in the case of pantothenic acid. In another study[72] it was found that the total choline content of normal skin varied in four individuals over approximately a 10-fold range: 127 to 1200 µg. per gm. The variation in the free choline in the same individuals was relatively small.

Hair

In a study of the mineral content of human hair[73] (of different colors) it was found that the over-all range of iron concentration in about 15 selected individuals was 1.79 mg. per cent to 10.8 mg. per cent. Red hair had the highest iron content, but one sample of black hair had 4.95 mg. per cent iron whereas another sample of black hair had only 1.92 mg. per cent iron.

The copper content of hair varied from a low value of 2.17 mg. per cent for one sample of black hair up to 5.15 mg. per cent for another sample of the same color. The total ash content of hair from different individuals varied at least through more than a 2-fold range (0.455 per cent average for gray hair, 0.943 per cent for a sample of red hair). As hair becomes gray, its ash content tends to diminish. This is an indication of a change in mineral metabolism with age, a change which may be local or may extend throughout the body.

Calcium Content of Umbilical Cord

An investigation of the effect of vitamin D administration during pregnancy on the calcium content of the umbilical cords of the infants[74] inadvertently yielded some information regarding individual variations. Samples of 51 cords from women who had *not* received extra vitamin D during pregnancy had a calcium content varying from 0.077 to 0.178 gm. per 100 gm. of tissue (dry weight). This more than 2-fold range is strongly suggestive of significant inter-individual differences not due to chance fluctuations or experimental error. Even more striking were the inter-individual differences among the women who had received vitamin D supplement; there was in some cases a substantial increase in the calcium content, and the range was over 4-fold (0.091 to 0.375 gm. per 100 gm. dry tissue).

Miscellaneous Observations on Compositional Variation

In a series of analyses of the tissues of individual rabbits, cats, and guinea pigs[75] it has been found that the phosphocreatine content of liver and other tissues varies from animal to animal over very wide ranges, in some cases up to 100-fold or more.

The copper content of human sperm in 10 individuals was found to vary from 6 μg. to 24 μg. per cent.[55] The DNA content of spermatozoa was found to vary from 1.18 to 1.30 arbitrary units in 13 males of proven fertility, but among males of suspected infertility 6 individuals out of 18 exhibited values lower than 1 (0.76 to 0.98). Repeated tests on the fertile individuals gave closely concordant values.[76] "Normality" with respect to fertility and spermatozoa composition is obviously something that cannot be established by any routine examination.

Analyses of the livers of four autopsy specimens showed the following variations:[77] Sodium: 121 to 266 mg. per cent, iron: 1.0 to 32.5 mg. per cent, and copper: 0.17 to 0.78 mg. per cent. For three spleens the variation in iron content was 3.4 to 72.1 mg. per cent; and for zinc, 1.51 to 5.29 mg. per cent.

REFERENCES

1. Helen Kirby Berry, Louise Cain, and Lorene Lane Rogers, *Univ. Texas Publ.*, 5109, 150–156 (1951).
2. Paul R. Schloerb, Bent J. Friis-Hansen, Isidore S. Edelman, A. K. Solomon, and Francis D. Moore, *J. Clin. Invest.*, **29**, 1296–1310 (1950).
3. Norman Deane, *J. Clin. Invest.*, **30**, 1469–1470 (1951).
4. Leone Lattes, *Individuality of the Blood*, Oxford University Press, London, England, 1932.
5. Alexander S. Wiener, *Blood Groups and Transfusion*, C. C. Thomas, Springfield, Ill., and Baltimore, Md., 3rd ed., 1943.
6. William C. Boyd, *Genetics and the Races of Man*, Little Brown & Co., Boston, Mass., 1950.
7. R. R. Race and Ruth Sanger, *Blood Groups in Man*, Blackwell Scientific Publications, Oxford, England, 2nd ed., 1954.
8. Ian Aird, H. H. Bentall, and J. A. Fraser Roberts, *Brit. Med. J.*, **1**, 799–801 (1953).
9. Ian Aird, H. H. Bentall, J. A. Mehigan, and J. A. Fraser Roberts, *Brit. Med. J.*, **2**, 315 (1954).
10. L. A. Pike and A. M. Dickins, *Brit. Med. J.*, **2**, 321–323 (1954).
11. R. B. McConnell, C. A. Clarke, and F. Downton, *Brit. Med. J.*, **2**, 323–325 (1954).
12. Robert M. Hill and Virginia Trevorrow, *J. Phys. Chem.*, **46**, 1125 (1942).
13. N. Hallman, J. Kauhtio, A. Louhivuori, and E. Uroma, *Scand. J. Clin. Lab. Invest.*, **4**, 89–97 (1952).
14. E. G. Young and R. V. Webber, *Can. J. Med. Sci.*, **31**, 45–63 (1953).
15. Peter Bernfeld, Virginia M. Donahue, and F. Homburger, *Proc. Soc. Exptl. Biol. Med.*, **83**, 429–434 (1953).
16. Errett C. Albritton, ed., *Standard Values in Blood*, W. B. Saunders Co., Philadelphia, Pa., and London, England, 1952.
17. M. E. Lahey, C. J. Gubler, G. E. Cartwright, and M. M. Wintrobe, *J. Clin. Invest.*, **32**, 322–328 (1953).
18. Standley E. Kerr, *J. Biol. Chem.* **117**, 227–-235 (1937).
19. Robert G. Tucker and Ancel Keys, *J. Clin. Invest.*, **30**, 869–873 (1951).
20. David M. Kydd, Evelyn B. Man, and John P. Peters, *J. Clin. Invest.*, **29**, 1033–1040 (1950).
21. S. B. Barker, and M. J. Humphrey, *J. Clin. Endocrinol.*, **10**, 1136–1141 (1950).
22. T. S. Danowski, Shirley Hedenburg, and Jean H. Greenman, *J. Clin. Endocrinol.*, **9**, 768–773 (1949).
23. G. E. Cartwright, "Copper Metabolism in Human Subjects," in William

D. McElroy and Bentley Glass, eds., *Copper Metabolism,* Johns Hopkins Press, Baltimore, Md., 1950, pp. 274–314.
24. Clark W. Heath *et al., What People Are,* Harvard University Press, Cambridge, Mass., 1946.
25. F. William Sunderman and F. Boerner, *Normal Values in Clinical Medicine,* W. B. Saunders Co., Philadelphia, Pa. and London, England, 1949.
26. Abraham Saltzman, Wendell T. Caraway, and Irving A. Beck, *Metabolism, Clinical and Experimental,* 3, 11–15 (1954).
27. W. H. Fishman, M. Smith, D. B. Thompson, C. D. Bonner, S. C. Kasdon, and F. Homburger, *J. Clin. Invest.,* 30, 685 (1951).
28. Harold H. Scudamore, Louis J. Vorhaus, II., and Robert M. Kark, *J. Lab. Clin. Med.,* 37, 860–866 (1951).
29. E. Haworth and A. D. Macdonald, *J. Hyg.,* 37, 234–242 (1937).
30. Irvine H. Page, Esben Kirk, William H. Lewis, Jr., William R. Thompson, and Donald D. Van Slyke, *J. Biol. Chem.,* 111, 613–639 (1935).
31. Maurice T. Fliegelman, Charles F. Wilkinson, Jr., and Eugene A. Hand, *Arch. Dermatol. and Syphilol.,* 58, 409–429 (1948).
32. V. Posborg Petersen, *Scand. J. Clin. Lab. Invest.,* 2, 44–47 (1950).
33. E. S. Aleksintseva, *J. Physiol. U.S.S.R.,* 27, 132–138 (1939).
34. Philip K. Bondy, *J. Clin. Invest.,* 31, 231–237 (1952).
35. William N. Valentine, Morton Lee Pearce, and John S. Lawrence, *Blood,* 5, 623–647 (1950).
36. D. Eckert and G. Tötterman, *Scand. J. Clin. Lab. Invest.,* 2, 58–61 (1950).
37. William E. Ehrich, *Science,* 118, 603 (1953).
38. Charles F. Code, *Physiol. Revs.,* 32, 47–65 (1952).
39. Evelyn B. Man and Edwin F. Gildea, *J. Biol. Chem.,* 119, 769–780 (1937).
40. Warren M. Sperry, *J. Biol. Chem.,* 117, 394 (1937).
41. Irvine H. Page, Esben Kirk, William H. Lewis, Jr., William R. Thompson, and Donald D. Van Slyke, *J. Biol. Chem.,* 111, 638 (1935).
42. Harold A. Harper, Maxine E. Hutchin, and Joe R. Kimmel, *Proc. Soc. Exptl. Biol. Med.,* 80, 768–771 (1952).
43. Lilli Hofstatter, Philip G. Ackermann, and William B. Kountz, *J. Lab. Clin. Med.,* 36, 259–265 (1950).
44. P. Astrup and I. Munkvad, *Scand. J. Clin. Lab. Invest.,* 2, 133–137 (1950).
45. Helen Kirby Berry and Louise Cain, *Univ. Texas Publ.,* 5109, 71 (1951).
46. Harold W. Woodson, Stanley W. Hier, James D. Solomon, and Olaf Bergeim, *J. Biol. Chem.,* 172, 613–618 (1948).

47. Esben Kirk and Margaret Chieffi, *J. Nutrition*, **38**, 353–360 (1949).
48. Harold L. Rosenthal and Herbert P. Sarett, *J. Biol. Chem.*, **199**, 443–442 (1952).
49. P. N. Joshi and R. G. Desai, *Indian J. Med. Research*, **40**, 277–287 (1952).
50. B. Josephson and G. Dahlberg, *Scand. J. Clin. Lab. Invest.*, **4**, 216–236 (1952).
51. Irvine H. Page, Esben Kirk, William H. Lewis, Jr., William R. Thompson, and Donald D. Van Slyke, *J. Biol. Chem.*, **111**, 619–620 (1935).
52. Jozef Cohen and Donald P. Ogdon, *Science*, **110**, 532–533 (1949).
53. Helen Kirby Berry, *Univ. Texas Publ.*, **5109**, 157–164 (1951).
54. Ralph E. Bernstein, *J. Lab. Clin. Med.*, **40**, 707–717 (1952).
55. S. Munch-Petersen, *Scand. J. Clin. Lab. Invest.*, **2**, 335–336 (1950).
56. Samuel Dreizen, Henry A. Spies. Jr., and Tom D. Spies, *J. Dental Research*, **31**, 137–142 (1952).
57. Arnold E. Osterberg, Frances R. Vanzant, Walter C. Alvarez, and Andrew B. Rivers, *Am. J. Digestive Diseases*, **3**, 35–41 (1936).
58. Walter C. Alvarez, Frances R. Vanzant, and Arnold E. Osterberg, *Am. J. Digestive Diseases*, **3**, 162–164 (1936).
59. Frances R. Vanzant, Walter C. Alvarez, George B. Eusterman, Halbert L. Dunn, and Joseph Berkson, *Arch. Internal Med.*, **49**, 345–359 (1932).
60. J. Lerman, F. D. Pierce, and A. J. Brogan, *J. Clin. Invest.*, **11**, 155–165 (1932).
61. E. Rissel and F. Wewalka, *Klin. Wochschr.*, **30**, 1065–1069 (1952).
62. E. Rissel and F. Wewalka, *Klin. Wochschr.*, **30**, 1069–1073 (1952).
63. R. J. Williams, V. H. Cheldelin, and H. K. Mitchell, *Univ. Texas Publ.*, **4237**, 97-104 (1942).
64. Lucie Randoin and André Perroteau, *Lait*, **30**, 622–629 (1950).
65. R. A. Collins, A. E. Harper, M. Schreiber, and C. A. Elvehjem, *J. Nutrition*, **43**, 313–321 (1951).
66. Richard H. Follis, Jr., *J. Biol. Chem.*, **194**, 223–226 (1952).
67. Arild E. Hansen, *Am. J. Diseases Children*, **50**, 132–157 (1935).
68. Pauline Beery Mack, Personal Communication.
69. Pauline Beery Mack, Walter N. Brown, Jr., and Hughes Daniel Trapp, *Am. J. Roentgenol. Radium Therapy*, **61**, 808–825 (1949).
70. George V. Alexander, Ralph E. Nusbaum, and Norman S. MacDonald, *J. Biol. Chem.*, **192**, 489–496 (1951).
71. Teh H. Lee, Aaron Bunsen Lerner, and R. John Halberg, *J. Investigative Dermatol.*, **20**, 19–26 (1953).
72. Bertha Ottenstein, N. Boncoddo, A. Walker, and Francis M. Thurmon, *J. Investigative Dermatol.*, **19**, 105–108 (1952).

73. Thomas F. Dutcher and Stephen Rothman, *J. Investigative Dermatol.*, **17**, 65–68 (1951).
74. M. Lévy, M. Sapir, P. Walter, P. Vellay, and S. Mignon, *Bull. soc. chim. biol.*, **33**, 170–173 (1951).
75. A. H. Ennor and H. Rosenberg, *Biochem. J.*, **51**, 606–610 (1952).
76. Cecilie Leuchtenberger, Franz Schrader, David R. Weir, and Doreen P. Gentile, *Chromosoma*, **6**, 61–78 (1953).
77. E. M. Widdowson, R. A. McCance, and C. M. Spray, *Clin. Sci.*, **10**, 113–125 (1951).

V

Individual Enzymic Patterns

On the basis of the hypothesis already developed, it may be presumed that in the organs and tissues of every individual there will be found more or less distinctive enzymic patterns. This concept does not suggest that the *assortment* of enzymes present would actually be different and qualitatively distinctive for different individuals, but that for genetic reasons the efficiencies of the different enzymes and enzyme systems would vary from individual to individual.

In order to obtain comprehensive evidence bearing upon the question of this variation and the degree to which it is significant and important, it would be necessary to have extensive data regarding the enzymatic make-up of different individuals including that from repeated biopsy samples and autopsy material. A large part of the pertinent data which are at present available have to do with the enzymic composition of the blood.

Plasma Alkaline Phosphatase

In a recent study[1] of over 600 children and adults from birth to 27 years of age, Clark and Beck found that the levels for each individual are characteristic and tend to remain about the same year after year. They conclude that "a single sampling every year would, generally speaking, be sufficient to classify a child regarding plasma alkaline phosphatase activity." The over-all range in the tabulated data

77

for over 600 subjects was from 1.29 to 14.00 units. Although males and females differed somewhat in the progressive changes with age and the largest ranges were observed for the period 10–14 years, large ranges appeared in both boys and girls.

A number of other investigations corroborate the fact that alkaline phosphatase values exhibit wide variance from individual to individual.[2,3,4] In certain pathological conditions—Paget's disease, hyperparathyroidism, and obstructive jaundice—the values may rise to 10 or 50 times the average normal value.[2] In normal individuals the levels of alkaline phosphatase are not affected significantly by an 18-hour fast, a high protein meal, or a 40-hour period of very high fat intake.[5] In rickets the values are high and subside slowly but definitely when the condition is treated nutritionally.

We shall not go into the question of the existence of different alkaline phosphatases in the blood or their origin. From the standpoint of our discussion the conclusion is clear: Wide inter-individual differences exist with respect to this type of enzyme as it appears in the blood. On the basis of observations cited above, it is apparent that these inter-individual differences are significant in relation to metabolism and disease.

Acid Phosphatase of Blood

In one investigation Gutman and Gutman[2] found the range of acid phosphatase in 10 normal adults to be from 0.6 to 2.0 units. In certain diseased conditions the values were high, up to 5.0 in an advanced case of Paget's disease. The substrate used was monophenyl phosphate.

Using adenosine phosphate as the substrate at pH 4.8, Meister[6] found for 24 individuals a range of 0.20 to 0.66 units. These units, of course, are not the same as those in the previous citation.

In a third investigation, in which sodium-β-glycerophosphate was used as the substrate, Tuba, et al.,[3] have found both the spring and fall acid phosphatase values for adults to vary through the same range, 0.0 to 1.2 units. For children, boys and girls alike, the range was 0.0 to 1.6 units. No attention was paid to inter-individual differences.

Acid phosphatase is widely distributed in tissues. Male prostate glands[7] are extraordinarily rich, and this enzyme is implicated in the physiology of sex. Men excrete in the urine about 3.5 times as much acid phosphatase as women.[8] The prostate glands of individual well men vary in acid phosphatase content per unit weight through at least a 4-fold range.

Blood Arginase

The amount of arginase in blood has been studied in enough different individuals and with enough samples to demonstrate that activity of this enzyme in erythrocytes varies widely from individual to individual, but is, to quote Clark and Beck, "remarkably constant for a given individual."[9] The range found in a group of about 200 normal children was from 2.0 to 8.4 units per 100 ml. of blood. When a group of 81 children was tested twice in consecutive years, the one who had the lowest value (2.5) the first year exhibited the lowest value the second year (2.0). The individual child who exhibited the highest value the second year (7.6) also showed a correspondingly high value (7.1) the first year. There were individual children who showed substantial variation, the maximum being that of a child who exhibited a value of 3.0 one year and 6.5 the next, but most children did not vary more than a half unit.

In the case of this enzyme there is a highly significant, though not large, sex difference (of the order of 10 to 20 per cent) which appears even before pubescence. Females tend to have higher arginase values. Adult values are substantially like those for children. There is no significant change during pregnancy. We have found no reports indicating that elderly people have been studied specifically in this connection.

Cholinesterase in Blood

Sawitsky, et al.,[10] have shown that the cholinesterase activity of corpuscles in 15 normal individuals varied through a range of 7.25 to 10.34 units per ml. and of the plasma from 1.5 to 5.0 units per ml., but that for a given individual the values were relatively constant. The relative constancy of intra-individual values and the variation between individuals have been confirmed by other investigators.[11] Females show more variation than males, but otherwise there is no significant sex difference. Age appears not to be an important factor. A logical assumption is that the variation is a reflection of genetic differences.

Hall and Lucas[12] found a variation of 2.7 to 7.24 units of cholinesterase in the blood serum of 25 normal human individuals. Variations between different samples from the same individual were small.[13] They also found similar inter-individual differences in other species— horses, dogs, guinea pigs, cats, rabbits, and chickens. Interspecies differences were apparent as well; the range for cats, for example, was from 1.84 to 2.80 units, whereas for rabbits it was 0.35 to 0.70 units. More recently Mann, *et al.*,[14] found more than a 3-fold range in cholinesterase in the serum of normal humans and practically a 10-fold range when patients with hepatic cirrhosis were included. In viral hepatitis the cholinesterase decreases with the onset and increases with convalescence. De la Huerga, *et al.*,[15] using a colorimetric method, found an inter-individual range of 130.0 to 310.0 micromoles per 1 ml. per hour for 132 normal individuals. Serial determinations in 20 normal persons over a period of 1 month did not show any significant variation in serum cholinesterase activity.

The sum total of the observations is in line with the supposition that genetic factors are highly important in determining the activity of this enzyme in the bloods of different individuals and that the level has physiological significance.

Serum Amylase

The activity of this enzyme was found to vary in "healthy normal" subjects from 40 to 179 units per 100 ml. of serum.[16] In "normal" hospitalized patients the variation was from 10 to 500 units per 100 ml. Regarding the constancy in a given individual, Somogyi says that "if the normal level for a given person is known, even moderate changes are significant, for the diastase content of the blood in any healthy person is maintained at a fairly constant level."

Among medical technologists the normal limits, using an iodometric method, are considered to be from 0 to 320 units. In a series of 23 individuals the range was from less than 80 up to 1070. Five of these individuals were judged to be abnormal, and one was considered borderline. Two cases of acute pancreatitis yielded values on admission of 1600 and 3200 units, respectively.[17]

The level of this enzyme is practically unchanged from childhood to adulthood; there are apparently no sex differences, and the level is not affected by the amount or type of food, by fasting, diuresis, dehydration, exercise, or sleep. This enzyme, therefore, constitutes another example in which variations between individuals are large (up to 50-fold including a hospital population), but those exhibited by a single individual are small. Since high serum amylase levels appear to be associated with pancreatic impairment,[18] there is ample reason to suppose that differences have a functional signficance.

Plasma Catalase

Study of plasma catalase activity on an individual basis has been limited in scope. For 50 adults the range was found to be from 4.2 to 9.5 per ml. of plasma.[19] One of the normal individuals was studied for five days, and the following values were obtained: 9.5, 8.5, 9.5, 7.0, 9.5. Further study is required before one could conclude definitely that there are significant inter-individual differences. The available evidence points in that direction. In various anemias the values may be 50 or more. In one "diagnostic problem case" the value was 42. It seems highly probable that "normal" differences have physiological significance.

Serum Phenolsulfatase

The activity of this enzyme in the serums of 24 different individuals[20] varied from 0.3 to 15.5 units per ml. No study has been made of the constancy of the value for specific individuals. The wide range noted above is accompanied by a correspondingly wide range in excretion values: 0.9 to 19.7 units per ml. of urine.

Serum Lipase

The range of values for this enzyme corresponds to 0.0 to 1.5 ml. $N/20$ sodium hydroxide required to neutralize the fat acids released by 1 ml. of serum under controlled conditions.[18] Since 0.05 ml. of $N/20$ sodium hydroxide solution should be easily detectable, this corresponds to at least a 30-fold range and is in line with the large range in the blood lipids which is known to be inter-individual (p. 58). Because of lack of interest in the question, apparently no investigation has been made regarding the constancy or lack of constancy of the lipases in the blood of specific individuals.

Peptidases of Human Erythrocytes

Using four different peptides as substrates, Adams, *et al.*,[21] found for 10 normal individuals the following ranges in activity (proteolytic coefficient $\times 10^4$).

Substrate	Range
Glycyl-L-proline	13–23
L-Leucinamide	2–12
Glycylglycine	2–12
Triglycine	6–19

These ranges, which average over 4-fold, have not been investigated for intra-individual constancy.

Aldolase in Blood

The aldolase activity of human serum has been investigated and found to range slightly over 2-fold in 68 normals and up to 10-fold if diseased individuals are included.[22] No special attention has been paid to the constancy of the values for specific individuals. The tissues of laboratory rats show on the average a little less than a 2-fold variation from animal to animal.

Dehydropeptidase

Meister and Greenstein[23] found the mean activity of 22 normal serums to be 3.59 ± 0.84 units per ml. Albritton and co-workers have calculated that the normal range is from 191 to 527 units per 100 ml.[24] The question of the constancy of the values for specific individuals has not been studied.

Vitamin B_c Conjugase

Wolff and co-workers[25] found this enzyme activity in plasma to vary over a 3-fold range in an unspecified number of normal cases. From 0.5 to 1.5 µg. of folic acid per ml. of plasma was liberated under specified conditions in 90 minutes. In asystolic patients the corresponding values were from 0.2 to 0.7 µg.

β-Glucuronidase in Blood

The β-glucuronidase activity of human blood has been studied by Fishman and co-workers.[26] The range in 230 normals was found to be from 41 to 1285 units per 100 ml. of serum. In the diseased subjects studied, the minimum values tended to be higher and the maximum values were up to 2340 units.

The β-glucuronidase levels in normal healthy individuals are rather constant. Differences in glucuroic acid metabolism were observed which undoubtedly were connected in some way with the enzyme activity of the blood.

In mice there are large strain differences in tissue content of glucuronidase which must be genetically determined. In the livers of male white mice Fishman[27] found that in Swiss mice the β-glucuronidase activity was about 12 times as great as in C3H mice. Cohen and Bittner[28] found in 13 strains of mice a variation from 4 units per mg. of tissue nitrogen for C3H mice up to 125 units per mg. of tissue nitrogen for AX strains. This 30-fold difference between strains of mice suggests that the investigation of a human population would show substantial genetic differences between individuals with respect to the β-glucuronidase activity of their tissues.

Enzymes in Digestive Juices

In the previous chapter we have given some data on the wide variation of the pepsin content of samples of gastric juices from different individuals. Limited information is available with respect to the enzyme content of other digestive juices. Berkman[29] has reported that for small children the enterokinase content of the intestinal juice varies from 130 to 670 units per ml. and the phosphatase from 4 to 83 units. This investigator, like most others, was not interested particularly in the subject of variation but was concerned with establishing norms. It would appear that the gastric juice (p. 65) is not unique in exhibiting extreme variations in its enzyme content.

ENZYMES IN TISSUES

For obvious reasons the data on the amount of enzymes in human tissues and their constancy in the tissues of individuals are limited.

Some pertinent data are available, however, having to do both with human and animal material.

Arginase Activity of the Skin

It has been previously noted that the arginase activity of human blood corpuscles varies over at least a 4-fold range and that the values are highly characteristic of the individuals. The arginase activity of the skin of 8 individuals (surgical female breast samples)[30] was determined and found to vary from 202 to 562 units. The range, of course, would be expected to be wider if the number of individuals had been larger. It would be interesting to know whether the concentrations of the enzyme in blood and skin run parallel, but, of course, this has not been determined.

Carbonic Anhydrase Activity of Human Aorta Tissue

Segments of human aorta obtained fresh at autopsy were freed from blood and covering connective tissue and analyzed manometrically for carbonic anhydrase activity. Twelve specimens from 7 males and 5 females yielded nearly a 9-fold spread in values (0.12 to 1.05 units).[31] This is interesting in view of the zinc content of carbonic anhydrase and the extremely wide variations in the zinc content of blood plasma and spleens which have been observed (pp. 55 and 72).

ATPase Activity in the Vascular System (Dogs)

Carr and co-workers[32] have found that the ATPase activity of arterial tissue in dogs varied as indicated in Table 12.

It should be noted that these ranges might be wider if the number of individual animals were larger. It is interesting that venous tissue showed no ATPase activity. It may be pointed out that for the purpose of studying variability, dogs which are available for laboratory study are more suitable than inbred rats because, like humans, they usually have a mixed ancestry.

Enzymes Involved in Utilization of D-Phenylalanine

Albanese and co-workers[33] have carried out a series of investigations on the utilization of D-amino acids by humans. In the investigation of the utilization of D-phenylalanine, individual differences appeared which were so striking as to call for special attention. Vari-

Table 12.
ATPase in Arterial Tissues

Tissue	Number of Animals	Range	High/Low
Aorta	21	7 –16.5	2.3
Carotid	21	1.5– 8.5	5.7
Coronary	32	1 – 8.1	8.1
Renal	19	2 – 7.7	3.8
Femoral	20	1 – 7.3	7.3

From C. Jeleff Carr, Frederick K. Bell, and John C. Krantz, Jr., *Proc. Soc. Exp. Biol. and Med.,* **80,** 324 (1952).

ability was observed throughout the study; this was taken as a matter of course, but in the case of this amino acid the range of utilization was extraordinarily wide and relatively constant for the individuals, as is shown in Table 13. One of the four individuals was an infant, and the test was made only once.

Table 13.
Utilization of D-Phenylalanine

		Per Cent Utilized
L, ♀, 6 kg.	in 3 tests	90.1, 93.9, 98.8
C, ♂, 6 kg.	in 1 test	60.9
I, ♀, 60 kg.	in 2 tests	34.4, 28.0
A, ♂, 70 kg.	in 3 tests	7.5, 1.2, 1.6

Just what enzyme or enzymes are involved in these differences is not obvious, but it is clear that marked inter-individual differences (presumably genetic in origin) exist with respect to them. Here we see also a distinct gradation in the utilization figures which seem to bear out the principle of genetic gradients referred to earlier (p. 13).

The fact that enzymes necessary to bring about the oxidation of L-phenylalanine were absent in the livers of two phenylpyruvics and were present in three controls[34] has been demonstrated, but there is inadequate evidence as to a wide gradation of enzyme efficiencies with respect to this metabolic step. The condition involving phenyl-pyruvic acid excretion is, of course, known to be genetically controlled.

Pyruvate Metabolism in Different Strains of Rats

Anker,[35] using isotope tracer technique, found in a mixed laboratory strain of rats (Wistar) no significant conversion of pyruvic acid to acetic acid. This was in contrast to the results obtained with the Sprague-Dawley strain of rats in which either such a conversion did take place or else pyruvic acid was utilized directly for acetylation. Exactly what constitutes the enzymic difference between the two strains is not known, but it is clear that a striking and potentially important difference exists. From the genetic standpoint one should not expect precisely the same metabolic results from rats of different strains or even from individual rats within the same strain, but the difference here reported is perhaps more fundamental than one might anticipate. If this difference is real, presumably other differences exist which have not been looked for, and one should be extremely careful about accepting the results from one strain as applicable to another.

Summary

The cumulative evidence that each individual human being has a distinctive pattern of enzyme efficiences is hard to refute on any rational basis. Furthermore, inter-individual variations in enzyme efficiencies in normal individuals, insofar as they have been determined, are not of the order of 20 to 50 per cent, but are more often at least 3- or 4-fold. Differences of 10- to 50-fold (!) have been observed in a substantial number of cases even when the number of normal individuals tested was small.

Certainly these differences are far from trivial. Even to the author, who has been interested in variability for some years, the extent of the variability comes as a surprise. He, therefore, cannot blame his colleagues if they seem incredulous. We have included in our discussion every enzyme for which we have found substantial data, and the least inter-individual variation we know of appears to be about 2-fold.

Inter-individual differences related to metabolism come to light only when *detailed items* are compared. When two individuals of the same height and weight yield total metabolism values that are about the same, it is easy to conclude that their metabolisms are substantially identical. The evidence presented in this chapter, however, indicates that the details of metabolism in two such individuals may be very different indeed. The extent to which specific reactions may take place may vary 10-fold! This idea is admittedly difficult to accept, but it appears to be substantiated by concrete and cumulative evidence.

REFERENCES

1. Leland C. Clark, Jr., and Elizabeth Beck, *J. Pedia.*, **36**, 335–341 (1950).
2. Alexander B. Gutman and Ethel Benedict Gutman, *Proc. Soc. Exptl. Biol. Med.*, **38**, 470–473 (1938).
3. Jules Tuba, Max M. Cantor, and Herman Siemens, *J. Lab. Clin. Med.*, **32**, 194–195 (1947).
4. J. R. McKerrow, R. E. Lau and E. W. McHenry, *Can. J. Pub. Health*, **41**, 322–326 (1950).
5. Otto A. Bessey, Oliver H. Lowry, and Mary Jane Brock, *J. Biol. Chem.*, **164**, 321–329 (1946).
6. Alton Meister, *J. Clin. Invest.*, **27**, 263–271 (1948).
7. Alexander B. Gutman and Ethel Benedict Gutman, *Proc. Soc. Exptl. Biol. Med.*, **39**, 529–534 (1938).
8. Leland C. Clark, Jr., Elizabeth Beck, and Haskell Thompson, *J. Clin. Endocrinol.*, **11**, 84–90 (1951).
9. Leland C. Clark, Jr., and Elizabeth I. Beck, *J. Applied Physiol.*, **2**, 343–347 (1949).
10. Arthur Sawitsky, Howard M. Fitch, and Leo M. Meyer, *J. Lab. Clin. Med.*, **33**, 203–206 (1948).
11. Leland C. Clark, Jr., and Elizabeth Beck, *Child Development*, **21**, 163–167 (1950).
12. G. E. Hall and C. C. Lucas, *J. Pharmacol. and Exptl. Therap.*, **61**, 10–20 (1937).
13. G. E. Hall and C. C. Lucas, *J. Pharmacol. and Exptl. Therap.*, **59**, 34–42 (1937).
14. Joseph D. Mann, William I. Mandel, Peter L. Eichman, Marjorie A. Knowlton, and Victor M. Sborov, *J. Lab. Clin. Med.*, **39**, 543–549 (1952).

15. J. de la Huerga, Charlotte Yesinick, and Hans Popper, *Tech. Bull. of the Registry of Med. Technologists*, **22**, 248–255 (1952).
16. Michael Somogyi, *Arch. Internal Med.*, **67**, 665–679 (1941).
17. Mildred Rose Tolluto, *Am. J. Med. Technol.*, **20**, 69–75 (1954).
18. Mandred W. Comfort and Arnold E. Osterberg, *Med Clinics N. Amer.*, **24**, 1137–1149 (1940).
19. Roger S. Dille and Charles H. Watkins, *J. Lab. Clin. Med.*, **33**, 480–486 (1948).
20. Charles Huggins and Dwight Raymond Smith, *J. Biol. Chem.*, **170**, 391–398 (1947).
21. Elijah Adams, Mary McFadden, and Emil L. Smith, *J. Biol. Chem.*, **198**, 663–670 (1952).
22. John A. Sibley and Albert L. Lehninger, *J. Natl. Cancer Inst.*, **9**, 303–309 (1949).
23. Alton Meister and Jesse P. Greenstein, *J. Natl. Cancer Inst.*, **8**, 169–171 (1948).
24. Errett C. Albritton, ed., *Standard Values in Blood*, W. B. Saunders Co., Philadelphia, Pa., and London, England, 1952.
25. R. Wolff, L. Drouet, and R. Karlin, *Science*, **109**, 612–613 (1949).
26. W. H. Fishman, M. Smith, D. B. Thompson, C. D. Bonner, S. C. Kasdon, and F. Homburger, *J. Clin. Invest.*, **30**, 685 (1951).
27. William H. Fishman, *Ann. N. Y. Acad. Sci.*, **54**, 548–557 (1951).
28. Saul L. Cohen and John J. Bittner, *Cancer Research*, **11**, 723–726 (1951).
29. E. N. Berkman, *Pediatriya*, **5**, 31–34 (1951).
30. Eugene J. Van Scott, *J. Investigative Dermatol.*, **17**, 21–26 (1951).
31. John Esben Kirk and Per From Hansen, *J. Gerontol.*, **8**, 150–157 (1953).
32. C. Jelleff Carr, Frederick K. Bell, and John C. Krantz, Jr., *Proc. Soc. Exptl. Biol. Med.*, **80**, 323–325 (1952).
33. Anthony A. Albanese, Virginia Irby, and Marilyn Lein, *J. Biol. Chem.*, **170**, 731–737 (1947).
34. George A. Jervis, *Proc. Soc. Exptl. Biol. Med.*, **82**, 514–515 (1953).
35. H. S. Anker, *J. Biol. Chem.*, **176**, 1337–1352 (1948).

VI

Endocrine Activities

If the general hypothesis developed in the first chapters of this book is valid, we would presume that each human individual has, for basic genetic reasons, a distinctive pattern with respect to his various endocrine glands and their interrelationships. The *existence* of such patterns involving the gross and microscopic anatomy and physiology of each gland can hardly be questioned. *How different* individual patterns may be is another question; it has often been assumed that in normal individuals these differences are relatively inconsequential. The material to be presented in this chapter has to do with the validity of this assumption.

Stockard's extensive but unfortunately uncompleted studies on *The Genetic and Endocrine Basis for Differences in Form and Behavior*[1] indicate clearly that different breeds of dogs have characteristically different sizes of thyroids, pituitaries, etc., and that these endocrine differences are transmitted to offspring and are related to behavioral differences. In dealing with large numbers of dogs of 12 different pure breeds and their hybrids, he observed tremendous variations in temperament which were in no way related to early handling. Some dogs were observed which from puppyhood were untrainable. In addition to the interbreed variations in size of endocrines, there were substantial intrabreed variations, which fact presumably is related to the high degree of individuality often exhibited by dogs even of the same breed. The anatomical findings with the dogs are in line with the variations in the weights of endocrine glands of rabbits already mentioned (p. 20).

Riddle's extensive study (p. 21) which included numerous breeding experiments showed clearly that the endocrines, as well as other anatomical features, of pigeons and doves showed wide inter-individual and interstrain differences.

Despite the numerous advances that have been made in endocrinology, we are not in a position to discuss human endocrine *patterns* intelligently because such individual patterns have never been studied. Our scientific way of doing things involves studying a group of individuals from one standpoint, another group from another standpoint, etc., but we almost never study the same individuals from many standpoints. The tools necessary for studying individual endocrine patterns are likewise not simple nor are they well developed at the present time.

We may, however, gain some insight into how much potential significance endocrine patterns have, by considering the magnitude of the variations related to endocrine function which commonly occur. Whether or not endocrine patterns are important will hinge on the question of the extent of the inter-individual variation in specific hormonal activities which exists among so-called normal people. If these differences involve only minor variations from a norm, then quite possibly they are insignificant.

Variations Related to the Thyroid Gland

Anatomically, normal thyroid glands are said to vary in weight from 8 to 50 gm.,[2] and the shapes are extremely variable. Often there are two distinct glands connected by an isthmus; in other cases the whole structure is relatively compact. So-called aberrant thyroid tissue is sometimes found in interrupted masses along the path of the thyroglossal duct or in the thoracic cavity; sometimes it is present in the ovaries. In 3 out of about 20,000 cases, the thyroid was found to be located at the base of the tongue.[3] In "normal" cases the thyroids have a blood supply from three to five arteries. "Misplaced" thyroid tissue produces thyroid hormone just as does thyroid tissue in its more usual location. Sometimes individuals are born virtually without thyroid glands (cretins). In animals as well as humans there is wide inherited variation with respect to the thyroid glands. In rabbits we have already noted a 25-fold range. In Stockard's study on dogs[1] the milligrams of thyroid gland per kilograms of body weight varied in different animals from about 50 to nearly 1000, approximately a 20-fold range. In the P.V.G. strain of mice (Glaxo Laboratories), for example, about 5 per cent of the animals have only one thyroid gland.[4] Riddle (p. 21) made extensive genetic studies which showed that different strains of doves differ markedly in the size of their thyroid glands. Different strains of white Leghorn chicks were found to exhibit a 4-fold difference in their response to thyreotropic hormone.[5]

Although the *size* of the thyroid gland is only one factor and there is no assurance that the largest thyroid glands are always the most active, a study of thyroid function in humans by means of metabolic rates, by the amounts of protein-bound iodine in the serum (p. 56), and by the retention of administered radioactive iodine[6,7] shows that a wide variation in thyroid activity exists among "normal" human beings. We have earlier indicated (p. 56) that in a population of about 400 well individuals the variation in protein-bound iodine was from 2.5 µg. to 11.5 µg. per cent and relatively constant for each individual. In unwell individuals, including many who had known thyroid difficulties, the variation was from 0 to 48.2 µg. per cent.

Evidence of a different sort also indicates wide variability with respect to thyroid function. In endemic areas not all of the individuals exhibit endemic goiters, only *certain* individuals. These, it would be assumed, are individuals who for some reason connected with the production of thyroid hormone need more iodine than their fellows. Similarly, it may be noted that in areas where sea food is abundantly used and iodine is therefore relatively plentiful, there are still some individuals who develop simple goiter.

In another factor related to the thyroid gland, wide variation has been observed with respect to the thyroid-stimulating hormone (TSH) of the pituitary. D'Angelo[8] and co-workers, using tadpoles as a tool, have studied the thyroid and TSH activity of the serums of normal and diseased individuals. Both limb growth (metamorphosis) induced by thyroid hormone and the development of thyroid tissue induced by TSH were measured.

Normal individuals were found to range in TSH activity from 0.000 to 0.001 Junkmann-Schoeller units per ml. of serum. In cases of "pituitary dysfunction" the range was 0.003 to 0.005, in hypothyroid cases from 0.000 to 0.005, in hyperthyroid cases 0.000 to 0.002, and in cases of exophthalmus 0.000 to 0.005 Junkmann-Schoeller units per ml. It is not clear just how sensitive the method is and how little TSH activity can be detected, but it would appear that the range may be 10-fold among "normals" and 50-fold if others are included. It is interesting that the authors state: "Rarely, however, have both the thyroid and TSH levels been determined in the blood of the same individual."[9] This corroborates our earlier reference to the fact that endocrine patterns have not been investigated. It is also interesting to note that the findings of these authors indicate that the thyroid activity and the TSH activity of the blood vary somewhat independently. For example, in 10 cases of hypothyroidism the thyroid activity of the blood was low, but the TSH values varied widely—0.000 to 0.005. In 10 hyperthyroid cases, the thyroid hormone levels were high but the TSH levels showed a "normal" variation. It appears, therefore, that high thyroid activity may be promoted in some cases by high TSH activity, but that in other cases the thyroids are active without outside stimulation of a high order. Likewise, it would seem plausible to suppose that low thyroid activity is due in some cases to deficiencies in the thyroid gland itself, but that in other cases the thyroid glands are ample and would function satisfactorily were it not for a deficiency of TSH.

Evidence for variability in thyroid function as observed in different species of animals is suggestive. The fact that thyroidectomized dogs can utilize diiodotyrosine in lieu of the thyroid hormone indicates that species differ with respect to the means of building the hormone or the form in which it can be utilized, presumably as a catalyst. Another striking observation is that rhesus monkeys appear to exhibit *no deficiency symptoms* when their thyroid glands are removed;[10] these monkeys evidently either have little or no need for the thyroid hormone or are able to produce it outside the thyroid gland. In view of the wide occurrence of "aberrant" thyroid tissue in humans, one might suspect that the latter possibility might account for the observation. In any case, however, it appears that the need for the hormone on the part of rhesus monkeys must be unusually low. This, of course, could be due to the utilization by the monkeys of metabolic pathways which avoid the need for thyroid hormone. In Stockard's study of dogs,[1] some were found which did not respond in the usual manner to thyroidectomy.

Such observations as these should inject caution into those who speak glibly about what metabolism is like in *the* mammalian organism. Furthermore, if differences such as these exist among different species of higher mammals, it lends credence to the idea that, *within* the human species, quantitative differences of a similar nature may exist. Because of differences in enzyme systems and the extent to which different metabolic pathways are utilized in different individuals, it is not at all unreasonable to conclude that different individuals probably have fundamental needs for quite different levels of the thyroid hormone.

Variations Related to the Parathyroids

The variation in the anatomy of the parathyroid glands is well illustrated by the fact that, although the standard (normal?) number of glands for human beings is 4, there may be anywhere from 2 to 12.[2] The positions are also highly variable. One investigator found among 25 cadavers only 6 which had 4 glands. Other anatomists estimate that about one-half the population have four. It seems probable to the writer that the number may be found to vary from one population to another, depending on ethnic origin. The total weight of the glands is said to vary in individuals from about 50 to 300 mg.

The parathyroid hormone content of blood has not been studied sufficiently to yield any data with regard to variation. The functioning of the glands is so closely related to other factors which regulate calcium and phosphorus metabolism that it is impossible to assign differences in these areas to variation in parathyroid function. The variation of the calcium (and phosphorus) in the blood has been noted (p. 55), and this variation, of course, may be due in a substantial degree to differences in parathyroid functioning.

One of the reasons for suspecting that variations in parathyroid functioning are great is the fact that experimental animals have striking individual sensitivity to administered hormone. This fact has been noted particularly in dogs which have been used for assay animals. Also, in one study involving humans it was found that four normal individuals had their phosphate clearance increased 60 per cent, 190 per cent, 150 per cent, and 110 per cent, respectively, when 200 units of the hormone was administered intravenously, while two individuals who had previously undergone thyroidectomy and were known to be hypothyroid showed corresponding increases of 430 per cent and 400 per cent.[11] The fact that thyroidectomy may interfere with parathyroid functioning needs to be taken into account in interpreting these results.

The effects of gland extirpation in different species of animals are worthy of note.[12] In dogs from 0 to 5 per cent survive, in cats 20 to 50 per cent, in rabbits 67 to 97 per cent. The fact that some dogs survive, while most do not, suggests that in the surviving animals the metabolic machinery involving calcium is such that only minimal amounts of the hormone, if any, are needed. The failure to survive on the part of some of the rabbits suggests that these particular animals needed larger amounts of the hormone than did most of the rabbits tested.

Both hypo- and hyperparathyroidism have been observed in human beings, and, if the principle of genetic gradients (p. 13) is valid, various intermediate levels of hormone activity will be found in the general population. Although the data on the subject, with the exception of that concerning anatomy, are not definitive, there would seem to be little doubt as to the existence of several-fold variation in the parathyroid activities of "normal" individuals.

Variations with Respect to Insulin

Insulin production takes place in the islet tissue of the pancreas, and the individual variation in the amount of this tissue is large. It is estimated that a substantial percentage of the pancreases in a population (78 per cent in one study)[13] have from 0.9 to 3.5 per cent of islet tissue. Those individuals having less than 0.9 per cent are likely to be diabetics, and those having more than 3.5 per cent are likely to be actual or potential sufferers from hyperinsulinism.[14]

Obviously the percentage of the islet tissue would be only one factor; the total size of the pancreas might be another (65 to 160 gm.) and the specific activity of the islet tissue another. The total number of islets constitutes a possible measure of the ability to produce insulin. This number is estimated to vary normally from 200,000 to 2,500,000.[15]

That the islet tissue is not uniform in its make-up and hence may show variation in its ability to produce insulin is indicated by the varying percentages of the three types of cells: A cells, 10 to 40 per cent; B cells, 60 to 90 per cent; D cells, 2 to 8 per cent.

The obvious interpretation of these facts is that, although every individual is born with the anatomical and physiological machinery for producing insulin, the potential rates of production probably vary through a 10-fold or greater range. In some diabetics, for instance, the insulin-producing capacity becomes a limiting factor early in life; in others the machinery may limp along, and diabetes may not appear until the individuals become adults; in still others the individuals may be nondiabetic through middle age only to have the deficiency show up when the aging process is well along. Some individuals probably have throughout life the capacity for producing just about the right amount of insulin; in others the tendency may be to produce too much with a resulting hyperinsulinism which may be mild or severe. The existence of this enormous gradation in the capability for producing insulin—which may, of course, be modified by various environmental influences and particularly by aging—seems to square with all the known facts. The fact that some chronically thin people have been successfully treated with insulin so that they have gained weight (fat deposits) suggests that these individuals may tend to be deficient in insulin production. It is well known, however, that obesity and diabetes are often associated with each other, and this association is in line with the conclusion that diabetes may have several etiologies depending upon the endocrine pattern of the individual who becomes afflicted.

This discussion should not imply that the problem of diabetes revolves wholly around the ability to produce insulin. There is evidence that such other organs of the body as the pituitary, the thyroids, the adrenals, and the liver all have their effects on carbohydrate metabolism and influence the prevention, onset, and progress of diabetes. A clear-cut case is that of the pituitary gland, which was shown to be concerned initially by Houssay and Biasotti.[16] When the supply of the carbohydrate metabolism hormone of the pituitary is cut off by hypophysectomy, depancreatized dogs are greatly relieved with respect to their diabetic condition. Injecting them with pituitary extracts may bring back the diabetes. It is clear that the two hormones are opposing each other. If the pituitary hormone activity is decreased, less insulin is needed; if the supply of the pituitary hormone

Table 14.
Blood Sugar Levels after Pancreatectomy

	Number of Animals	Survival, Days	Blood Glucose, mg. per cent
Dogs	4	10	310–345
Cats	10	5	212–788
Pigs	5	9	30–232
Goats	4	up to 44	58–194
Ducks	12	41–163	100–200
Monkeys	12	7–305	14–410

From Cyril Norman Hugh Long, "Diabetes Mellitus—Etiology," in Garfield G. Duncan, ed., *Diseases of Metabolism*, W. B. Saunders Co., Philadelphia, Pa., and London, England, 1943, p. 713.

is augmented, the insulin supply must be increased, too. This balance appears to be very real, regardless of exactly how one wishes to interpret it.

Theoretically, diabetes could be as readily caused by overproduction of the pituitary hormone as by the underproduction of insulin. Actually both activities probably vary greatly, and the diabetes results from an imbalance. Even when diabetes has its origin in an overactivity of the pituitary in producing the diabetogenic hormone, insulin may still be an effective remedy. Actually, of course, diabetes is sometimes insulin-resistant, which fact reveals that the disease does not always have the same origin.

There is not room here to discuss the complex problems and complications involved in diabetes. We are limiting our discussion largely to the question of insulin production without attempting to discuss fully its exact role in diabetes. There are a number of environmental factors including nutrition which influence the disease. Exercise, for example, lessens one's insulin requirement.

In keeping with the variability which we have noted in human beings, there is in animals wide interspecies and intraspecies variability in relation to insulin. When the supply of insulin was cut off by removal of the pancreas, the blood sugar levels listed in Table 14 were found in different animals of different species.[17]

The most striking intraspecies variation in blood levels observed

(29-fold) is that between different monkeys. Unless other unknown factors seriously complicate the interpretation, it appears that some monkeys require vastly different amounts of insulin than others. This might be due to differences in pituitaries, thyroids, or adrenals, etc. That the endocrine patterns of rhesus monkeys differ greatly from those in humans is shown by the fact that their thyroids can be removed without inducing observable evidence of thyroid deficiency (p. 92).

Variation with Respect to Estrogens

To discuss the numerous facets of the physiology of sex would be far too space-consuming for the purposes of this book. We shall therefore limit ourselves to relatively simple and measurable phases of the subject on the supposition that variability similar to what we find in such investigations probably also exists with respect to other aspects of the broad subject.

The principal source of estrogens in females is thought to be the ovaries. Anatomically these vary greatly in size in "normal" individuals,[2] weighing from 2 to 10 gm. At birth they have been estimated to contain from 30,000 to 400,000 ova.[2] During embryological development the original bisexual gland is female in the cortex and male in the medulla. When an ovary develops from the bisexual gland, the cortex becomes dominant, and the medulla subordinate. The opposite happens when a testis develops from the bisexual gland. Presumably ovaries, in addition to varying in size, also vary in the proportions of cortex and medulla, but this has apparently not been studied.

In view of the wide variation in the weight of ovaries and the number of ova present, one would suppose that the amount of estrogens produced by the glands of different individuals would vary greatly. On this matter we have little satisfactory information. No information is available as to the range of concentration of estrogens in the blood of normal women and only a little with respect to the urinary excretion. Gallagher and co-workers[18] found wide daily variations in estrogen excretion in both men and women. In women there was little excreted during menses and much more between periods of menses. The over-all variation among the women (4 subjects) was from 18 to 36 µg. of theelin per day as determined by biological tests. In men (4 subjects) the variation was less, 9 to 12 µg. per day.

Reifenstein and Dempsey[19] using Talbot's colorimetric method found the urinary "estrone" to vary from 10 to 39 µg. per day in 5 normal women and from 27 to 40 µg. per day for 5 normal men. Attention was not paid to the question of whether the observed differences were primarily inter-individual. In another study[20] involving 3 men and 2 women, Pincus found about a 12-fold variation between the two women. One woman excreted over a period of several days estradiol + estrone + estriol to the extent of 155.2 µg. per day; for the other woman and the 3 men, the corresponding values were respectively 13.4 µg., 12.4 µg., 7.6 µg and 16.8 µg.

Clearly not enough cases have been studied individually to establish a range of excretion for normal populations of either males or females. On the basis of the rather unsatisfactory excretion data coupled with the incontrovertible anatomical differences, it appears very likely that the estrogen output of the ovaries of different individuals varies through a wide range. Estrogens excreted by males may be presumed to arise in the cortex (female portion) of the testis, though this fact has not been demonstrated. It is interesting that stallion urine has been reported to be a very rich source of estrogens, though some investigators have not found it to be. On the face of it, it would appear that individual stallions probably differ greatly in this regard. The ranges observed for men would probably be greatly increased if a larger number of cases were examined, and it could easily be that extremely wide ranges would be found if looked for. This probability seems even more likely in the light of the enormous variations in sexual activity observed in men by Kinsey and his co-workers.[21]

Variations Related to Androgens

In males the androgens arise predominantly from the testes which are said to vary from 10 to 45 gm. in weight.[2] Actually eunuchoid individuals may have testes weighing as little as 1 or even ½ gm. for the pair. In this case as well as many others the dividing line between normal and abnormal is difficult to draw. No dependable data are available as to the inter-individual ranges of concentration of androgens in human blood. Urinary excretion has been studied, however, and ranges for normal men have been reported up to 11-fold, i.e., 20 to 225 I.U. of androgens per day. That this difference is wholly inter-individual has not been adequately established.[22]

In a study in which individual urinary components were determined and repeated samples from the same individuals analyzed, Dobriner and co-workers[23] found that the androsterone excretion in twenty normal males 21 to 76 years of age varied from 0.2 to 7.0 mg. per day, a 35-fold range. Age was a factor in contributing to the wideness of this range, since older individuals tended to excrete less, but each individual's androsterone excretion was distinctive, and large differences which were truly inter-individual were observed. One man of 72 excreted, for example, more than twice as much as one who was 21 years old. This study will be referred to further in a later discussion (p. 101).

Ovaries contain and produce androgens also. It is interesting that androgen excretion in preschool boys and girls is at very low levels, but that in both sexes at 7 or 8 years of age there is a marked rise at about the same rate and to the same levels, on the average. For adult women the amounts of androgens excreted appear to vary through wide limits. Dorfman[24] cites four ranges by different investigators: 20 to 68, 22 to 85, 2 to 50, 7 to 35, all expressed as I.U. per day. If the extreme values are taken at their face value, the range is 44-fold, but it is not certain that this wide range is due wholly or primarily to inter-individual variations.

It appears that an important basic factor which determines the rate at which ovaries can produce androgoens is the temperature. If mouse ovaries are transplanted to the ears of castrated male mice where the temperature is maintained at lower levels, the ovaries produce androgens which tend to counteract the effects of castration. If, however, the ovaries are grafted into the *abdomen* of the male mice, where the temperature is higher, the counteracting effect is largely absent. Since testis tissue in mammals also requires a lower-than-body temperature for normal functioning, the above facts point to an important similarity between the male and female gonads.

It seems probable from our discussion that individual normal males, for example, vary through wide limits (possibly 10-fold or more) in their production of both androgens and estrogens. If we classify individual men roughly as (1) *low*, (2) *intermediate*, and (3) *high* producers of each of the two types of hormones, we find that an individual may belong in one of nine groupings. Placing the androgen production first and the estrogen production second, these groupings are: (1) *low-low*, (2) *low-intermediate*, (3) *low-high*, (4) *intermediate-low*, (5) *intermediate-intermediate*, (6) *intermediate-high*, (7) *high-low*, (8) *high-intermediate*, and (9) *high-high*. Exactly the same classifications could apply to women.

It seems obvious that if one wishes to deal intelligently with problems of sex (which involve *real* people) we should take account of these variations and not think in terms of a population the members of which are "normal" or about average in estrogen and androgen production. The *intermediate-intermediate* group may be larger than any other, but it constitutes only one group out of nine possibilities and may conceivably include only those who have no acute sex problems.

The above discussion should not be taken as implying that all the problems of sex revolve around the two types of hormones, estrogens and androgens. Other endocrine glands besides the gonads, particularly the adrenals and pituitary, are doubtless involved in highly complex patterns. The understanding of psychogenic and cultural factors in sex should be based upon a knowledge of the physiological elements, and these cannot be appreciated unless there is consistent investigation of the wide and all-prevading endocrine variation. How little attention has been paid to this variation may be illustrated by pointing out that not one reader (at most) in a thousand knows how he or she would be classified in the nine groupings listed above.

Variations Concerned with Steroid Excretion

The urinary excretion of steroids is closely related to the gonadal and adrenocortical production of hormones. Because they can be determined quantitatively on the basis of color reactions, for example, with *m*-dinitrobenzene, a relatively large amount of data is available with respect to the excretion of 17-ketosteroids. Exactly what is included in this group in specific instances must be ascertained by consulting the original publications.

It is estimated that, of the total 17-ketosteroids excreted by men, about 60 per cent come from the adrenal cortices and 40 per cent from the testes. Anatomically the adrenal glands are said to vary in weight from about 7 to 20 gm. Some authors merely state that the weights are highly variable, and it may easily be that they vary even more than 3-fold. More important than adrenal size, however, is the variation in the thickness of the adrenal cortex. This is said to range from 0.5 to 5.0 mm., and a 10-fold range of activity of the adrenal cortex on this basis may be expected.[25]

Although a number of studies have pointed to substantial variation in the 24-hr-urinary 17-ketosteroid excretion of men and women, the most definitive work dealing with inter-individual differences is that of Dobriner and co-workers[23] which was referred to earlier (p. 99). In this study samples were collected from individuals over long periods of time and analyzed separately by exhaustive research methods involving the use of chromatography and infrared spectrometry in addition to the more usual techniques.

The range of *crude* ketosteroids is not particularly large in comparison with other ranges we have encountered: 9.5 to 29.8 mg. per day. But when the data for individual steroids are examined, the ranges are much larger, and the excretion patterns are seen to be distinctive for each individual. In the case of androsterone (already mentioned) and etiocholanolone, which are thought to constitute the main metabolic products of testosterone, the ranges are 35- and 15-fold, respectively. Age differences are *in part* responsible for these ranges. However, in the case of 11-ketoetiocholanolone and 11-hydroxyandrosterone, which are thought to be the principal metabolic products of hydrocortisone from the adrenal cortex, the ranges are 9- and 29-fold, respectively. These latter ranges are surely inter-individual and not due to age differences, as indicated below. In the case of 11-hydroxyandrosterone, the largest excretion appeared in the case of a man 72 years old and the least, a "trace," was from a man of 76. If the "trace" referred to is taken as one-half the least amount tabulated, the range becomes 58-fold instead of 29-fold as stated above. Since hydrocortisone is one of the principal products of adrenocortical activity,[23] it seems that there may be among normal individuals, over a considerable period of time, *at least* 10-fold inter-individual differences with respect to the production of this hormone. An alternative interpretation would involve wide differences in the metabolism of this hormone. It should be pointed out that the Dobriner study, monumental as it was, involved only 20 normal males. It appears safe to assume that larger segments of the population would yield larger ranges, and that if "unwell" individuals were included the ranges would be even greater.

Inter-individual Variations Relating to the Pituitary Gland

In Table 15 is given pertinent information with respect to the anatomical variations in human pituitary glads.[26, 27,28] Detailed comparative study of the patterns of individual glands has not been attempted, but there is nothing in the available data to preclude the existence of wide inter-individual differences with respect to the detailed anatomy and the machinery for the production of each specific hormone.

Just as two human beings of the same weight, age, and sex may appear alike when examined in a cursory manner and yet be very different when examined in detail, so may two pituitary glands appear outwardly alike but be found very different when subjected to detailed study. We have just noted in the previous section a case involving the same principle. The *total* ketosteroid excretion for each of two individuals may be about the same, but the excretion of specific substances may be very different for the two.

In view of the fact that pituitary glands (both lobes) produce at

Table 15.
Normal Variation in Human Pituitary Glands

Total weight, 350–1100 mg.[a]		
	Per Cent of Weight of Whole Gland	Per Cent of Chief Cells
Anterior lobe	56–92[a]	37–64 chromophobes[b]
		23–43 acidophiles[b]
		9–27 basophiles[b]
Posterior lobe	7–41.3[a]	
Epithelium (pars intermedia)	0.13–3.6[c]	
Colloid (pars intermedia)	0.02–10.4[c]	

[a] As low as 130 mg. and as high as 1800 mg. have been reported [A. T. Rasmussen, *Endocrinology*, **8**, 511 (1924)].[a] A. T. Rasmussen, *Am. J. Anat.*, **42**, 21 (1928).
[b] A. T. Rasmussen, *Endocrinology*, **8**, 522 (1924).
[c] A. T. Rasmussen, *Endocrinology*, **12**, 143 (1928).

least eight entirely different hormones, two glands could have exactly the same "total" hormone output and yet be very different in their functioning. We shall therefore look for evidence of variability in connection with specific hormones.

We have already noted (p. 92) that the blood levels of the thyreotropic hormone (thyroid stimulating hormone TSH) appear to vary by a factor of 10 or more. This is one of the better-known pituitary hormones since it has been obtained in nearly pure form.

The lactogenic hormone of the pituitary is one that has been known for a relatively long time and has been purified. The hormonal control of lactation and of the development of the mammary glands is complicated by several endocrine interactions, but the lactogenic hormone is a potent and highly important agent.

The well-known variability as milk producers among cows of different breeds and among individual cows of the same breed, as well as the differences between different species of mammals in this respect, is obviously based upon genetic differences. In view of the fact that the development of the mammary glands and the production of milk in virgin animals can be brought about by hormone administration and that the amount of milk produced by a lactating animal can be augmented by similar means, it is clear that the genetic variability is concerned, at least in part, with hormone production.

That wide variability in lactogenic hormone production and in its effectiveness for different individual animals is common, and genetically determined, is shown by the fact that Riddle[29] found one strain of doves that required twenty times as much lactogenic hormones as did another strain to induce crop milk secretion. When compared on the basis of their response to low levels of prolactin administration, there were 8-fold racial differences in doves and 12-fold racial differences in pigeons. Since crop milk production is necessary for the rearing of young, it seems probable that the pituitaries of some strains produce vastly greater amounts than the pituitaries of others.

When this hormone was administered to a series of rabbits, it was found that the amount required to elicit milk secretion varied from 0.75 to 3.0 I.U. for different animals. This 4-fold variation indicates a substantial variation in the abilities of the pituitaries of the different rabbits to produce prolactin. Another evidence of variability in prolactin production is found in fowls. It is well known that in a flock of hens, unless the characteristic has been successfully "bred out," there will be some individual broody hens, those that are determined year after year to set and raise a flock of chicks. An assay[30] of the pituitaries of such hens has shown that the content of prolactin is approximately 2 to 3 times higher than in nonbroody hens. It is well known that prolactin administration, in addition to causing milk secretion, engenders mothering instincts in virgin rats. The results with the hens are thus in line with other known facts.

That prolactin is produced in highly variable amounts in different human beings is indicated by the fact that its urinary excretion varies tremendously from individual to individual. In five women the urinary prolactin excretion per 24 hours varied from 52 to 210 units when tested on pigeons by intravenous injection. A series of 12 males excreted from 0 to 305 units in 24 hours when tested in the same manner.[31] Omitting the individual who exhibited a zero value, the variation was still nearly 40-fold.

The gonadotrophic hormones of the pituitary include the interstitial cell stimulating hormone (ICSH), which is present and effective in both males and females, and the follicle stimulating hormone (FSH), which stimulates the development of multiple follicles in females and apparently in males induces spermatogenesis.

When young animals have their pituitaries removed, they remain sexually undeveloped. In hypophysectomized male rats, the testes may develop to only $\frac{1}{16}$ the usual size and in females the ovaries are similarly affected. When young animals are furnished an extra amount of pituitary gonadotrophins by injection, they become sexually precocious, and the sex functions become exaggerated. Corresponding effects, degeneration of the gonads and the reversal, can be brought about in mature animals by hypophysectomy and administering gonadotrophic hormones.

It is clear, therefore, that although there are interrelations between the gonadal sex hormones and the pituitary sex hormones involving also the adrenals, thyroids, etc., the effective hormonal impetus to sexual development arises in the pituitary.

Perhaps the best evidence for wide variation in humans in the production of pituitary gonadotrophins is the existence side by side, in the human family, of sexual precocity and exaggerated sex development and activity on the one hand, and sexual impotence and underdevelopment on the other. At one end of the scale, for example, are girls who have been known to menstruate regularly beginning at 2½ years of age. At the other extreme is eunochoidism, which is accompanied by failure of the sex structures, both primary and secondary, to develop. These extreme cases are not necessarily the result of pituitary deficiency, but they may be. There is an obvious tendency to dismiss such cases as being "not normal." The dividing line, however, is very hard to draw, and application of the idea of genetic gradients (p. 13) would lead one to suppose that there would be a graduation of cases intermediate between the two extremes. The study of sex behavior by Kinsey and co-workers[21] supports this idea since variation to a most remarkable degree is abundantly evident.

Again our discussion should not be taken to imply that sex phenomena are simple and easily understood. Whatever factors are involved, and there are many, the element of variation is always present. If we were to consider exhaustively the details of sex physiology and psychology, we would probably see the importance of variation more clearly than when we consider the subject in a more cursory way.

The growth hormone is another product of pituitary glands which has been purified. Overproduction of this hormone results in gigantism and underproduction leads to dwarfism. Dwarfism in mice, for example, is inherited and has been shown to be accompanied by a deficiency of the acidophile cells in the pituitary. When growth hormone is administered to such mice, however, they grow to "normal" size. This indicates that the genetic difference involves the machinery for producing the growth hormone.

Since in the human family not only do dwarfism and gigantism exist but all intermediate statures in between, the existence of wide variation in the production of the growth hormone is indicated. This is not to imply that growth is controlled by the growth hormone alone. Other hormones act synergistically or antagonistically, and this makes any simple interpretation impossible. Little definitive evidence is available on which to base conclusions regarding the interindividual variability of growth hormone production. We must rely largely on circumstantial and indirect evidence.

Concerning other endocrine activities of the pituitary gland, including the posterior lobe, not enough data appear to be available to make discussion of individuality of production profitable. Certainly, however, there are no data which throw doubt on the existence of wide variability in the areas not discussed.

Summary

In concluding our discussion on inter-individual variability in hormone functions, we may well point out that with respect to hormone after hormone we have cited evidence of wide variability. Furthermore, the hormones for which the evidence is most convincing are those which have been studied in greatest detail and for the longest time. It may therefore be presumed that, as study of other individual hormone activities progresses, the role and importance of variation will become more widely evident.

It appears on the basis of our discussion that the idea that normal people have about average hormonal levels and that only "freaks" depart significantly from the average is untenable. Each individual, normal or not, it appears, must have a distinctive endocrine pattern which is based upon the anatomical and physiological potentialities of each gland and the intricate balances which exist between the different endocrine agents. The distinctiveness of these patterns involves differences in single items not of the order of 10, 20, or 50 per cent, but often differences of as much as 10-fold or more. The endocrine patterns of different people appear to be fully as diverse as are the habitations in which human beings live.

In later discussions we shall have more to say regarding the interpretation of these facts and the possibility of attacking problems which arise because of their existence.

REFERENCES

1. Charles Rupert Stockard, *The Genetic and Endocrinic Basis for Differences in Form and Behavior,* Wistar Institute, Philadelphia, Pa., 1941.
2. Arthur Grollman, *Essentials of Endocrinology,* J. B. Lippincott Co., Philadelphia, Pa., 2nd ed., 1947.
3. Shields Warren, Personal Communication.
4. A. L. Bacharach, Personal Communication.

5. Robert W. Bates, Oscar Riddle, and Ernest L. Lahr, *Endocrinology,* **29,** 492–497 (1941).

6. Rulon W. Rawson and Janet W. McArthur, *J. Clin. Endocrinol.,* **7,** 235–263 (1947).

7. F. Raymond Keating, Samuel F. Haines, Marschelle H. Power, and Marvin M. D. Williams, *J. Clin. Endocrinol.,* **10,** 1425 (1950).

8. Savino A. D'Angelo, Karl E. Paschkis, Albert S. Gordon, and Abraham Cantarow, *J. Clin. Endocrinol.,* **11,** 1237–1253 (1951).

9. *Ibid.,* p. 1238.

10. Walter Fleischmann, Harris B. Shumacker, Jr., and William L. Straus, *Endocrinology,* **32,** 238–246 (1943).

11. Charles R. Kleeman and Robert E. Cooke, *J. Lab. Clin. Med.,* **38,** 112–127 (1951).

12. Lester Dragstedt, *Physiol. Revs.,* **7,** 499–530 (1927).

13. Robertson F. Ogilvie, *Quart. J. Med.,* **6,** 287–300 (1937).

14. William Susman, *J. Clin. Endocrinol.* **2,** 97–106 (1942).

15. Gregory Pincus and Kenneth V. Thimann, eds., *The Hormones,* Academic Press, Inc., New York, N. Y., 1948, Vol. I.

16. See B. A. Houssay, *Endocrinology,* **30,** 884–897 (1942).

17. Cyril Norman Hugh Long, "Diabetes Mellitus—Etiology," in Garfield G. Duncan. ed., *Diseases of Metabolism,* W. B. Saunders Co., Philadelphia, Pa. and London, England, 1943, p. 713.

18. T. F. Gallagher, D. H. Peterson, R. I. Dorfman, A. T. Kenyon, and F. C. Koch, *J. Clin. Invest.,* **16,** 695–703 (1937).

19. Edward C. Reifenstein, Jr., and Eleanor F. Dempsey, *J. Clin. Endocrinol.,* **4,** 326–334 (1944).

20. Gregory Pincus, *J. Clin. Endocrinol.,* **5,** 291–300 (1945).

21. Alfred C. Kinsey, Wardell B. Pomeroy, and Clyde E. Martin, *Sexual Behavior in the Human Male,* W. B. Saunders Co., Philadelphia, Pa. and London, England, 1948.

22. Elizabeth Dingemanse, Helene Borchardt, and Ernst Laqueur, *Biochem. J. (London),* **31,** 500–507 (1937).

23. Konrad Dobriner, Attallah Kappas, C. P. Rhoads, and T. F. Gallagher, *J. Clin. Invest.,* **32,** 940–949, 950–951 (1953).

24. Ralph I. Dorfman, "Biochemistry of Androgens," Gregory Pincus and Kenneth V. Thimann, eds., *The Hormones,* Vol. I, pp. 467–548.

25. Max A. Goldzieher, *The Endorcrine Glands,* D. Appleton-Century Co., New York, N. Y. and London, England, 1939.

26. A. T. Rasmussen, *Am. J. Anat.,* **42,** 1–27 (1928).

27. A. T. Rasmussen, *Endocrinology,* **8,** 509–524 (1924).

28. A. T. Rasmussen, *Endocrinology,* **12,** 129–150 (1928).

29. Oscar Riddle, *Endocrines and Constitution in Doves and Pigeons*, Carnegie Institution of Washington, Washington, D.C., 1947.
30. William H. Burrows and Theodore C. Byerly, *Proc. Soc. Exptl. Biol. Med.*, **34**, 841–844 (1936).
31. Richard L. Coppedge and Albert Segaloff, *J. Clin. Endocrinol.*, **11**, 465–476 (1951).

VII

Excretion Patterns

Some of the first clues as to the importance of biochemical individuality date back to the pioneer interest of Sir A. E. Garrod in "Inborn Errors of Metabolism." These "errors" were often detected because of differences in urinary composition. The idea, which has often come to be held, that these "errors" are isolated freaks of nature and perhaps primarily of interest to geneticists because of the light they can throw on gene action, was not in Garrod's mind in the early days of his interest in the subject. In 1902 he wrote:[1] ". . . the thought naturally presents itself that these [alkaptonuria, etc.] are merely extreme examples of variations of chemical behavior which are probably everywhere present in minor degrees and that just as no two individuals of a species are absolutely identical in bodily structure neither are their chemical processes carried out on exactly the same lines." This statement might have led, but unfortunately did not, to an early testing of his hypothesis. A serious testing of this hypothesis leads inevitably to the observation that the variations among "normal" individuals are major rather than minor.

Most conclusive evidence of the biochemical individuality of every human specimen—not restricted to those who exhibit marked idiosyncrasies—has been obtained by the recent studies of urinary excretion patterns using paper chromatography and other methods.[2,3,4] Typical results from one study[2] illustrating how various items in the patterns vary from individual to individual are shown in Figure 13.

It will be noted that the two identical twins included in the study exhibit patterns which show a strong resemblance, but that each of the other patterns is distinctively different. This study was made with the idea of individual differences definitely in mind; the intra-individual as well as the inter-individual differences were carefully studied statistically and otherwise. The graphs in Figure 13 represent averages for each individual; the number of samples in a few cases was as low as 7 to 12, but more often it was 25 to 50. Such results as these have been obtained so many times in our laboratory that there can be no possible question as to the distinctiveness of the urine of each individual.

Similar extended studies from the Institute for the Study of Human Variation at Columbia University involving twins indicate that genetic factors are operative in the control of the excretion of certain amino acids.[5,6] Sutton and Vandenberg[4] have also studied variation in human excretion patterns.

With respect to interpretation, the question arises whether the observed urinary differences are based merely upon renal differences (which fact would be interesting itself) or whether they are more far-reaching in their significance. An indication that kidney differences are not wholly responsible is the fact that salivary patterns are likewise distinctive and, in one case at least, a correlation exists between the urinary and salivary pattens. Female *A* (Fig. 13), whose urinary excretion of lysine is many times higher than that of female *B*, has shown in her saliva (21 samples) 10 times as much lysine as that of female *B* (24 samples). The importance of kidney differences in causing variations in the excretion of specific substances should not be minimized, as has been brought out by the excellent discussion by Harris.[7]

Much of the material presented in previous chapters relating to compositional and enzymic differences has a bearing on this problem, and it tends to support the concept that these urinary patterns arise, in part at least, because of the differences in the fundamental body chemistry (differing specific reaction rates) of each individual concerned.

Another question involving interpretation is whether these patterns are merely a reflection of different "food habits" of the individuals concerned, since all the individuals were on self-selected diets. The answer to this question appears to be that, although dietary differ-

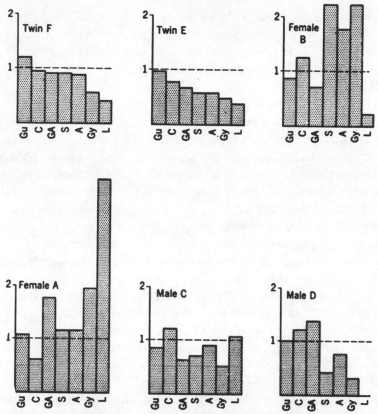

Figure 13. Urinary excretion patterns of six individuals. Gu = glucose; C = creatine; GA = glutamic acid; S = serine; A = alanine; Gy = glycine; L = lysine. Broken line represents group average excretion (mg. constituent per mg. creatinine), and vertical bars represent ratio of individual average to group average. From Helen K. Berry, Louise Cain, and Lorene L. Rogers, *Univ. Texas Publ.*, **5109**, 153 (1951).

ences are influencing factors, they are not crucial. If the differences were solely due to differences in self-selection of foods, they would still be interesting. Food selection is not necessarily based upon whim or habit, but may be based on differences in physiological need.

The twin variance studies cited above[5,6] indicate that dietary differences are not primarily responsible for the differences in the urinary excretion patterns. Additional evidence is of several sorts. Two experiments,[8,9] each involving placing individuals on uniform diets, have been done in our laboratory with the result that individuals' excretion patterns remain distinctive and unchanged with respect to at least certain items. Furthermore, babies only a few months old, largely on a milk diet, exhibit patterns that are just as distinctive as those of adults.[10]

Even more conclusive evidence as to the existence of excretion patterns which are not based upon dietary differences was obtained using animals fed exactly the same diets.[11] The urinary excretion patterns of seven individual rats are shown in Figure 14, and it may be noted that the differences with respect to the excretion of certain items, particularly phosphorus, aspartic acid, taurine, and lysine, are extreme even when the animals are getting exactly the same food. These particular patterns were selected from a larger number because of the interesting divergences exhibited. In another study[12] it was found that, although there are intrastrain differences with respect to excretion patterns, there are marked similarities within closely inbred strains; each closely inbred strain exhibits a characteristic pattern (Fig. 15). Thus, one strain (Iowa 65–76) was found to excrete practically no taurine in the urine; one (Fisher 344) excreted relatively very large amounts of taurine; one (Iowa 25–32) excreted (unlike all other strains tested) practically no lysine, while another (Piebald), unlike all the others, excreted almost no leucine.

These findings show clearly that even when the animal diets are uniform, highly distinctive urinary excretion patterns are exhibited. The results with different inbred strains show that inheritance is the basic reason for the differences in pattern. It would require extremely extensive genetic studies to demonstrate the inheritance process for each item, but this does not seem crucially important from the standpoint of elucidating the phenomenon of individuality.

Another question regarding the excretion patterns exhibited by humans concerns their consistency over a life span. This question we cannot answer directly because the methods have not been available long enough. One individual in our group, however, has been studied over a period of about five years during which time she has married and borne a child. The outstanding features of her pattern, notably her high excretion of lysine, have remained essentially the same. During pregnancy there were notable changes with respect to certain items (histidine excretion, for example), but these changes reverted

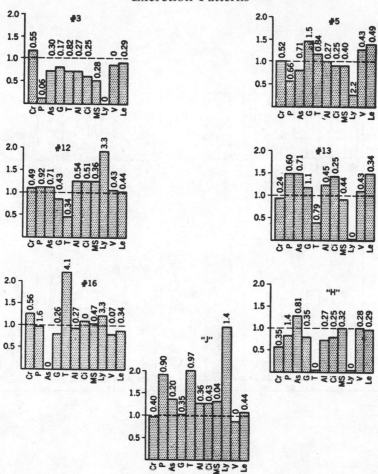

Figure 14. Excretion patterns of individual rats. Vertical bars represent the ratio of the average excretion of urinary constituents (expressed as mg. constituent per mg. creatinine) for individual rats divided by average excretion for the group. The broken line indicates average excretion for the group. The number at top of bar shows standard deviation (σ) on the same scale. Cr = creatinine; P = phosphorus; As = aspartic acid; G = glutamic acid; T = taurine; Al = alanine; Ci = citrulline; MS = methionine sulfoxide*; Ly = lysine; V = valine; Le = leucine. From Janet G. Reed, *Univ. Texas Publ.*, **5109**, 142 (1951).

afterwards. We have reason to presume that serious illnesses may temporarily change an individual's patterns materially, and, of course, it is possible that some of these changes may be irreversible.

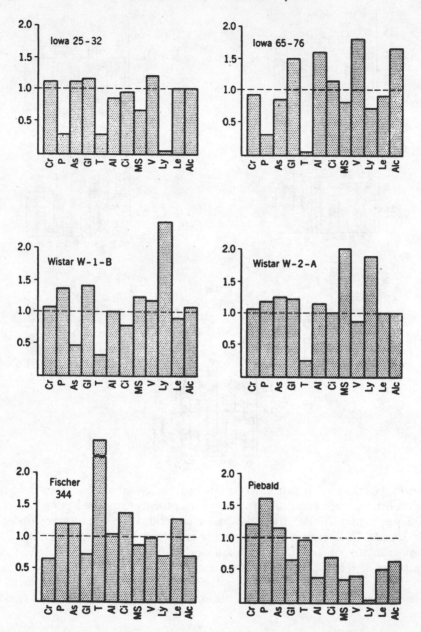

Figure 15. Excretion patterns of rats of different strains. Vertical bars represent the ratios of average excretions of urinary constituents (expressed as mg. constituent per mg. creatinine) by the rats in each strain divided by the average

Our evidence leads us to conclude, however, that these patterns tend to remain about the same in reasonably well individuals, at least over a period of years. That very young babies have highly distinctive patterns and that closely inbred strains of rats have close resemblances in their patterns (as do also human identical twins) strongly indicate that the pattern which an adult human being exhibits has not been produced merely as a result of the various illnesses and environmental experiences through which he has passed.

There are numerous reports from other laboratories which are in line with these findings respecting individuality in urine composition, though seldom has attention been paid to repeated samples from the same individuals.

With respect to amino acid excretion Woodson and co-workers[13] and others[14,15] have found by microbiological methods large variations. Stein[16] obtained evidence of wide variations in the amino acid excretion of cystinurics. Further data are also available with respect to creatine and creatinine excretion which bear out our conclusion regarding individuality of excretion patterns.[17,18,19]

That individuality in excretion patterns may be exhibited with respect to minerals is suggested by the work of Ryssing and Ehrnrooth. Ryssing[20] found in three subjects almost a 7-fold variation in the sodium content of the urine; Ehrnrooth[21] found a 9-fold variation in 22 women in the rate of excretion of potassium during pregnancy. Macy[22] reported that the pH values of the urine of children varied not only diurnally but also from child to child, even when the children were consuming the same food and living in the same environment. Similar results have been obtained in our laboratory and elsewhere.[4]

---

excretion for the rats in all strains. Broken line indicates average excretion for all strains. Cr = creatinine; P = phosphorus; As = aspartic acid; Gl = glutamic acid; T = taurine; Al = alanine; Ci = citrulline; MS = methionine sulfoxide*; V = valine; Ly = lysine; Le = leucine. *Since the material for the Bulletin was prepared, it has become probable that the substance originally identified by Dent as methionine sulfoxide is actually β-aminoisobutyric acid. *Nature* (London), **167**, 307 (1951).

Alc = average alcohol consumption by all rats in each strain expressed as ml. ethanol/100 g. rat/day. From Janet G. Reed, *Univ. Texas Publ.*, **5109**, 146–147

Excretion of thiamine appears to vary from individual to individual,[23] and some other data are available regarding the other better-known B vitamins.[24] The differences in the excretion of nicotinic acid-like compounds strongly suggest the existence of individual patterns.[25,26] The urinary excretion of vitamin B_{12}, folic acid, and the citrovorum factor by different individuals, even on controlled diets, was found to vary through rather wide ranges (2- to 9-fold) though the study was not concerned with individual differences and individual patterns were not established.[27]

Rather voluminous data are now available regarding steroid excretion. These are all in line with the idea that there is a high degree of individuality[28,29,30,31] though the individual patterns, especially of so-called "normals," have not often been studied. We have already referred p. 101) to the extensive and conclusive work of Dobriner and co-workers in which attention was paid to each individual's steroid excretion and in which it was shown that, when individual steroids are considered, extremely wide variations are present, and each individual's excretion constitutes a highly distinctive pattern.

Pepsinogen appears to be excreted in characteristic amounts by each individual. The range in excretion of pepsinogen by normals was found to be from 0 to 136 units per hour.[32] The acid phosphatase activities of male urines show a range of 5 to 310 units. Women excrete less, 5 to 70 units.[33]

The existence of excretion patterns is apparently not limited to urine. In a recent study it was found that normal individuals on constant dietary intakes excreted a characteristic percentage of the nitrogen in the feces. In successive years, one individual excreted in the feces 7.02 and 7.89 per cent, respectively, of the nitrogen consumed. In another individual the percentages were 8.72 and 10.02 per cent; in still another, 8.52 and 8.93 per cent; and in a fourth, 13.0 per cent (1 year only).[34]

In summary, we may say that excretion studies point to the existence of marked differences in specific reaction rates in different individuals and to the probability that each individual exhibits a highly distinctive pattern with respect to his internal chemistry.

REFERENCES

1. Sir Archibald E. Garrod, *Lancet,* December 13, 1902, p. 1620.
2. Helen Kirby Berry, Louise Cain, and Lorene Lane Rogers, *Univ. Texas. Publ.,* **5109,** 150-156 (1951).
3. Helen Kirby Berry, *Am. J. Physical Anthropology.,* **11,** (n.s.), 559–576 (1953).
4. H. Eldon Sutton and Steven G. Vanderberg, *Human Biology,* **25,** 318–332 (1953).
5. H. K. Berry, Th. Dobzhansky, S. M. Gartler, H. Levine, and R. H. Osborne, *Am. J. Human Genet.,* **7,** 93–107 (1955).
6. S. M. Gartler, Th. Dobzhansky, and H. K. Berry, *Am. J. Human Genetics,* **7,** 108–121 (1955).
7. Harry Harris, *An Introduction to Human Biochemical Genetics,* Cambridge University Press, London, England and New York, N.Y., 1953.
8. Roy C. Thompson and Helen M. Kirby, *Arch. Biochem.,* **21,** 210–216 (1949).
9. Harry Eldon Sutton, *Univ. Texas Publ.,* **5109,** 173–180 (1951).
10. Helen Kirby Berry and Louise Cain, *Univ. Texas Publ.,* **5109,** 165–172 (1951).
11. Janet G. Reed, *Univ. Texas Publ.,* **5109,** 139–143 (1951).
12. Janet G. Reed, *Univ. Texas Publ.,* **5109,** 144–149 (1951).
13. Harold W. Woodson, Stanley W. Hier, James D. Solomon, and Olaf Bergeim, *J. Biol. Chem.,* **172,** 613–618 (1948).
14. Stanley W. Hier and Olaf Bergeim, *J. Biol. Chem.,* **163,** 129–135 (1946).
15. C. E. Dent, *Biochemical Society Symposia* (Cambridge, England), No. 3, 34–51 (1949).
16. William H. Stein, *Proc. Soc. Exptl. Biol. Med.,* **78,** 705–708 (1951).
17. Violet M. Wilder and Sergius Morgulis, *Arch. Biochemistry and Biophysics,* **42,** 69–71 (1953).
18. Leland C. Clark, Jr., Haskell L. Thompson, Elizabeth I. Beck, and Werner Jacobson, *Am. J. Diseases Children,* **81,** 774–783 (1951).
19. Leland C. Clark, Jr., Haskell L. Thompson, and Elizabeth I. Beck, *Am. J. Obstet. Gynecol.,* **62,** 576–583 (1951).
20. E. Ryssing, *Scan. J. Clin. Lab. Invest.,* **3,** 17–32 (1951).
21. C. A. Ehrnrooth, *Scan. J. Clin. Lab. Invest.,* **2,** 217–227 (1950).
22. Icie G. Macy, *Nutrition and Chemical Growth in Childhood,* Charles C. Thomas, Springfield, Ill., and Baltimore, Md., 1942, Vol. I.
23. Olaf Mickelsen, W. O. Caster, and Ancel Keys, *Proc. Soc. Exptl. Biol. Med.,* **62,** 254-258 (1946).
24. Herbert P. Sarett, *J. Nutrition,* **47,** 275–287 (1952).

25. Daniel Melnick, William D. Robinson, and Henry Field, Jr., *J. Biol. Chem.*, **136**, 131–144 (1940).
26. Daniel Melnick, William D. Robinson, and Henry Field, Jr., *J. Biol. Chem.*, **136**, 145–156 (1940).
27. U. D. Register and Herbert P. Sarett, *Proc. Soc. Exptl. Biol. Med.*, **77**, 837–839 (1951).
28. S. L. Tompsett, *J. Clin. Endocrinol.*, **11**, 61–66 (1951).
29. Elizabeth Dingemanse, Leonora G. Huis in 'T. Velt and S. Lore Hartogh-Katz, *J. Clin. Endocrinol.*, **12**, 66-85 (1952).
30. Avery A. Sandberg, Don H. Nelson, E. Myles Glenn, Frank H. Tyler, and Leo T. Samuels, *J. Clin. Endocrinol. Metabolism*, **13**, 1445–1464 (1953).
31. William Duane Brown, M.A. thesis, The University of Texas, 1951.
32. Henry D. Janowitz, Milton H. Levy, and Franklin Hollander, *Am. J. Med. Sci.*, **220**, 679–682 (1950).
33. Mark D. Altschule, Barbara H. Parkhurst, and George R. Zager, *Tech. Bull. of the Registry of Med. Technologists*, **21**, 480–483 (1951).
34. Vincent Toscani and G. Donald Whedon, *J. Nutrition*, **45**, 119–130 (1951).

VIII

Pharmacological Manifestations

Variability in responses to drugs has been observed as long as drugs have been tested systematically. These variations have been designated as "biological" and have been considered a necessary evil by those who have sought to develop a systematic science of pharmacology. Much attention has been paid to the mathematical treatment of the data obtained from such tests, but little to the basic reasons for the variability. Krantz and Carr[1] state frankly: "The mechanism of idiosyncrasy is not understood."

It is not always fully appreciated that, when a drug produces a physiological effect, there is always an *interaction* between the drug and some constituent(s) of the affected system. The chemistry of the drug itself is often fairly well understood, but the chemistry of the living systems with which it interacts is much more obscure. Especially is this so if biochemical variations are as large as our discussions have indicated. It is most often impossible in specific cases to designate with precision just what enzyme or enzymes are interfered with or what metabolites are involved in the interactions. In the case of a complex organism with many organs and tissues it is frequently impossible to know precisely what tissues and organs are most involved.

It is interesting, as noted by Clark,[2] that the dosage-response relationships when intact animals are used appear simpler than when specific tissues, such as the epidermis, are used as test objects. He suggests that this simplicity is apparent rather than real because, in an intact animal, the effect of a drug is the summation of a large number of variable activities. The situation here parallels, in principle, that previously discussed (p. 101) in connection with the excretion of ketosteroids in general as contrasted with the excretion of individual well-defined ketosteroids. Between individuals, the *total* ketosteroid excretion varied about 3-fold while the androsterone excretion varied 35-fold.

On the basis of this concept, one might expect a poison to be *relatively* uniform in its toxic effect on a series of intact animals because, in the different animals, many different tissues and organs would be involved and the chance exists that the resistance of one tissue might be compensated for by the susceptibility of another. Since from our previous discussions we realize that every individual animal is made up of a coordinated set of organs and tissues, each distinctive (quantitatively) in size, composition, and enzymic make-up, we should expect the greatest inter-individual differences to be observed when single tissues from different animals are tested in parallel. This exemplifies the principle which appears to be an important one for our discussions. We expect to find the most striking evidences for biochemical individuality when we look at *details,* rather than at crude summations.

The use of closely inbred animals in pharmacological testing tends, of course, to lessen observed variability. Another factor which operates in the same manner is the selection of drugs for investigation. Investigators have always been influenced in their study of drugs by the ultimate possibilities of practical use, and it seems inevitable that drugs which are relatively uniform in their action should have been studied more thoroughly than those which yield erratic results. If such a thing were possible as a random selection from all possible drugs, one would doubtless find in this group greater variability in action than would be observed in a series of accepted useful drugs.

When simple substances, even those that are intimately associated with living processes, are tested upon organisms, the results may be highly variable depending on the genetics of the organism tested. Thus, there are strains of *Drosophila* which are sensitive and resistant, respectively, to carbon dioxide. Some can stand hours of contact with pure carbon dioxide without permanent injury, while others either do not recover from the narcosis or, if they do, their movements remain incoordinated and some of the legs may show more or less complete paralysis.[3] The thoracic ganglion seems to be the seat of the intoxication; there seems to be marked biochemical differences in sensitivity between the two strains. The fact that the inheritance mechanism involved is obscure should not cause one to question the fact of striking biochemical individuality. There is some clinical evidence, including deaths from carbon dioxide administration, which indicates that human beings also vary in their response to this substance.

An interesting series of observations grow out of an accidental exposure of mice to chloroform. It was found, for example, that the female mice are much more resistant to chloroform poisoning than males; no females were killed under the accidental conditions, whereas all the breeding males in one colony (C3H and C3Hf strains) were lost. Male mice in other strains were more resistant, but there were many casualties.

In experimental trials on C3H mice, individual animals also showed some variance; males after 2-hour exposure at a given level lived from 2 to 11 days, while females exposed in a similar manner lived from 42 to 60 days.[4]

Individual differences were observed resulting from the accidental exposure of 78 men to carbon tetrachloride vapors. The author concludes: "It is not apparent why 15 men out of the 78 exposed to carbon tetrachloride fumes were poisoned and why 6 of these became so ill as to require hospitalization. All were white men within 5 to 8 years of the same age and in good general health. . . . All 15 of the men poisoned were exposed from 3 to 8 hours; however, many of those who developed no symptoms were exposed for a similar length of time or longer."[5] In the light of our discussions, a basis for the differences in responses may be the ever-present phenomenon of biochemical individuality.

A relatively simple substance which is known to have vastly different effects on different individuals is ethyl alcohol.[6] Nagle found that 0.25 oz. of alcohol had the same effect on some individuals as did 10 times this amount on others.[7] Jetter[8] studied 1000 cases and found as a result of objective tests that 10.5 per cent were intoxicated when the blood level of alcohol was 0.05 per cent and 6.7 per cent were *sober* when the blood level was 0.40 per cent, leaving 82.8 per cent for which intermediate levels were effective. Some of such differences are due to adaptive changes, but it seems likely that substantial innate differences exist.

A striking phenomenon which probably involves biochemical individuality is that of pathological intoxication. Occasionally an individual, who may be a habitual drinker or not, is afflicted. In a typical case the individual goes berserk and may commit all sorts of crimes and cause damage to property. After a subsequent long sleep he has no memory of his acts.[9] This very special type of drunkenness is not caused by any special type of alcohol or necessarily by large amounts; it fortunately happens only rarely, and involves only a few individuals. Whether certain individuals are peculiarly susceptible and have repeated typical attacks (these would be classed, no doubt, as alcoholic psychotics) is not clear; in any event only certain rare individuals ever are in such a condition as to be susceptible.

It appears likely that the term "pathological intoxication" may be applied only to extremely acute cases, and that less acute examples of essentially the same disease exist without getting special notice. It is well known that the effect of alcohol on different individuals is often characteristic: some become drowsy, some sad, some happy, some pugnacious. Pathological intoxication may occur in certain individuals, whose make-up predisposes to it, when they are in a particular metabolic and endocrine state.

The rate at which alcohol disappears from the blood was found to vary through nearly a 2-fold range when only six individuals were tested.[10] Presumably a larger and more diverse sample population would yield a much larger range. The tendency of alcohol to produce pylorospasm and vomiting is so strong in certain individuals that they are protected from drunkenness by this means because small amounts of alcohol are sufficient to elicit the symptoms.

An interesting way in which individuals differ in their response to alcohol is the reaction when a small amount (0.03 cc.) of 60 per cent alcohol is injected into the skin.[11] In all individuals there is produced a localized wheal about 1 cm. in diameter, but the reaction in the surrounding area varies greatly from individual to individual. In about 18 per cent of the cases tested, the surrounding area was unaffected; in the others the inflammation graded from a small, very slightly pink corona to a highly inflamed area 4 cm. in diameter.

Richter[12] found among 72 children 4 to 10 years of age a striking difference in their reactions to alcohol solutions. Most of them did not like solutions in concentrations above 10-15 per cent, but six liked the taste of samples containing up to 50 per cent alcohol.

The chronic effects of alcohol consumption are also highly varied. Fleming[13] cites the case of a man who died at the age of 93, having drunk a quart of Scotch whiskey every day for the last sixty years of his life, all the while managing a successful business. This individual was evidently highly resistant to the toxic effect of alcohol. At the other extreme are alcoholics who sometimes drink themselves to death in their thirties. The compulsion to drink as well as the tolerance for alcohol varies greatly with individuals, and all kinds of psychoses may develop as a direct result of alcohol consumption in individuals whose make-up predisposes them.[14,15]

It should be noted that our direct knowledge, based on experiments, about innate inter-individual human differences in response to alcohol is relatively meager. Such data must be collected as a result of repeated tests on the same individuals, and this is not often done. A study of the "normal" response to alcohol may be relatively fruitless if, as we suspect, innate human differences are basic to all the health problems which exist in connection with alcohol consumption.

An interesting case involving a simple poison illustrates how wide variability may be when human beings are tested in a systematic way. Percival[16] measured the minimum concentrations of mercuric chloride required to produce skin irritation in a series of individuals. Thirty-five subjects were used. Of these, one subject responded to the application of 1 part per 100,000; another to 3 parts per 100,000; 5 more responded to 10 parts; 11 more to 30 parts, 13 more to 100 parts; and 4 failed to respond to any of the concentrations tested. Here in a group as small as 35 individuals we find 100-fold variations, even excluding the 4 for which some unknown higher concentration was required. An adequate sampling of a representative human population would doubtless exhibit a variation wider than 100-fold. A complete understanding of the reasons for this variability in skin reactions to mercuric chloride does not exist, but clearly this is an exhibition of individuality which must have its roots in histological and biochemical differences.

Recent evidence has indicated that for certain babies boric acid may exhibit toxic properties when applied locally. Although such preparations have been used with infants for many years, reports of 5 cases[17] and 3 cases (1 fatal),[18] respectively, have recently been published. Some quantitative differences in the metabolism of the babies must cause them to vary in susceptibility. On the basis of experiments with fowls it is clear that genetic differences are responsible for the wide variation in their response to boric acid when solutions are injected into embryonated eggs. There are striking breed differences. In this case it appears that boric acid interferes with riboflavin-containing enzymes and that fowls which have a higher riboflavin requirement were more susceptible to boric acid poisoning under the conditions used.[19]

Racial differences have been observed in the susceptibility to the effects of chromate on industrial workers exposed to this hazard. Among non-white workers less than 55 years of age, the frequency of sickness lasting over 8 days was 156.7 per thousand, whereas for white workers the rate was 86.2 per thousand.[20]

The importance of biochemical individuality is emphasized by a consideration of the variable effects of various alkaloids. These agents have been used for a long time, and their pharmacology is relatively well known.

An illustration of the variable responses to nicotine concerns aphids. In an experiment, 2 per cent of an insect population died or became moribund when exposed to 0.0001 M nicotine solution, 48 per cent were affected when the concentration was 0.0025 M, and 98.5 per cent when the concentration was 0.012 M. The concentrations of nicotine required to affect all the insects alike varied more than 120-fold.[21] The pharmacology of nicotine as studied in mammals is notably complex and unpredictable, partly because many sites of action are involved. Its effect on different human individuals is also diverse, but it has not been adequately investigated, particularly in view of the fairly well established fact that amblyopia and Buerger's disease occur in relatively rare cases directly because of its use.[22]

Physostigmine is an interesting alkaloid because it is generally recognized that it acts by inhibiting a specific enzyme, cholinesterase. This enzyme has been found to be at characteristic levels in the corpuscles and blood plasma of different individuals (p. 79), and it would be expected that the action of the alkaloid in different individuals might vary with their characteristic cholinesterase levels. Although the alkaloid often causes objectionable side reactions, its effects on individuals have not been studied adequately, particularly with relation to the cholinesterase content of the individual's tissues.

Morphine is known to produce in human beings a multitude of different side reactions which vary from individual to individual. In a study in which several drugs were compared for their effects on 29 healthy students, using saline control tests, it was found that morphine caused nausea in 18, sleep in 16, drunkenness in 9, dizziness in 13, itching in 9, and indistinct speech in 7.[23] The proneness to addiction to morphine is also known to vary from individual to individual; and sometimes this drug excites instead of depressing the individual to whom it is administered.

In a study of chronic morphine poisoning in dogs, wide variability was noted not only with respect to the direct effects of the alkaloid but also the effects observed when it was withdrawn after a period of months.[24] The variability in the initial response of dogs to morphine is illustrated in another study[25] in which one dog (No. 15) showed pupillary contraction (8 to 5 mm), a slight decrease in pulse rate (130 to 108), and a marked decrease in respiration rate (150 to 40). Another dog (No. 20) showed no contraction of the pupil (6 to 6 mm), a marked decrease in pulse rate (120 to 50), and a marked *increase* in respiration rate (42 to 96). Still another dog (No. 45) showed slight pupillary *expansion* (7 to 8 mm.), decrease in pulse rate (138 to 96), and over a 4-fold increase in respiration rate (43 to 180).

One of the most revealing examples of biochemical individuality in relation to alkaloids is the variable response of rabbits to atropine, and particularly the fact that rabbits vary greatly in the ability of their blood and tissues to destroy atropine by hydrolysis.[26] Some rabbits are able to hydrolyze it readily, however, and can eat belladonna leaves ad libitum without being poisoned. This case is particularly interesting because the genetics of this situation have been investigated sufficiently so that it is certain that the ability of the rabbits to produce the atropinesterase is inherited.[27] When human beings are given atropine in sublethal doses, they are said to excrete most of it promptly in unchanged condition.

In a recent study[28] involving atropine and human beings, it was found that only one-fourth of the peptic ulcer patients tested had their gastric secretion reduced by atropine administration. Various toxic symptoms accompanied the action of the alkaloid. The authors concluded that these symptoms did not depend upon the dosage or the phase of activity of the affected cells, but rather upon the sensitivity of the entire human organism to the action of the drug. This appears to be a clear-cut case where biochemical individuality plays a highly significant role. It seems probable that human differences with respect to the action of this alkaloid are inherited. It is interesting, however, that infants and unweaned animals often appear to tolerate relatively large doses of atropine. In baby rabbits the enzyme causing hydrolysis does not appear in the blood until two months after birth. These facts emphasize the point that developmental changes may be accompanied by metabolic changes and that both may be under genetic control.

In an earlier chapter we have noted that wide variability of endocrine patterns exists. It would therefore be expected that hormone preparations and drugs known to affect hormone systems would show corresponding variability.

Methyl thiouracil, which is used to treat hyperthyroidism, is a case in point. Stirrett, et al.,[29] found recently that out of 70 cases, 7 gave toxic responses to the drug: nausea (2), jaundice (3), vomiting (2), fever (1), leucocyte changes (1), hair loss (1), vaginal bleeding (1), joint swelling (1). The amount of the drug needed to bring the protein-bound iodine to "normal" varied from 0.05 to 0.6 gm. per day.

Adrenaline, when administered to humans at 20 μg. per min. levels, caused increases in pulmonary ventilation of 13 to 153 per cent. The percentage increases in oxygen consumption resulting from the same administration were 19 to 56 per cent.[30] Noradrenaline at the same level caused increases in pulmonary ventilation of 39 to 70 per cent and changes in oxygen consumption from −23 percent up to +31 per cent. Funkenstein, et al.,[31] have tabulated the differences in the pharmacological action of these two substances and have adduced good evidence that two different types of psychotic patients tend to secrete excessive amounts, respectively, of the two types of hormones. Those who appear to secrete excess epinephrine-like hormone are more likely, at better than the 0.01 level of probability, to be benefited by electric shock therapy. If there are, as indicated, wide differences in the amounts of these related hormones secreted by different individuals, the wide variation in their effects on individuals cited above would be expected.

Kalter[32] has shown that the susceptibility to the production of cleft palates by cortisone administration is not the same in different strains of mice. For example, 10 mice of the A strain were treated four times with 2.5 mg. of cortisone beginning on the eleventh day of gestation. Every one of the 36 mice born had cleft palates. When strain C57BL mice were treated in the same way at the same time, 22 females gave birth to 75 young only 14 of which had cleft palates. The difference between the strains when injection was at three different periods during gestation was always significant with a P value less than 0.001.

One of the difficulties in assessing individual differences in response to hormone preparations lies in the lack of uniformity of these preparations. Thus, when different brands of ACTH were studied, they appeared to differ substantially from one another.[33]

Histamine is a substance to which there are known variable responses. When 4 dogs were injected with histamine in the same way, the range in the hydrochloric acid produced in the stomach was 4-fold.[34]

It has been known for some time that mice receiving injections of pertussis vaccine develop a very high sensitivity to histamine poisoning. In Table 16 are given the total deaths divided by the total number of mice injected with histamine at different levels for five different strains of mice.[35] The most marked resistance is shown by the CF strain which has not been rendered materially susceptible to histamine by the pertussis vaccine. The LD_{50} for this treated strain is about 200 times that for the TF strain. It should be noted that there are intrastrain differences also. For example, in the BF strain, 2 animals out of 10 were *killed* with 0.125 mg. of histamine, whereas 5 out of 10 *survived* a dosage 64 times as high. This shows that for different individual mice within this strain differences in the amounts of histamine required to kill may be of the order of 100-fold.

The existence of the medical speciality of anesthesiology is itself an indication that inter-individual variation in anesthesia is important. As Nelson[36] says in connection with anesthesia, "If a series is large enough there will inevitably be a number of dangerous or even fatal reactions from what are ordinarily considered safe doses." Of course,

Table 16.
Histamine Poisoning in Pertussis Vaccine Treated Mice

Histamine Base, mg./mouse	Strain of Mice				
	TF	CF	BF	SD_1	SD_2
0.031	0/10[a]	0/10	0/10	0/0	0/5
0.125	10/10	0/10	2/10	7/10	0/10
0.5	9/10	1/10	6/10	10/10	1/10
2.0	10/10	1/10	6/10	10/10	3/10
8.0	.....	1/10	5/10	10/10	....

TF, Swiss Webster strain from the Tumblebrook Farms. CF, CF_1 strain (white) from the Carworth Farms. BF, N.H.I. strain from the Beverly Farms, SD_1, Sharp & Dohme colony of mice originated from the Webster strain. SD_2, another Sharp & Dohme strain also originated from the Webster strain.

[a]Deaths/total injected.

From J. Munoz and L. F. Schuchardt, *J. Allergy,* 24, 331 (1953).

there are other variables in the total situation, variations in the anesthetic preparations, variations in the mode and rate of administration, variations in the particular condition of the patient at the time of administration, etc., but superimposed upon all these is the fact that individuals may react very differently when all other variables are held as constant as possible. Relatively little research has been directed toward finding the cause of this inter-individual variability, and some students of anesthesia are inclined to minimize its importance. The subject of anesthesia is, however, far too large to be treated here in more than a cursory manner.

Variability, which must have a biochemical basis, has also been observed with respect to antibiotics. In some individuals, after the administration of penicillin, a detectable blood level is maintained much longer than in others.[37] A substantial percentage of individuals experienced side reactions when they were given 50,000 units of penicillin during 2½ days.[38] The side reactions of 28 normal individuals were graded as follows: 41 "slight," 2 "moderate," 7 "severe." Out of the 28 individuals, 26 showed some reactions; this figure should be discounted, however, because some individuals given placebos showed a few "slight" and "moderate" reactions, but no severe ones.

In the same study aureomycin (150 mg.) was administered to 27 normal young men during 2½ days. There were 67 reactions: 58 "slight," 6 "moderate," 3 "severe." Twenty individuals out of 27 showed some kind of reaction. When 50 control individuals received placebos, there were 11 "slight" and 3 "moderate" reactions. Seven individuals out of 50 showed some reaction.

When individuals were administered 800 mg. per day of phenylbutazone (Butazolidin) for 14 days or more, each developed a characteristic plasma level.[39] For 60 subjects this level ranged from 60 to 150 mg. per liter and was constant from day to day for individuals. It was concluded that the rate at which the drug was metabolized under the conditions used varied from 17 to 35 per cent per day for different individuals. It is interesting that the "biological half-life" of this substance varies from species to species—3 hours for rabbits, 6 hours for dogs and rats, 72 hours for man. It is also clear from the above that its rate of disappearance varies widely for individual human subjects.

Studies of the plasma levels of phenylindanedione after injection of 400 mg. in 10 individuals showed that after 8 hours the plasma concentrations varied from 6 to 29 mg. per liter.[40] The time necessary for the levels to reach 5 mg. per liter ranged from 9 to 33 hours. Repeated tests on the same individual showed his levels behaved in the same manner each time.

A study of the effects of administering isonicotinic acid hydrazide to 173 tuberculosis patients for 3 months resulted in the following observations: no toxicity, 62 per cent; increased reflexes, 13 per cent; tremor of limbs, 12 per cent; twitching of legs, 1 per cent; drowsiness, 8 per cent; difficulty in urination, 2 per cent; constipation, 5 per cent; nervousness, 2 per cent; flushing of face, 2 per cent; skin rashes, 2 per cent.[41]

Antihistaminics are rather notorious from the standpoint of the diverse reactions which they elicit from individuals. Benadryl, according to a typical report,[42] caused side reactions in 133 out of 217 patients to whom it was administered. Drowsiness was reported for 93 patients, dry mouth for 44, parasthesias of the hands for 32, headache for 21, dizziness for 15, nervousness for 8, tinnitus for 8, vomiting for 4, confusion for 3, narcolepsy for 2, weakness for 2, and diarrhea for 1. Even if the complete accuracy of such reports is questioned (some of the patients might have responded similarly to place-bos, either due to suggestion or to some other independent cause), the observations cannot be wholly discounted. The symptoms are often too definite and too closely tied to the administration of the antihistaminic for the relationship to be denied.

Pyribenzamine is reported to elicit side reactions in a smaller pro-portion of patients than does benadryl and the pattern is somewhat different.[43] Gastrointestinal symptoms topped the list with 19 out of 200 patients being affected in this way. Insomnia was reported in 6 cases, and dry mouth in only 4. Drowsiness was noted for 18 cases and vertigo for 16. One case of urticaria was found definitely to be caused by the drug.

All other antihistaminics produced side reactions.[44] One, dra-mamine, is often very effective for the prevention of motion sickness, but it is not effective for all individuals. A recently tested antihista-minic, vibazine,[45] was found to have effects that lasted from 1 hour to over 8 hours in different individuals. Of the 545 patients tested, 31 showed effects after 8 hours or more. Of the whole group, 33 (6 per cent) showed moderate to severe side reactions.

In all of the examples of individuality in relation to drug action so far discussed, we have sought to avoid what might be regarded as typical cases of allergy. In allergy we see clearly evidences of bio-chemical individuality which is related, no doubt, to the individuality of body proteins, concerning which there is abundant evidence of various sorts (pp. 53, 54). Since the field of allergy involves a volumi-nous and special literature, we will make no attempt to survey the field. We will merely suggest that in this area there is abundant evi-dence of biochemical individuality. Furthermore, there is evidence that allergic tendencies are inherited. Since the capabilities for build-ing specific body proteins are inherited, this seems inevitable. It may also be noted that the dividing line between allergic and nonallergic reactions is not always easy to draw on any scientific basis. If one is inclined to use the word allergy loosely to designate any *unusual* reaction to a chemical agent, then the term can be used in connection with any and every known drug.

Individuality is exhibited not only with respect to the responses to drugs and chemicals but also to radiations. Radiologists have long been puzzled by the fact that one patient may be greatly benefited and another not by the same radiation treatment. There is also a wide spread in tolerance to radiation.

Variation in different strains of mice to X radiation has recently been studied.[46] The percentage depression of growth (below the controls) produced by radiation of different strains was as follows: Z, 24 per cent; RI, 27 per cent; S, 35 per cent; E, 59 per cent; LWG, 85 per cent, BALB/GW, 161 per cent. Heavier strains tended to be more resistant, and females were more resistant than males. In another study, a 4-fold decrease in head sensitivity (to radiation) was observed, in the following order: dba, Marsh, C57 black, and C3H. Sensitivity seems to be related to the adrenal hormones.[47]

Radiation, of course, affects specific chemical substances present in biological systems. It appears evident that when the enzymic and hormonal levels of two individuals differ markedly in pattern by inheritance, there will be corresponding differences (as there are in mice) to radiation effects.

Summary

Krantz and Carr[1] quote a parody attributed to Dragstedt which goes as follows:

> Build me newer molecules,
> O my Soul—
> As the swift seasons roll
> Let each new compound
> Safer than the last
> Avoid the reactions observed in the past
> Till all at length are free
> From vexing idiosyncrasy.

If our interpretation is correct, it will be quite impossible to find a drug that will act with complete uniformity on all human beings. In order for this to be accomplished, variation, the cornerstone of evolution, and biochemical individuality would have to be abolished.

Regardless of the drug or chemical (or radiation) used, wide human variability in response may be noted. For some drugs, the more useful ones, the variations are less extreme, and the extreme reactions are relatively rare. For all agents, however, the variation may be substantial. These facts are known and have been recognized for decades, but relatively little attention has been paid to them in the form of research effort. The probable connection between variation in drug responses and biochemical individuality has not been generally recognized, nor has any substantial amount of data been collected which is directly pertinent to this interpretation.

REFERENCES

1. John C. Krantz, Jr., and C. Jelleff Carr, *The Pharmacologic Principles of Medical Practice*, Williams & Wilkins Co., Baltimore, Md., ed., 1954, p. 64.
2. A. J. Clark, *The Mode of Action of Drugs on Cells*, Edward Arnold & Co., London, England, 1933.
3. Ph. L'Heritier, *Cold Spring Harbor Symposia on Quant. Biol.*, XVI, 99–112 (1951).
4. Margaret K. Deringer, Thelma B. Dunn, and W. E. Heston, *Proc. Soc. Exptl. Biol. Med.*, 83, 474–479 (1953).
5. Freidrichs H. Harris, *U.S. Armed Forces Med. J.*, 3, 1023–1028 (1952).
6. Roger J. Williams, *Quart. J. Studies Alc.*, 7, 567–587 (1947).
7. John M. Nagle, *J. Allergy*, 10, 179–181 (1939).
8. W. W. Jetter, *Am. J. Med. Sci.*, 196, 475 (1938).
9. Ralph S. Banay, *Quart J. Studies Alc.*, 4, 580–605 (1944).
10. E. M. P. Widmark, *Physiological Papers Dedicated to Professor August Krogh*, Levin & Munksgaard, Copenhagen, Denmark, 1926.
11. Douglas McG. Kelley and S. Eugene Barrera, *Psychiat. Quart.*, 15, 224–248 (1941).
12. Curt P. Richter, *Quart. J. Studies Alc.*, 1, 650–662 (1941).
13. Robert Fleming, "Medical Treatment of the Inebriate," in *Alcohol, Science, and Society*, Journal of Studies on Alcohol, Inc., New Haven, Conn., 1945, pp. 387–402.
14. Samuel Henry Kraines, *The Therapy of the Neuroses and Psychoses*, Lea and Febiger, Philadelphia Pa., 3rd ed., 1948.
15. Charles C. Hewitt, *Quart. J. Studies Alc.*, 4, 368–386 (1943).
16. See reference 2, p. 107.
17. R. B. Goldbloom and A. Goldbloom, *J. Pediatrics*, 43, 631 (1953).
18. J. Ducey and D. B. Williams, *J. Pediatrics*, 43, 644 (1953).
19. Walter Landauer, *Genetics*, 38, 216–228 (1953).

20. Hugh P. Brinton, Elizabeth S. Frasier, and A. Link Koven, *Public Health Repts.*, 67, 835–847 (1952).
21. F. Tattersfield and C. T. Gimingham, *Ann. Applied Biol.*, 14, 217–239 (1927).
22. Louis Goodman and Alfred Gilman, *The Pharmacological Basis of Therapeutics*, The Macmillan Co., New York, N.Y., 1941.
23. Jane E. Denton and Henry K. Beecher, *J. Am. Med. Assoc.*, 141, 1051–1057, 1146–1153 (1949).
24. O. H. Plant and I. H. Pierce, *J. Pharmacol. Exptl. Therap.*, 33, 329–357 (1928).
25. Ardrey W. Downs and Nathan B. Eddy, *J. Lab. Clin. Med.*, 13, 739–745 (1928).
26. Sydney Ellis, *J. Pharmocol. and Exptl. Therap.*, 91, 370–378 (1947).
27. Paul B. Sawin and David Glick, *Proc. Natl. Acad. Sci. U.S.*, 29, 55–59 (1943).
28. Erwin Levin, Joseph B. Kirsner, and Walter L. Palmer, *J. Lab. Clin. Med.*, 37, 415–424 (1951).
29. Robert L. Stirrett, Donald W. Petit, and Paul Starr, *J. Clin. Endocrinol. Metabolism*, 12, 719–724 (1952).
30. R. F. Whelan and I. Maureen Young, *Brit. J. Pharmacol.*, 8, 98–102 (1953).
31. Daniel H. Funkenstein, Milton Greenblatt, and Harry C. Solomon, *Am. J. Psychiat.*, 108, 652–662 (1952).
32. Harold Kalter, *Genetics*, 39, 185–196 (1954).
33. Henry D. Kaine, *Proc. Soc. Exptl. Biol. Med.*, 81, 412–415 (1952).
34. W. D. M. Paton and M. Schachter, *Brit. J. Pharmacol.*, 6, 509–513 (1951).
35. J. Munoz and L. F. Schuchardt, *J. Allergy*, 24, 330–334 (1953).
36. Erwin E. Nelson, *J. Am. Med. Assoc.*, 113, 1373–1375 (1939).
37. John F. Waldo and Jeanne T. Tyson, *J. Lab. Clin. Med.*, 37, 272–277 (1951).
38. Austin H. Kutscher, Jack Budowsky, Stanley L. Lane, and Neal W. Chilton, *J. Allergy*, 24, 164–171 (1953).
39. J. J. Burns, Rose K. Rose, Theodore Chenkin, A. Goldman, Arthur Schulert, and Bernard B. Brodie, *J. Pharmacol. Exptl. Therap.*, 109, 346–347 (1953).
40. Arthur R. Schulert and Murray Weiner, *J. Pharmacol. Exptl. Therap.*, 110, 451–457 (1954).
41. Daniel E. Jenkins, *Southern Med. J.*, 46, 1052–1057 (1953).
42. Emanuel Schwartz, *Ann. Allergy*, 7, 770–777 (1949).
43. Alex S. Friedlaender and Sidney Friedlaender, *J. Lab. Clin. Med.*, 31, 1350–1354 (1946).

44. Howard T. Simpson, Master's Thesis, University of Tennessee, 1950.
45. American Academy of Allergy, Committee on New Drugs, Dr. Carl E. Arbesman, Chairman, *J. Allergy,* 25, 288–289 (1954).
46. Douglas Grahn, *J. Exptl. Zoöl.,* 125, 39–61 (1954).
47. M. C. Reinhard, E. A. Mirand, H. L. Goltz, and J. G. Hoffman, *Proc. Soc. Exptl. Biol. Med.,* 85, 367–370 (1954).

IX

Miscellaneous Evidences
of Individuality

There are numerous diverse evidences of individuality which have some bearing on the general theme of this book. Of these we will discuss briefly only a few.

Basal Metabolism

A basal metabolism measurement which constitutes a summation of the oxygen consumption of every cell and tissue in the body cannot be expected to reveal anything regarding the intricate details of the metabolism of the individual under examination. It is a fact, however, that the metabolism of normal children 2 to 4 years old, for example, varies from about 45 to 65 cal. per sq. m. of body surface per hour,[1] and that intra-individual measurements show far less variation than do inter-individual measurements. Although any value within the range ±15 per cent of the average is commonly regarded as "normal" clinically, it is not safe to conclude that variations within the normal range are meaningless. Although a high value (+10), even if exhibited regularly by an individual, may be difficult or impossible to interpret clinically, it is not without meaning; it denotes individuality even with respect to the summation of all the oxygen consumption taking place in the tissues. Such a summation, of course, tends to weight heavily those tissues which are relatively abundant like muscle and to neglect variations in metabolism in such structures as endocrine glands which are relatively small.

In the area related to total metabolism as in many other areas it is difficult to find data pertaining to individuals and inter-individual variation. In a pioneer nutrition experiment involving restricted diets from the Carnegie Institution, some interesting data of this sort were included.[2] Groups of healthy male adults were placed on highly restricted (starvation) diets for a period of months, and from three tables the following information regarding five individuals are selected (Table 17).

Table 17.
Metabolic Data on Restricted Diet

Individual	Weight, kg.		Daily Caloric Intake for Maintenance at Low Weight Level	Average Daily Loss of Nitrogen, gm.
	Control	Minimum		
Kon	69.0	60.3	1600	4.09
Pec	64.3	57.8	1600	2.91
Tom	59.5	54.3	1600	0.62
Can	79.8	68.8	2500	1.85
Pea	69.3	60.0	2400	2.40

From "Carnegie Nutrition Laboratory Experiment," Chap. 3 in Ancel Keys, *et al.*, *Biology of Human Starvation*, University of Minnesota Press, Minneapolis, Minn., 1950, Vol. I, pp. 34–62.

On the basis of their total metabolisms, one might conclude that Kon and Tom were alike metabolically; however, the average loss of nitrogen per day was nearly seven times as high in Kon as in Tom. On the basis of their practically identical initial and final weights, one might suppose that Kon and Pea would be very similar; however, the calorie requirement of Pea was 50 per cent higher than that of Kon, and he lost 40 per cent less nitrogen.

These data illustrate the fact that individuals of the same weight or those with identical total metabolisms can differ materially in various aspects of their metabolism.

One study indicates what might be expected, namely, that there is variation in ability to adapt metabolism to changed climatic conditions.[3] Of 21 women examined, 13 showed a 6 to 11 per cent drop in basal metabolism when they moved from a temperate climate into the tropics; 8 on the other hand showed little or no change. When certain individuals find it difficult to accommodate themselves to a warm climate, there is a temptation to blame it on to their "attitude of mind" and neglect the fact that there are substantial physiological differences between individuals.

Growth Patterns

We have already noted (p. 43) that even in a newborn baby, the width of the bone, muscle, and fat layers of the calf of the leg are distinctive for each individual and different for the two sexes. The developmental patterns of individual children are also distinctive and are observable even in gross measurements, such as body weight. Wetzel has pioneered in this field and has worked out practical grids for evaluating the physical fitness of growing children.[4] He finds that all children tend to follow one of nine "channels" of growth and that, if they stray away from the channel in which their physique places them early in life, something is wrong—perhaps infection or malnutrition. The older idea that a "normal" child of a certain age should have a certain height and weight is absolutely indefensible in the light of present-day knowledge.

If we were able to scrutinize growth in a more detailed manner—that is, to give attention to the growth and development of each organ and tissue—we would doubtless find characteristic patterns of growth which encompass the entire body. Certainly in the growth and development of bones and teeth distinctive patterns are present.[5,6]

The development of the brains of different species of animals, as judged by the accumulation of DNA, follows very different patterns which are without question genetically determined.[7] It needs to be stressed that genetic factors (as well as environmental factors, notably nutrition) are strong determinants of the progress of development or of change. Two children of the same age who have the same over-all dimensions may possess entirely different genetic potentialities for growth and development, as well as for subsequent degeneration. Pattern change with time may be genetically controlled.

Temperature-Control Patterns

Body temperature, as determined orally, undergoes diurnal variations; but if a series of well young men are tested at the same time of day, considerable variation is observed. In 276 medical students, between 8 and 9 A.M. the variation was from 96.6° to 99.4°F.[8] In a group of 260 normal males (Grant Study)[9] the variation when the temperatures were taken in midmorning or midafternoon was from 97.0° to 100.1°F. Although the temperature of well individuals taken repeatedly at different times of day is not usually recorded in permanent form, some studies indicating variable patterns have been made. Kleitman and Ramsaroop found in a small series (some of the original group were "temperamentally unfit for regular hours" and were not included) three types of temperature variation curves. Only one individual of the group had the "normal" temperature (98.6°F.) in 40 per cent of the measurements between 10 A.M. and 10 P.M.[10] The diurnal variation is related to sleep patterns which are often distinctive, sometimes easily modified and sometimes not.[11]

The oral temperature is the resultant, *for that region*, of all the heat-producing and heat-dissipating agencies in the entire body and is, thus, an attempted summation. Since biochemical activity is accompanied by increased heat production, local activities tend to produce local temperature rises. Blood flow, of course, tends constantly to diminish any differentials which are built up by local activity. Muscular activity may, partly because muscle is so abundant, increase the temperature of the whole body until there is a high fever of 103°F. or more.

If it were possible to get simultaneous readings of the temperature of every organ and tissue of resting individuals, it seems probable that highly distinctive individual patterns would be observable. The probability that this is so is indicated, for example, in a study by Pennes[12] who measured the tissue and arterial blood temperatures in the resting forearms in 14 subjects. He found in 8 subjects a higher temperature in the distal forearm or hand than in the proximal arm. In 4 subjects the distal portion had a lower temperature than the proximal; in 2 subjects there were negligible differences.

It is evident that temperature measurements, when critically made, reveal inescapably the existence of biochemical individuality. Even overall temperatures, though fundamentally summations, often reveal substantial differences.

Sensitivity to Pain

The subject of pain is a very complicated one on which we can touch only briefly, but the existence of a high degree of variability with respect to pain sensitiveness can hardly be questioned.

At one end of the scale are those individuals who lack all sensitivity to the usual pain stimuli—burns, cuts, bruises, etc. Such a person was a boy at Johns Hopkins who could have pins thrust into him; his skin could be pinched until it became bloodshot; his Achilles' tendon could be squeezed with full force without any indication of discomfort. He did have a normal sense of touch and was sensible to cold and heat throughout his body surface, but nowhere was there a response to pain.

Next in the scale of variation are numerous individuals who are subnormal in their pain sensitivity. Dr. Emanuel Libman found among his patients 30 to 40 per cent who belonged in this category. Dr. Leon J. Saul tested 97 pugilists and found only 10 who were significantly responsive to painful stimuli.[13]

Still higher in the scale of sensitivity are the "normal" individuals who are about average in their reactions to painful stimuli. They experience moderate pain when the stimulus is moderate. Admittedly there is no adequate measure of the intensity of pain, and hence it cannot be described in quantitative terms.

At the sensitive extreme are those who experience pain of an acute nature even when the stimulus is only moderate. Those hypersensitive individuals are perhaps those for whom even suggestion may cause pain and who exhibit referred pain in a most striking manner. A recent observation would make it appear likely that *hyposensitive, average* and *hypersensitive* individuals are about equal in number. Papper, *et al.,*[14] state that only about one-third of a group of 286 unselected patients complained of severe postoperative pain, one-third had moderate pain, and one-third no pain at all.

Actually, the situation is not as simple as our discussion might imply. Different sites differ in their sensitiveness to various stimuli. Heat, for example, does not ever induce pain when applied to intestinal tissues so far as is known.[15] In this region severe burns would be painless, yet distention of intestines by gas, for example, can cause severe abdominal pain. One's internal organs can be badly diseased without there being any feeling of pain in the affected area. Not all lesions induce pain. Yet some of the children referred to above who did not experience pain from ordinary outside stimuli experienced abdominal pain, in one case from kidney disease.

Studies of "pain thresholds" by the Wolff, Hardy, Goodell technique indicate that these thresholds do not vary widely in normal individuals, nor are they readily modified by changing conditions.[16] The technique involves focussing light of definite intensity on the blackened forehead of the subject and noting the length of the exposure required to cause a sensation of pain. This procedure gives reasonably duplicable results and has been used in testing the analgesic effects of drugs. It appears, however, to be measuring something quite different from the general pain sensitivity. This is not unexpected since the stimulus is of only one kind and is applied only to one area. Furthermore, *intensity* of pain does not enter into this test.

When pain thresholds are determined by other methods involving, for example, the application of measurable pressure to the calf of the leg, the range of variability is several-fold.[17] No one method can be expected to give a complete picture of the pain thresholds, much less the more subtle matter of pain sensitivities. Presumably tests for the pain-inducing effect of heat applied to intestinal tissue of different individuals would yield uniformly negative results, but this, of course, does not mean that individuals are uniform in their pain sensitivity.

Whatever mechanisms may be involved in producing variable sensitivity to pain, they must have a genetic origin, and it would appear that all gradations of sensitivities from zero up to the highest level exist in the tissues of different individuals.

Effects of Oxygen Deprivation

Aviation has stimulated interest in the effects of oxygen lack (anoxia) on human beings and has brought the realization that some individuals are affected much more readily than others. The literature on the subject is full of allusions to the ever-present variation, but it is difficult to find definitive data. In connection with training of Air Force personnel, it is, of course, desirable to select individuals who are as little hampered as possible by untoward susceptibilities. In connection with anoxia, however, the tendency has been to make conditions such that all trainees would be out of danger in this respect, rather than to have marginal conditions that might be deleterious to some and, thus, make it necessary to select for nonsusceptibility.

One experiment which shows up the variation and its importance was that reported by Halstead in which impairment of peripheral vision was studied. Anoxia, or more properly hypo-oxia, causes all sorts of changes in metabolism, respiration, nerve responses, etc., but one of the most sensitive sites of disturbance is in vision.[18] Halstead found that when 20 young men selected to meet the physical and mental standards of the Service Air Corps were exposed for a few hours a day to a simulated atmosphere of 10,000 feet, 13 out of the group developed, after 3 or 4 weeks, a marked progressive impairment of peripheral vision. Seven of the group were unaffected. In some subjects the impairment of peripheral vision was accompanied by similar alteration of the central vision. In others there was no similar accompaniment. The effect was rapidly reversed in some of the subjects when the intermittent hypo-oxia was discontinued but in others it took days or weeks before the peripheral vision could be brought back to the pre-anoxia level. The impairment of peripheral vision was evaluated by briefly exposing targets in the peripheral field and noting the ability of the subjects to see the targets. The effect of intermittent exposure to low oxygen atmosphere was insidious in that the subjects were wholly unaware of the progressive impairment of their peripheral vision. This impairment is particularly important because of the potential importance of peripheral vision in flying (as well as in automobiling and many sports) and because so-called "normal" individuals may vary greatly in their initial endowments. Among 28 young men with 20-20 vision who were tested,[19] the one with the best peripheral vision could see an object's movement when its relative speed was 2.15 miles per hour; the one with the poorest visual equipment for this particular purpose could not see the movement of the object until its relative speed was 90.95 miles per hour.

Another study[20] involved 8 individuals who were subjected to an altitude of 44,800 feet. There was a wide range of reactions. The range in the arterial oxygen saturation was 58 to 84 per cent; the range in the carbon dioxide pressure in the arterial blood was from 12 to 34 mm. of mercury. One of the individuals experienced anoxia aftereffects. The aftereffects of anoxia may be mild and transient or severe and lasting, depending on the individual.

Oxygen is a substrate for enzymes located in every cell of the body; and, since the corresponding participating enzymes are not of the same efficiency in different individuals, variability in the effects of oxygen lack should be expected. As Nims says: "It is obvious that anoxia affects many functions and that these are not affected in the same degree from one individual to another."[21]

Because of its tie-up with aviation, decompression sickness, or aero-embolism, may be mentioned at this point. Some individuals are highly susceptible, while others are highly resistant, and the symptoms vary from case to case.[22,23] As with air sickness[24] there is up to now no way of telling in advance who will be resistant and who will be susceptible.

Air training programs have brought forth strong evidence indicating that individual cadets have in general vastly different characteristics and potentialities. The appreciation that these differences are often inborn, genetically determined, and closely related to physiological and biochemical individuality is limited. Even more limited is the appreciation of the probability that related inborn differences are highly important, not only in pilot, bombardier, or navigator training, but also in every walk of life.

Variations Related to Blood Pressure, Blood Flow, Etc.

There are a number of ways in which people differ markedly from one another which we will pass over without more than a brief mention because they lie primarily in the field of the physiology of the circulation.

In the *cold pressor test*,[25] for example, the blood pressure is taken on one arm while the opposite hand is immersed in ice water for about a minute. The blood pressure change due to the immersion of the other hand in cold water may vary in various "normal" individuals from 0 to about 30 mm. of mercury.

The blood flow through different regions of the body takes place at vastly different rates.[26] On the basis of what is known about variations in blood vessel patterns, it is apparent that individual patterns must exist and variations must be great. We have not been able, however, to find suitable raw data which would give us a definite idea as to what these patterns are like or how large the variation is in individuals of the same age.

The splanchnic blood flow was found in one study to range from 845 to 5260 ml. per minute in different individuals.[27] Such differences should not be surprising in view of anatomical and other differences already mentioned (p. 30). Coronary blood flow and cardiac oxygen consumption have also been found to vary widely in dogs.[28]

Related to blood flow are the spontaneous variations in volume of finger tips, top tips, and pinna.[29] There are five separate rhythms, two of which are directly related to heart beat and respiration; the other three are designated as α, β and γ rhythms. In twelve subjects, three different types of α rhythms were exhibited, and these are thought to be related to the excitability of the individual subjects.

Studies on the changes in blood distribution in the body after release of previously occluded circulation in the leg showed marked individual differences. In five different individuals the percentage of blood taken up by the abdomen, for example, varied from +11 per cent down to −7 per cent. In each individual the measurements were carried out three times so that the observed differences were truly inter-individual.[30]

The movement of cutaneous interstitial fluids varies from a 3- to 4-fold range in normal individuals as determined by injecting ribo-flavin intradermally and recording the time required for one-half its fluorescence to disappear.[31] When repeated tests were made on three individuals it was found that one gave relatively highly variable results. (S.D. 48.4), and the others gave relatively constant results (S.D. 9.5 and 5.8).

It seems inevitable in view of our discussion on variations of anatomy and of heart outputs that normal individuals should have circulatory peculiarities. An extreme case of what *may be* a circulatory peculiarity has been called to my attention. This individual continually has a problem of cold feet; he uses a heating pad under his working desk, carries one around with him and on social occasions sits near an electric outlet, plugs it in, and attempts to be comfortable. It seems likely that this individual suffers because of unrecognized anatomical and/or neurological differences rather than for psychogenic reasons.

One of the most interesting reactions to cold (which probably has its circulatory implications) is that of "cold allergy." Individuals afflicted with this difficulty may have a welt raised across their bodies merely by tracing a line with a piece of ice. Such manifestations would appear to call for an intensive study of the differences in the reactions of people who are more nearly normal in this respect.

Effects of Electricity

As might be expected on the basis of all the facts about variability which we have mentioned, individuals differ in their responses to electricity.

Dalziel has made an extensive study of the quantitative effects of electricity on man.[32,33] He found that the amount of direct current which could be perceived varied among 115 men from 2 to 12.5 ma.—a 6-fold range. For 60-cycle current the corresponding range was from 0.4 to 1.8 ma.—a 4.5-fold range. The "let go" current (60 cycle) varied from 7.5 to 22 ma. for 162 individuals, of which 28 were women. Very interesting was the fact that there was a distinct sex difference. The "let go" currents for 134 men varied from 9.5 to 22.0 ma., whereas those for the 28 women varied from 7.5 to 14.0 ma. The sex difference strongly suggests genetic variation.

Taste Sensitivities

One of the earlier recorded observations indicating that people's taste reactions for a particular chemical substance may not by any means be uniform was made with respect to *creatine*, which was found to be quite tasteless to some individuals but bitter and biting to others.[34] About the same time it was found that individuals vary in their ability to taste phenylthiocarbamide (PTC) and related compounds.[35] To most it is either violently bitter or completely tasteless. A small minority however, assign to it various other tastes.[36,37,38]

The variable taste reactions to this particular substance have caught the interest of geneticists and others with a result that the phenomenon has been widely studied not only among various peoples and races but also in rats and chimpanzees. The ability to taste PTC is inherited and has become an important item in the repertoire of human geneticists.[39] An extremely interesting observation in connection with the ability of tasters to taste this substance is that unless the substance has an opportunity to dissolve in the taster's saliva it cannot be tasted.[40] If dissolved in water or in another individual's saliva and placed upon the dry tongue of a taster, it is tasteless. In nontasters, it is tasteless regardless of the medium.

Actually when the subject is studied carefully, it becomes evident that ability to taste PTC is not definitely a positive or negative matter; people differ widely in their taste thresholds for the substance. The tasters are able to taste low concentrations; the nontasters require much higher levels but are in general able to taste it in highly concentrated solution.

One might suppose on the basis of the amount of attention PTC has received that it is quite a unique substance in its ability to elicit different responses from different individuals. Actually this is not the case at all since wide inter-individual differences in taste threshold and taste reactions can be observed with almost anything that can be tasted. Hundred-fold variations in taste thresholds are very common (even when small groups are studied) with respect to substances like sodium or potassium chlorides or hydrochloric acid.[41] Saccharine, quinine, cascara, and mannose are among the substances, in addition to creatine mentioned above, for which individuals are known to show highly diverse taste reactions.[42] Richter found some children who could not taste 20 per cent sugar solutions.[43]

Fox, who discovered the variable taste reactions to PTC, has also studied variable taste reactions to sodium benzoate.[44] He finds that human beings in general can be divided into two groups depending on whether they are tasters or nontasters for PTC, and that furthermore each of these two groups can be subdivided into five subgroups depending on whether sodium benzoate is to them (1) salty, (2) sweet, (3) sour, (4) bitter, or (5) tasteless. He found after testing about 1500 people that practically every possible combination of tastes could be found except that in which PTC was tasteless and sodium benzoate bitter. The more numerous cases were (giving the tastes in the order: PTC-sodium benzoate): (1) bitter-salty, (2) bitter-sweet, (3) bitter-bitter, (4) tasteless-salty. It furthermore appears that the "bitter-salty" group finds the taste of a variety of foods which may be considered controversial (sauerkraut, buttermilk, turnips, spinach, etc.) more attractive than average, whereas those who are in the "bitter-bitter" group like the taste of such foods less than average. Among the 1457 people tested, Fox found, for example, that 56.6 per cent liked sauerkraut, 19.5 per cent disliked it, and the remainder registered no comment. Among the "bitter-salty" group (273 individuals) 82.4 per cent liked sauerkraut and 17.3 per cent disliked it. Among the "bitter-bitter" group, however, only 26 per cent liked sauerkraut, and 23.5 per cent disliked it. The same trend was observed throughout the various tests. It is interesting to note that the individuals in the "bitter-salty" group registered definite likes and dislikes much more consistently than did, for example, the "bitter-bitter" group. Of the "bitter-salty" group an average of 97 per cent registered their preferences for nine common test items, whereas only 47 per cent of the "bitter-bitter" group registered a definite like or dislike.

Such investigations as Fox's are not in vogue, and there is no ready outlet for the publication of such results as he obtained. Taste reactions are admittedly not easy to study and, of course, as soon as one begins to experiment he finds inconsistencies: People do not always agree with themselves. The fact that there are intra-individual differences makes those who are disinclined to look at inter-individual differences turn their attention to the environmental factors which may operate to cause the intra-individual differences. It is difficult, however, to avoid recognizing that each individual has his own taste characteristics and that these are doubtless related to his genetically determined biochemical individuality.

One of the interesting observations which may be made in connection with taste-testing is that some individuals appear to have higher stable taste thresholds and others show much greater variability when repeated tests are made. Sufficient studies have not been carried out to ascertain how general or how striking these differences in variability are.

The question of conditioning one's taste is a matter which needs to be considered in this connection. Because it has been repeatedly observed that people sometimes change their tastes (e.g., they like coffee with sugar but learn to like it without), it is sometimes tacitly assumed that almost any taste can be changed in any individual simply by "getting used" to a new taste. Several possibilities need to be considered in this connection; people vary greatly in their adaptability so that, because one individual can adapt some of his tastes readily, it may not be safely concluded that all can do the same. (The fact that a particular American individual learns to speak Chinese readily and fluently does not prove that all Americans are capable of doing this.) Another consideration is the fact that tastes are known to change with age,[45,46] and the fact that a person's tastes are different at different times in his life may not be due to adaptation alone—his internal chemistry is changing progressively also as he matures and as he ages. Although studies have not been directed in such a way as to answer the question with certainty, it seems highly probable that, whereas every individual's tastes are capable of some modification (some much more than others), this modification is *within a range* which is characteristic of the particular individual.

Certain miscellaneous observations have a bearing on our discussion of differences in taste reactions. For example, it is well recognized in hospitals that, although a barium sulfate emulsion is perfectly tasteless and innocuous to many individuals, to others it is very disagreeable. It would appear that the taste threshold for barium sulfate varies from individual to individual and that this substance is soluble enough to give a sensation of taste to some individuals.

Taste idiosyncrasies (for example, the dislike of butter) are related no doubt to taste sensitivities, and according to Davenport[47] there is evidence that such dislikes are inherited.

We shall not go into the question of variations in the sense of smell, although they are widespread,[48,49,50] except in the case of ability to smell the hydocyanic acid evolved from solutions of potassium cyanide.[51] For some individuals a potassium cyanide solution has an odor; for others, it has none and cannot be distinguished in smell from water. For some, it has a strong odor; for others, the odor is detectable but weak. There is a marked difference in the sexes; 24 males out of 132 were unable to distinguish by odor between water and potassium cyanide solution, whereas only 5 females out of 112 lacked this ability. The data suggest that the inability to smell hydrocyanic acid is a sex-linked recessive. There was a highly significant tendency for parents who were "strong smellers" to have children who were "strong smellers" and for parents who were "weak smellers" to have children who were also "weak smellers."

Parasites, Symbionts, Etc.

Biochemical individuality is exhibited in our relationships with bacterial and other parasites and symbionts.

Not only can dogs, which have a keen sense of smell, tell people apart by their odors, but insects also appear to have similar abilities. Two individuals can walk through the woods together; one may attract a large number of mosquitoes, whereas the other may attract few or none. Fleas are very discriminating in this regard, and in the same environment there are those individuals who tend to attract them and others who do not. Fleas also are discriminating as to species; those which commonly live on human beings do not thrive on dogs or cats. Dog fleas and cat fleas are also selective.

More interesting is the fact that each of us probably harbors a distinctive bacterial flora. The evidence for this is based on several different types of observations. Zinsser[52] says:

> Perfectly normal individuals may, on occasion, harbor organisms of many varieties which are capable of causing disease. In fact, the problem of the so-called bacterial carriers—persons who though themselves apparently well for the time being, harbor within their bodies and distribute to their environment bacteria capable of causing disease in others—is, as we shall see, one of the most important difficulties of sanitary prophylaxis.

It is well known, for example, that about 5 per cent of the people who become infected with typhoid germs become typhoid carriers and continue indefinitely to harbor an active colony (harmless to them) of typhoid bacilli in their intestinal tracts. There is abundant evidence of graded susceptibility; there are many mild cases, and the incubation time in different individuals may be from 3 to 30 days, indicating variable resistance. The fact that about 70 per cent of the carriers are women suggests that the constitutional characteristics which make it possible for individuals to endure the presence of the organisms are in some way sex-linked in their inheritance. The evidence with respect to typhoid carriers, diphtheria carriers, scarlet-fever carriers, poliomyelitis-virus carriers, etc., makes it seem probable that "carriers" enter into the dissemination of many other milder infections, and such phenomena contribute to our certainty with respect to the existence and importance of biochemical individuality.

There is reason to think that each of us also carries a distinctive assortment of bacteria which may not be pathogenic to man. It has long been known that individuals may carry in their saliva organisms which are capable of producing lethal infections in mice. Recently more than 50 individuals were tested in this regard, and several were found to be carrying bacteria of sufficient virulence and in sufficient numbers so that their saliva was highly lethal to mice when injected intraperitoneally. Several of these individuals were tested periodically over an interval of approximately 8 months, and in general all of them were found to maintain their mouse-virulent flora throughout the whole period of observation. Conversely, several individuals who possessed nonlethal saliva were retested periodically, and in no case did those individuals produce lethal saliva. All of these tests were made during times when the individuals had no recognizable form of upper respiratory infection or abnormal oral pathology.[53]

It is well known that intestinal bacteria contribute to the nutrition of mammals and that dietary changes may be accompanied by changes in intestinal flora.[54] Bacteria-free mammals appear to have more exacting nutritional requirements than those which are infected with microorganisms.[55] It seems reasonable to suppose that biochemical individuality, which causes the chemical reactions in each individual to follow a quantitatively distinctive pattern, produces in each individual's alimentary tract a peculiar climate which is favorable to the development of an assortment of bacteria peculiar to that individual. The facts cited above as well as many others having to do with susceptibility and immunity to bacterial infection are in line with this supposition. No one so far as I know has even taken the trouble to demonstrate directly that the intestinal population of bacteria (dead and alive) is relatively stable and distinctive for different well individuals; but from the facts cited above, this is probably the case.

In the whole field of immunity there is ample evidence of inborn biochemical individuality. Aside from acquired immunity there is natural immunity which is exhibited in species differences, race differences (in animals and in man), and in individual differences. Immunity is closely related to the individuality which has been demonstrated, for example, with respect to the protein composition of the blood (p. 53).

Transplantation Studies, Etc.

We have already called attention (p. 53) to the extensive literature dealing with blood groups and to the fact that in this area we find abundant and striking evidence of meaningful individuality. A high degree of individuality with respect to skin and other tissues has been established by transplantation studies. These are in a sense parallel to transfusion studies and have been described in detail by Leo Loeb.[56] Because the evidence is voluminous and has been treated fully, we will give it only brief mention here. It is clear from Loeb's monumental work that individuality appears even as low down in the evolutionary scale as the earthworms, but that it becomes more and more striking as we ascend the evolutionary scale.

REFERENCES

1. Robert C. Lewis, Anna Marie Duval, and Alberta Iliff, *J. Pediat.*, 23, 1–18 (1943).
2. Ancel Keys, Josef Brozek, Austin Henschel, Olaf Mickelsen, and Henry Longstreet Taylor, *The Biology of Human Starvation*, University of Minnesota Press, Minneapolis, Minn., 1950, Vol. I, pp. 34–62.
3. Eleanor D. Mason, *Am. J. Trop. Med.*, 20, 669–686 (1940).
4. Norman Carl Wetzel, *The Treatment of Growth Failure in Children*, NEA Service, Cleveland, Ohio, 1948.
5. Icie G. Macy, *Nutrition and Chemical Growth in Childhood*, Charles C. Thomas, Springfield, Ill., 1946, Vol. II.
6. Marion M. Maresh, *Am. J. Diseases Children*, 66, 227–257 (1943).
7. Paul Mandel and Robert Bieth, *Compt. rend.*, 235, 485–487 (1952).
8. E. F. DuBois, *Fever and the Regulation of Body Temperature*, quoted in *Clark's Applied Pharmacology*, The Blakiston Company, Philadelphia, Pa., 8th ed., 1952, p. 281.
9. Clark W. Heath, *et al.*, *What People Are*, Harvard University Press, Cambridge, Mass., 1945, p. 79.
10. N. Kleitman and A. Ramsaroop, *Endocrinology*, 43, 5 (1948).
11. N. Kleitman, *Sleep and Wakefulness*, University of Chicago Press, Chicago, Ill., 1939.

12. Harry H. Pennes, *J. Appl. Physiol.*, 1, 93–122 (1948).
13. George W. Gray, *The Advancing Front of Medicine*, Whittlesey House, New York, N.Y., 1941, p. 277.
14. E. M. Papper, Bernard B. Brodie, and E. A. Rovenstine, *Surgery*, 32, 107–109 (1952).
15. W. K. Livingston, *The Clinical Aspects of Visceral Neurology*, Charles C. Thomas, Springfield, Ill., and Baltimore, Md., 1935, p. 36.
16. George A. Schumacher, Helen Goodell, James D. Hardy, and Harold G. Wolff, *Science*, 92, 110–112 (1940).
17. G. A. Deneau, R. A. Waud, and C. W. Gowdey, *Can. J. Med. Sci.*, 31, 387–393 (1953).
18. Ward C. Halstead, *Science*, 101, 615–616 (1945).
19. C. J. Warden, H. C. Brown, and Sherman Rose, *J. Exptl. Psychology*, 35, 57–70 (1945).
20. D. B. Dill and K. E. Penrod, *J. Applied Physiol.*, 1, 409–417 (1948).
21. Leslie F. Nims, *Ann. Rev. Physiol.* 10, 306 (1948).
22. Ezra V. Bridge, Franklin M. Henry, Sherburne F. Cook, Owen L. Williams, William R. Lyons, and John H. Lawrence, *J. Aviation Med.*, 15, 316–327 (1944).
23. Herschel J. Rubin, *J. Aviation Med.*, 13, 272–276 (1942).
24. Paul A. Campbell, *J. Aviation Med.*, 14, 126–131 (1943).
25. Edgar A. Hines, Jr., and George E. Brown, *Am. Heart J.*, 11, 1–9 (1936).
26. Hardin B. Jones, *Advances in Biological and Medical Physics*, Academic Press, New York, N.Y., 1951, Vol. II, pp. 53–75.
27. Sheila Sherlock, A. G. Bearn, Barbara H. Billings, and J. C. S. Paterson, *J. Lab. Clin. Med.*, 35, 923–932 (1950).
28. F. C. Spencer, D. L. Merrill, S. R. Powers, and R. J. Bing, *Am. J. Physiol.*, 160, 149–162 (1950).
29. G. E. Burch, A. E. Cohn, and C. Neumann, *Am. J. Physiol.* 136, 433–447 (1942).
30. *Acta Physiol. Scand.*, 26, 312–327 (1952).
31. Ray W. Gifford, Jr., J. Earle Estes, Jr., Charles F. Code, Edward J. Baldes, and Grace M. Roth, *J. Lab. Clin. Med.*, 42, 299–309 (1953).
32. Charles F. Dalziel, "Quantitative Effects of Electricity on Man," University of California, mimeographed summary paper furnished by the author, 1953
33. Charles F. Dalziel, *Elec. Eng.*, *AIEE Transactions*, 69, Part II, 1162–1168 (1950).
34. R. J. Williams, *Science*, 74, 597–598 (1931).
35. Arthur L. Fox, *Proc. Natl. Acad. Sci. U.S.*, 18, 115–120 (1932).
36. Albert F. Blakeslee, *Science*, 81, 504–507 (1935).

37. Theodora Nussman Salmon and Albert F. Blakeslee, *Proc. Natl. Acad. Sci. U.S.*, 21, 78–83 (1935).
38. Albert F. Blakeslee and Theodora Nussman Salmon, *Proc. Natl. Acad. Sci. U.S.*, 21, 84–90 (1935).
39. William C. Boyd, *Genetics and Races of Man*, Little, Brown & Company, Boston, Mass., 1950, pp. 278 ff.
40. Jozef Cohen and Donald P. Ogden, *Science*, 110, 532–533 (1949).
41. Roger J. Williams, *Univ. Texas Publ.*, 5109, 10–12 (1951).
42. Roger J. Williams, *The Human Frontier*, Harcourt, Brace & Company, New York, N.Y., 1946, pp. 71–72.
43. Curt P. Richter, *Quart. J. Studies Alc.*, 1, 650–662 (1941).
44. Arthur L. Fox, Personal Communication.
45. P. T. Young, *Psychology Bull.*, 38, 129–164 (1941).
46. J. Warkentin, L. Warkentin, and A. C. Ivy, *Am. J. Psychol.*, 139, 139–146 (1943).
47. C. B. Davenport, File at University of Minnesota.
48. A. F. Blakeslee, *Science*, 48, 298–299 (1918).
49. A. F. Blakeslee and A. L. Fox, *J. Heredity*, 23, 97–106 (1932).
50. Roger J. Williams, *The Human Frontier*, Harcourt, Brace & Company, New York, N.Y., 1946, pp. 73–76.
51. R. L. Kirk, and N. S. Stenhouse, *Nature*, 171, 698–699 (1953).
52. Hans Zinsser, *Resistance to Infectious Disease*, The Macmillan Co., New York, N.Y., 1931. See also René J. Dubos, *Biochemical Determinants of Microbial Diseases*, Harvard University Monograph in Medicine and Public Health, No. 13, Cambridge, Mass., 1954.
53. Lemuel D. Wright, Personal Communication.
54. K. R. Johansson and W. B. Sarles, *Bacteriol. Revs.* 13, 25–45 (1949).
55. James Arthur Reyniers, *Micrurgical and Germ-Free Techniques*, Charles C. Thomas, Springfield, Ill., 1943.
56. Leo Loeb, *The Biological Basis of Individuality*, Charles C. Thomas, Springfield, Ill., 1947.

X

Individuality in Nutrition

Before discussing the broader aspects of nutrition and the possibility of its application to the solution of some of the problems that arise because of biochemical individuality, we will consider, in sequence, several nutritional items for which the evidence of inter-individual differences seems particularly worthy of attention. Rather than attempt the discussion of every known nutritional item from this standpoint, we will exercise some selection. The omission of a particular item from our discussion, however, should not carry the implication that inter-individual differences with respect to this item do not exist.

Potassium

It may be noted that the normal range in the potassium content of the blood serum, for example, as given in Albritton's compilation (Table 5, p. 55), is 3.6 to 4.8 meq. per liter. Sunderman and Boerner[1] cite two relatively recent studies in which the ranges found were larger, 3.6 to 6.2 and 3.1 to 5.3. In a recent study[2] involving individuals who had "disturbed potassium metabolism," it was found that the range of plasma potassium was from 2.4 to 9.0 meq. per liter. In view of the fact that there has been a universal predisposition in all areas to accept moderate or concordant values without question and to reject as "abnormal" those which appear extreme, it seems safe to conclude that for the general population (which includes people who are not completely well) the range of plasma potassium concentrations is at least 2- or 3-fold. That such ranges are real cannot seriously be questioned; that they may be genetically determined is indicated by indirect evidence involving animals. In genetically different strains of sheep, for example, the potassium content of the corpuscles was found to vary from strain to strain through a 9-fold range (Table 6, p. 56).

The most convincing evidence that there is substantial variation in the potassium *needs* of human individuals is the existence of familial periodic paralysis which is accompanied by hypopotassemia. During a paralytic seizure or prior to it, the plasma potassium values in afflicted individuals are from 2.6 to 3.0 meq. per liter[3] (values as low as 1.95 have been reported),[4] and the relief from the condition comes promptly within 30 minutes after the administration of 2 to 5 gm. of potassium chloride. Though the disease has evidently never been thought of in these terms, it seems to be due to inherited needs for augmented amounts of potassium. Presumably because of genetic differences in enzyme systems and possibly in excretion rates, there is a substantial variation in the potassium needs in any human population, and the existence of familial periodic paralysis is a manifestation of an extremely high requirement on the part of certain individuals. There are various enzyme systems in which potassium is needed, and partial genetic blocks involved in the production of any of these, as well as other causes, might be responsible for an augmented demand for potassium. It appears that the requirement for potassium in fat catabolism is substantial, and for this reason persons afflicted with familial periodic paralysis are less likely to have seizures if they are on a low-fat diet.

It may be taken for granted that, if there is a wide variance in the potassium needs of individuals, the sodium needs vary also. We shall, however, dismiss this subject by commenting that the human consumption of sodium chloride is said to vary from 2 to 30 gm. per day,[5] and that sodium salts become highly toxic when there is a potassium deficiency.[6] It seems to the writer extremely unlikely that variations in sodium consumption should be attributed wholly to differences in "habit." The whole subject of low-salt diets needs to be re-examined with these facts in mind.

Calcium

The position of calcium, from the standpoint of its importance in nutrition and the likelihood that diets may be deficient in it, is regarded as probably unequaled by any other element.

Although the accepted variations in the calcium content of plasmas are not particularly striking (p. 55), there is direct evidence for wide variation in individual nutritional needs. Macy[7] cites an example of two normal 5-year-old children living in the same environment and eating the same food; one retained an average of 264 mg. of calcium per day for 45 days, but the other retained 78 per cent more—469 mg. per day. That this observed difference underestimates the variation which exists is shown by a recent careful study[8] by Steggerda and Mitchell who were directly concerned with the problem of variation. In balance studies performed on 19 healthy males, they found that one man given 225 mg. of calcium daily was in calcium balance, while at the other extreme another individual given 261 mg. of calcium daily was losing 256 mg. per day. The total requirement for calcium balance varied for the 19 individuals in experiments of at least 20 days' duration from 222 to 1018 mg. per day. On the basis of the requirement per kilogram of body weight per day, the range was 3.52 to 16.16 mg. On either basis the range is over 4.5-fold. The situation with respect to calcium is such that the Food and Nutrition Board of the National Research Council (which must maintain a conservative attitude) says: "Wide variations among individuals prevail, suggesting metabolic differences not explained by intake or absorption."[9]

If a study were to include both sexes and a large sample of the population (including people who are not wholly well), the range would presumably be larger than 4.5-fold. Since in the study of 19 males referred to above all gradations of needs were exhibited even in this relatively small group, the significance of the *average* need is limited; there are too many individuals whose needs are far from average.

When the element calcium is mentioned, its function as a constituent of bone (and teeth) is likely to come to mind because most of the calcium of the body is in the bones. Calcium is, however, required for blood coagulation and is needed by muscle and other tissues of the body; its importance in these other tissues cannot be judged on the basis of its relative abundance. Bone must be built and maintained, but calcium is doubtless a factor in many enzyme systems and thus has indispensable functions quite aside from those involving bone. There is considerable evidence to indicate that health and longevity are conditioned by an adequate continuous nutritional supply of this element.

Various factors may be associated with variations in calcium needs: differences in vitamin D supply, differences in absorption and excretion, differences in activity of the parathyroid glands, differences in steroid hormone production, differences in thyroid function, differences in phosphate supply and utilization.[10] These we will not discuss, although these considerations may make it possible, in individual cases, to circumvent extra needs for calcium by removing the basis for the augmented need. We are here concerned primarily with the fact that individual people, under prevalent conditions, require amounts of calcium which may vary from individual to individual by a factor of 5.

There are numerous metabolic diseases, infantile and other tetanies, steatorrhea, osteomalacia, arthritis of old age, epilepsy, etc., in which calcium either is or may be implicated. Each of these diseases needs to be studied against a background of wide variability in calcium needs, probably genetically determined, and involving "normal" individuals as well as those having overt disease.

It is well recognized that in Oriental countries there are millions of people who never get calcium at a level comparable with what is regarded adequate in America. It is commonly supposed that such peoples have become *adapted* to living with a lower calcium intake. The mechanism whereby this adaptation takes place is unknown. If individuals who have high demands for calcium are placed in an environment where they cannot get as much as they need, they will either limp along in a deficient state or they will be eliminated from the population. It seems probable that in Oriental countries there has been a genetic selection and that individuals who have high calcium demands have, through the centuries, been eliminated. Although data are not available to answer the question one way or the other, it seems that the demands for calcium (and other nutritional elements) are probably not identical for different ethnic groups and that at least a part of the existing adaptation is genetic.

Unpublished work in the author's laboratory[11] indicates that individual experimental mice have calcium requirements which vary substantially. This is also true of rats,[12] and there is evidence of similar variation in cattle.[13] When cattle are pastured on wheat, an occasional animal will, after a time, first become antisocial by leaving the herd and later develop tetany, which may be completely cured by the administration of calcium salts. It is noteworthy that this does not happen to all the cattle in a herd, only a few. It would appear that some animals have a genetic need for more calcium than is furnished by the wheat pasturage. Others remain healthy and do not suffer from "wheat disease." It is also interesting that an exactly parallel situation seems to exist with respect to magnesium. On certain grasses in specific areas *some* individual cattle suffer from a tetany which results from an inadequate supply of magnesium. This condition is known as "grass disease."

Individual variation in calcium needs suggests the existence of similar variation in magnesium needs and phosphate needs, both of which are closely related. We will not, however, discuss these nutritional elements further at this point.

Trace Elements

We have already cited evidence to indicate that *iodine* needs vary substantially from individual to individual. Not only does the thyroid hormone content of the blood show high inter-individual variation, but in endemic regions not all individuals exhibit simple goiter due to iodine deficiency. And, in nonendemic regions where the iodine content of the foods is sufficient for most individuals, there are still some who suffer deficiency. Furthermore, even the iodine in iodized salt is said to be sufficient to yield unfavorable results for some individuals.

For other trace elements, about which relatively less is known, the evidence for substantial variability is on the whole less impressive though by no means nonexistent. With respect to *copper*, Vallee[14] says that "most investigators agree that the serum copper level of normal individuals is remarkably constant, and in our experience, in close agreement with previous observers, it varies from 84 to 137 μg. per 100 cc. of serum from one individual to another." Cartwright[15] gives a somewhat wider range, 68 to 161 μg. per cent for 128 normal individuals of both sexes, and indicates that hypocupremia is rarely observed, only twice in several hundred determinations. When the copper level deviates from the "normal," it is usually high, not low. Many conditions, most infections, even colds, anemias, myocardial infarctions, leukemia, and malignancy cause significant rise in the copper plasma levels. During pregnancy (40th week) the level averages about 260 μg. per cent. The fact that the plasma copper level is altered by numerous conditions mentioned above is ample evidence of its physiological significance. A large part of the copper of the plasma is combined to produce a specific protein which has been called *coeruloplasmin*.[16]

The interpretation of the above facts with respect to the copper levels of the plasma must be somewhat speculative. It appears likely that copper is mobilized from storage (or possibly assimilated from the food) as a result of various infections, etc., and that the higher blood levels of the copper-containing protein constitute a type of defense mechanism. If this is so, then it might be argued that copper requirements probably rise as a result of the various conditions mentioned. During pregnancy, for example, the need for copper is thought to be increased.[15] It is worthy of note that the urinary excretion of copper in 10 normal male subjects was found to vary from 0 (3 subjects) up to 26 μg. per 24 hours.[17]

The questions which we regard of primary interest as related to our discussion are: Do individuals vary substantially in their copper needs? Is there likelihood that some individuals, because of high requirements, suffer from copper deficiency when consuming diets which are generally accepted as good? Certainly there are not enough data to answer either of these questions with certainty. The copper needs of human beings are calculated to be about 2 mg. per day, but increased amounts are retained up to 8 mg. per day. About 80 μg. per kg. of body weight is needed daily by children. The daily intake of Americans is said to average about 2.26 mg. It seems unlikely that *severe* copper deficiency, comparable with that observed in cattle in Holland or sheep in certain other areas,[18] exists in the human population of the United States. On the other hand, milder deficiency may exist and be a contributing factor in diseases of obscure etiology. Let us suppose that a particular individual consumes and assimilates *one-half* as much copper as would be required to promote maximum good health, what deficiency symptoms would we look for? For all we know a priori, such a deficiency might cause impairment in any tissue or organ of the body, including nervous tissue,[18] sperm cells, or liver (p. 158), or it might cause a general impairment of all functions and a resulting general lack of efficiency and good health. Commonly observed clinical symptoms need to be supplemented by biochemical evidence in evaluating the nutritional status of individuals.[19]

The question of the possible existence of copper deficiencies of genetic origin is related to the dietary supply of other elements, notably molybdenum. It is known that in animals excessive ingestion of molybdenum imposes a state of copper deficiency.[18]

The *zinc* content of blood, particularly the plasma fraction, showed wide variations (50 to 650 μg. per cent) when determinations were made on 31 normal individuals. In one case only were repeated observations on the same individual reported; the values in this case showed a range from 90 to 330 μg. during fifteen consecutive days, and the magnitude of inter-individual differences, if present, cannot be ascertained.[20] It is the experience in our laboratory that some individuals may exhibit relatively wide fluctuations when specific values are being measured, but that other individuals in the same series may fail to exhibit substantial fluctuation with respect to the same item.

The fact that zinc is known to be a component of an enzyme carbonic anhydrase leaves no doubt as to its physiological significance. The amount of zinc in erythrocytes seems to parallel the carbonic anhydrase activity.[21] The leucocytes which appear to lack carbonic anhydrase contain about 25 times as much zinc (per cell) as do the erythrocytes.[20] It seems likely that an investigation of the zinc content of different types of white blood cells coupled with a study of individuals from the standpoint of the different types of white cells present (p. 35) would lead to the discovery of substantial inter-individual differences. The wide spread in the zinc concentrations in three human spleens has already been mentioned (p. 72). A recent study has been made of the intake and excretion of zinc by 13 college women on self-selected diets. Although the urinary excretions varied over a 3-fold range, in general the data do not suggest wide variability.[22]

One interesting observation relating to the possible existence of wide inter-individual differences in *cobalt* needs is the fact that, although cattle and sheep (ruminants) show cobalt deficiency on cobalt-deficient pasturage, horses, rabbits, marsupials, and rats seem to require cobalt at *much* lower levels.[18] If genetic differences of great magnitude exist between different species of mammals in this regard, it might be expected that substantial differences would exist among members of the human family. The cobalt retention of different individuals under comparable conditions was found in one study to vary through wide limits.[23]

Amino Acids

There are several reasons for anticipating that the quantities of the various amino acids required will be found to be distinctive for each individual. Many of the enzymes involved in the metabolism and inter-conversions of amino acids are known, and the differing efficiencies of these enzymes and those involved in protein synthesis in different individuals should be the basis for needs which are quantitatively distinctive for each individual.

The fact that amino acid excretion patterns (p. 111), amino acid salivary patterns (p. 65), and amino acid duodenal juice patterns (p. 68) are distinctive for each individual is in line with the idea of distinctive needs. That there are wide ranges (presumably distinctive for each individual) in the content of blood plasma (p. 60) with respect to individual amino acid points in the same direction.

Of course, it is well known that substantial interspecies differences in amino acid and protein needs exist, and that these are genetically determined. It is also notable that there are substantial differences between the maintenance pattern for adults and the growth pattern for infants.[24]

Little attention has been paid to the question of inter-individual differences in amino acid requirements. In the attempts to determine what the human adult requirements for individual essential amino acids are (for maintaining nitrogen equilibrium), studies have been made on individual young men. The following inter-individual ranges have been noted by Rose:[25] Tryptophane, 0.15 to 0.25 gm. per day; lysine, 0.4 to 0.8 gm.; leucine, 0.5 to 1.10 gm.; and threonine, 0.3 to 0.5 gm. In view of the fact that for most amino acids the number of individuals tested is small (even in the case of tryptophane, which has been studied more thoroughly than most, the number of cases is about 30), it is quite possible that the ranges for a large population are much wider than those indicated. Albanese[24] suggests, on the basis of the work of Murlin and co-workers[26] that the presumably safe estimates of Rose may be low by a factor of about 3.

That amino acids, which are not regarded as essential for maintenance of nitrogen equilibrium, may be "required" by certain adult individuals (probably for genetic reasons) is suggested by a study reported by Albanese[24] in which it appeared that the sperm count in an individual with "idiopathic hypospermia" was increased several-fold by administering 8 gm. of arginine per day. The rationale of this experiment was based upon the fact that about 80 per cent of the sperm protein protamine is made up of arginine. It seems reasonable to suppose that certain individuals would be found who would have partial genetic blocks which would, for example, make the production of arginine from other amino acids difficult. Such an individual might have "idiopathic hypospermia" for this reason (as well as others) and hence for normal functioning may be said to require arginine.

The extensive and conflicting findings with respect to the enhancement of "intelligence" in experimental animals and in mentally deficient children, by the administration of glutamic acid, are interesting in this connection because glutamic acid has never been considered an essential amino acid for mammals (though it is for chicks). Rose and co-workers[27] found that glutamic acid enhanced the growth of young weanling rats when it was used to supplement the 10 essential amino acids, but that removal of the glutamic acid from a mixture of 19 amino acids resulted in only slight decrease (of questionable significance) in growth.

It seems likely to the author, if not certain, that individual human beings and individual experimental animals possess substantial quantitative differences with respect to their utilization of glutamic acid and the conversion of other nonessential amino acids into glutamic acid, and vice versa. If this is the case, it could well be that certain individual human beings or experimental animals will have their physiological and psychological well-being enhanced by introducing substantial amounts of glutamic acid into the diet. This could explain the favorable effects on "intelligence" of glutamic acid administration. The results obtained in these studies are characterized by what seems to be clear-cut evidence that certain individuals show marked improvement which, however, may not be sufficiently large to affect the group averages significantly. Although it does not seem advisable to enter directly into this controversy, it does seem worthwhile to point out that, inasmuch as different strains of experimental animals (as well as different individual animals) have substantial differences in their metabolism of amino acids,[28] positive results obtained using one strain or set of individuals are not cancelled by negative results obtained using a different set of animals.

The subject of the effect of glutamic acid on "intelligence," as well as many related problems, needs to be investigated fully, bearing in mind the considerations we have presented here.

At this time when proteins are receiving so much attention from various angles, it is necessary to bear in mind the high probability that nutritional needs for proteins and specific amino acids vary substantially from individual to individual.

Vitamin A

Even though this vitamin was one of the earliest recognized and the chemical interrelations between the various available forms are relatively well known, the human needs are still uncertain from the quantitative standpoint. In 1932 Mead Johnson and Company offered a $15,000 award for which the following terms were set:

> The award will be made to the investigator (or group of investigators) who (1) determines the clinical value of vitamin A (if any) in human medicine, or (2) determines the vitamin A requirements of human beings, or (3) determines whether vitamin A in amounts more than obtained in a well-balanced diet is of benefit in human physiology.

After 13 years when four of the seven original judges were deceased and had been replaced, there were still no serious contenders for the award, and the judges advised the donors "that it is their considered opinion that no report or reports have been published which adequately answer any of the three stated requirements of the Award . . . no adequate answer to the problems as formulated will result from current research." They advised that the award be revoked, which was done.[29] Eight years later the situation had not changed materially, and the Food and Nutrition Board[30] thought it necessary to say, "The Board recognizes that allowances for this vitamin cannot at this time be stated precisely."

There are several factors which underlie what might seem to an impartial observer to be an extremely backward situation. These factors, in the author's opinion, are (1) inadequacy of provisions for clinical research in general, (2) minor difficulty because of the existence in nature of more than one form of the vitamin, and (3) serious difficulty in establishing human needs because these needs are probably *highly* variable from individual to individual.

One of the most revealing pieces of published evidence on this last point was obtained with respect to experimental animals (rats). Sherman and co-workers[31,32,33] first established a level of vitamin A intake (not necessarily the very lowest) which kept the animals free from signs and symptoms of deficiency for 58 generations. The food contained 3 units per gm. of air-dried weight. The investigators then provided groups of the animals with 2 to 4 times this amount of vitamin A in the food and found particularly that *variability* of growth was progressively decreased with the higher levels of intake. Though the authors appear not to have interpreted the results in this way, an obvious interpretation is that, with higher levels, a larger proportion of the animals (because of their variable needs) were supplied at optimal levels. The longevity and reproductive records, etc., of the animals as a group were improved with higher vitamin intake because of the distinct advantage to some of the animals.

It is well recognized that in biological assays of vitamin A with rats, high variability in response is continually encountered. For this reason as many as 10 to 15 carefully selected animals, generally males, are used for each testing level, and the responses averaged. Certain stocks of animals then yield concordant results, whereas other stocks cannot be used. Through the courtesy of H. J. Deuel, Jr., the writer has been furnished the raw data on which several satisfactory vitamin A assays were based.[34] When the level of intake was such that all the rats (males) grew substantially, there was at least a 3-fold variation in growth among 10 to 12 rats used in each test. At a lower level of intake one rat gained 31 gm., while at the other extreme on the same intake one lost 12 gm. Undoubtedly the variation would have been much larger if the rats had not been so carefully selected.

Paul and Paul[35] made a study of the effect of various levels of vitamin A intake, particularly on the eye and tooth development of albino rats. They found that 10 times the supposed minimum gave the best response of any of the levels tested. At this level (20 units per 100 gm. body weight daily) 18 of the 19 animals were "normal," both as to teeth and eyes, but one animal was listed as slightly abnormal as to teeth, and one definitely so with respect to eyes. At ⅕ of this level (4 units per 100 gm.) 20 per cent were normal as to teeth and 60 per cent were normal as to eyes. At ⅒ of the top level (2 units per 100 gm.) 26 per cent were normal as to eyes but none were normal as to teeth. It is apparent from these data that the 20 unit level *was not* sufficient for some of the rats, but that the 4 unit level *was* sufficient for about 20 per cent. This indicates a greater than 5-fold spread even among these relatively homogeneous albino rats.

There seems little doubt that, if a heterogeneous population of rats were tested, variability of vitamin A needs would be found to be at least 10-fold. There is good reason a priori to think that human populations would also vary as much as this.

When utilization tests were run on a group of 18 male and 7 female human subjects, wide variations in blood level responses were found, particularly among the males.[36] [Both in animals (rats) and humans the two sexes respond somewhat differently.] When 134,000 µg. of vitamin A in four different forms, viz., vitamin A alcohol, vitamin A acetate, vitamin A natural ester No. 1, and vitamin A natural ester No. 2, was fed to the group of 18 males on four different occasions, the serum levels found after 6 hours ranged from 178 to 1423 µg. per 100 ml., 122 to 1170 µg. per 100 ml., 110 to 1183 µg. per 100 ml., and 114 to 1230 µg. per 100 ml., respectively. These nearly 10-fold variations in serum levels do not, of course, indicate 10-fold variation in need, but they do show that the vitamin when given in relatively large doses does behave very differently in different individuals.

In line with the supposition that human vitamin A needs vary greatly from individual to individual are the findings of Popper and

Steigmann.[37] In a group of 92 individuals including 65 hospital controls (fracture cases, etc.), a 10-fold inter-individual range in the vitamin A plasma levels and 30-fold inter-individual range in plasma carotenoid levels were determined four times in 24 hours without significant intra-individual variations. In 7 cases of hospital controls daily determinations were made for 7 to 18 days without any considerable changes being found. Other workers had previously observed a similar constancy.

Admittedly the evidence for widely variable vitamin A needs in a human population is not as direct as could be wished, yet it seems that one would have to have a strong bias in favor of uniformity to overlook the facts that we have cited and to presume that the variation is small.

There is additional evidence of wide variation in needs in the fact that high vitamin A intakes (much higher than the supposed normal) have been found beneficial in the treatment, in certain individuals, of skin lesions, night blindness, etc., when lower doses failed. Part of the difficulty in some cases may have involved faulty absorption. Even so, a difference in need is involved, and if one individual needs to consume ten times as much as another because of difficulty in absorption, the augmented need is just as real as if the difficulty involved some other step in utilization.

The vitamin A needs of the body are by no means centered in any one organ or tissue. It is necessary for vision, for tooth and bone development, for maintenance of healthy epithelial tissue in the skin and in many organs, for reproduction, etc. It is to be expected that deficiency would be exhibited in many ways and that in different individuals the symptoms would not be the same. The benefits of vitamin A administration may thus appear very different in different individuals, and this helps to explain why many kinds of benefits (part of which are probably real) have been ascribed (by physicians as well as others) to vitamin A administration. A substance with such diverse functions is bound to show different effects in different individuals, and, of course, for some individuals who have low requirements and get plenty in their food, its administration will appear to be wholly without effect. Otto Bessey, in discussing the problem of nutrition, has used vitamin A as an illustration of how widely different levels are needed to maintain different functions in experimental rats. A chart showing this has been reproduced with his permission (Fig. 16). It will be noted that there is about a 30-fold difference between the level needed to produce "normal histology" and the level needed for maximum reproducibility (uniformity of response). These data are highly suggestive with regard to wide variability in tissue needs and in the needs of individual animals.

Vitamin D

Human adult needs for this vitamin (vitamins) are not established quantitatively. Most human studies have involved preventing or curing rickets in infants or children, and the recommended daily allowance of the Food and Nutrition Board is 400 units. Even among "normal" children, however, there is evidence of variation in vitamin D needs. According to Spies and Butt,[38] "The activated milk does not exhibit sufficient potency in vitamin D for the prevention of rickets in cases *in which a susceptibility exists*" (italics added). They note that "susceptible" children may require 5,000 to 10,000 units daily.

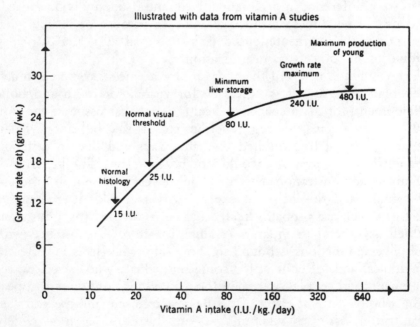

Figure 16. Growth rate relationship to vitamin A intake

Most convincing with respect to variable needs, however, are well authenticated cases of "vitamin D-resistant rickets" which respond only when enormous doses of vitamin D, sometimes up to 100,000, 500,000 or even 1,500,000 units, are administered.[39,40] Lower levels, which are wholly adequate even for mildly susceptible children, are without any beneficial effect on highly resistant cases so far as calcium and phosphorus retention is concerned. When extremely high levels are used, toxicity is liable to develop.[40]

On the basis of the concepts which we have developed, it appears most probable that, for various and diverse structural and biochemical reasons, the needs for vitamin D vary greatly from individual to individual. Children who are nonsusceptible to rickets require small amounts; susceptible children require many times more; children afflicted with vitamin D-resistant rickets require for a time, at least, extremely high doses. There are probably no sharp dividing lines between normals, susceptible individuals, and cases of vitamin D-resistant rickets. The susceptible individuals may make up an appreciable percentage of the population, for Park has found in postmortems on 230 children that about 46.5 per cent of children between 2 and 14 years have histological signs of rickets.[41]

Vitamin C

If one reads an account of the outbreak of scurvy on shipboard in the days of long voyages on sailing vessels, he finds indications of individual differences in vitamin C need. For example, in Dana's *Two Years before the Mast,* one member of the crew was described as suffering from severe scurvy and was about to die of the disease, while many of the crew were quite free from any symptoms. Since they had been living for the same length of time on vitamin C-deficient diets, they would, if uniformly constituted, have all been attacked at about the same time.

Mild vitamin C deprivation can cause many disturbances which are not the typical symptoms of scurvy. Dalldorf[42] discusses the following manifestations which may be caused by vitamin C deficiency: idiopathic hemorrhages, subperiosteal hemorrhages, petechial hemorrhages, rheumatism (in children), osteomyelitis, nonhealing of wounds, and hemorrhagic gingivitis. McLester[43] discusses dental disease, anemia, cryptogenic hemorrhages and cataract in the eye, endocrine disorders, gastrointestinal disorders (including achlorhydria) and susceptibility to infection and to arsenicals and other poisons as manifestations of vitamin C deficiency. The work of Javert[44] implicates vitamin C deficiency in abortions. Park[45] has observed that "even in the development of outspoken [deficiency] disease there is a long latent period during which, without recognizable symptoms, changes are taking place in the skeleton." It is well known that the bones of scorbutic guinea pigs become almost as thin and breakable as egg shells, but this happens progressively, and the first stages are not detectable by ordinary means.

There is, without doubt, a wide spread between the amount of vitamin C needed to prevent frank scurvy and that required for the maintenance of best health. In young growing guinea pigs about 0.5 mg. ascorbic acid per day will protect against scurvy symptoms, but there are distinct gains in health when the intakes are up to 10 times this amount.[46]

With respect to human beings there is some question as to what level of tissue saturation should ideally be maintained. In guinea pigs defects in developing incisors appear when the tissue concentrations are about 40 per cent of the maximum. Scurvy symptoms do not appear until the tissue saturation has reached a much lower level (about 20 per cent saturation). It seems logical to suppose that in different individuals the manifestations of mild vitamin C deficiency would be different and that a high degree of saturation would be safest from the standpoint of all the vulnerable tissues.[19]

Whether this supposition is justified or not, the evidence is clear that individual serum levels of ascorbic acid (in normal individuals) vary widely, from 0.02 to 3.1 mg. per cent according to a recent investigation,[47] and the requirement for tissue saturation ranges at least from 0.6 mg. or less per kg. of body weight up to 2.85 mg. per kg. One limitation (from our point of view) of the studies which have been conducted on this subject is the small numbers of individuals included. Too often, 3, 5, 7, 9, or 12 subjects have been studied. In one study involving 9 normal young women, 1 was found to require (for saturation) 0.6 mg. or less per kg., 6 had requirements from 1.4 to 1.8 mg., and 2 had requirements of 2.2 mg. or above.[48] This 4-fold range in a group of 9 individuals suggests that the range for a large population, including some individuals who are not perfectly well, might be very large.

In view of the probable differences in the vulnerability of different tissues in different individuals, it may well be that the vitamin C needs for best health could vary from individual to individual more than the amount of vitamin C necessary for tissue saturation. It may easily be the case, for example, that some individuals are healthy and free from minor symptoms when their tissues are 50 per cent saturated. Others, because of the greater vulnerability of specific tissues may require that their tissues be highly saturated at all times. Dalldorf[49] hints at something like resistant vitamin C deficiency when he says, "Even these large amounts [75 to 100 mg. daily], however, are inadequate to maintain saturation *in certain patients*" (italics added). He cites that in Hodgkins disease, protracted fever from various causes, active rheumatic heart disease, and tuberculosis, the vitamin C requirement may be "extremely high."

B Vitamins

Because of the fact that many of the B vitamins are implicated in recognized enzyme systems and the building of enzyme systems is known to be under genic control, it follows inevitably that the need, quantitatively speaking, for these raw materials for enzyme building must vary from organism to organism depending on genetic constitution. It will be recalled (p. 00) that it was in connection with riboflavin that partial genetic blocks were discovered and that for the organism concerned the range of needs could vary widely depending upon the conditions of growth, notably temperature.

The only reasonable question of doubt with respect to individual variation of needs for B vitamins is this: In mammals and specifically in human beings, *how wide are the variations* in needs? In the following pages we will cite specific evidence with respect to several of the individual B vitamins. Each one, of course, has its own peculiar enzymic relationship and must be considered separately.

Thiamine is chronologically the first B vitamin to be discovered, but, in spite of this, the evidence with respect to the extent of the variability of individual human needs is not as definitive as one could wish. This is primarily due to lack of interest or attention to the subject.

Light and Cracas[50] demonstrated clearly in 1938 that different strains of white rats have inherently different levels of need for thiamine. The B strain used in these studies responded with less growth at the 4 µg. of thiamine per day level than did the A strain at the 2 µg. level. This shows, therefore, at least a 2-fold variation in the two strains. It should be pointed out that these were not closely inbred strains (e.g., brother-sister mated for many generations) but ordinary rat colonies such as have been used for nutritional investigations. If the authors had been interested in inter-individual differences in needs, they would doubtless have found in their data evidence that *within each strain* there were individual animals which exhibited high and low thiamine needs. If the rats of strain A with the least requirements of any in the group had been compared with the rats of strain B which had the highest requirements of any in that group, the spread in thiamine needs (even among relatively homogeneous white rats) would doubtless have been much more than 2-fold.

Similarly it has been found that different breeds of chickens appear to have different thiamine needs.[51]

The question of how much thiamine human beings need has been subjected to a great deal of study, and the literature on the subject will not be reviewed here. Most of the investigation has been based upon the assumption that "normal man" has a requirement at the adult level which is subject to relatively small variation and that "the normal infant" has likewise a fairly definite requirement. If this assumption is valid, it is easy to see that, when three or a half-dozen individuals have been found to give reasonably concordant results, an investigator may be satisfied that he has found the answer.

A further assumption is also often made, namely, that even a mild thiamine deficiency, if it is a *real* deficiency, will make itself known by outward signs. This, in the author's opinion, is probably far from true. In animal experiments, for example, deficiencies require weeks to develop, and long before an animal shows overt symptoms of deficiency, an analysis of its tissues would show that deficiencies are present and metabolism is being impaired. The importance of considering other evidence about the nutritional state besides overt symptoms is stressed in a recent review by Lowry.[19]

An interesting experiment directed specifically at the question of human thiamine needs was that of Najjar and Holt.[52] Nine adolescent young males, 16 to 23 years of age, were induced to subsist on a basal diet much like those which have been used in animal experiments, containing vitamin-free casein, Crisco, dextrimaltose, a mineral mixture, and a vitamin mixture. At the outset of the experiment the vitamin mixture contained thiamine enough so that each individual received 1 mg. per day. This amount was to be gradually reduced until deficiencies developed. Thiamine deficiency, as judged by the development of neuritis or edema associated with anorexia and sometimes vomiting, did not appear in any of the individuals for a period of many months of diminished thiamine supply. Eventually, when the individuals had remained on thiamine intakes between 0.1 and 0.2 mg. for months without exhibiting the aforementioned symptoms, thiamine was eliminated from their diet altogether. In the course of the next 3 to 5 weeks, four out of the nine developed clinical thiamine deficiency, one was borderline, and the other four showed no signs of deficiency during 7 weeks of observation.

Seeking for possible sources of thiamine for these resistant individuals, the investigators analyzed the feces of the eight individuals (four susceptible and four resistant) and found on the average that those who exhibited no symptoms had about 20 times as much free thiamine in the feces as did those who showed symptoms. This pointed rather unmistakably to the importance of the synthesis of thiamine by intestinal organisms in these cases on this specific diet.

Many pertinent comments suggest themselves in connection with this experiment. First, it should not have been too great a surprise that clinical deficiencies did not show themselves promptly or even during the period of the experiment. If one were to repeat the same experiment on a group of nine young *adult* rats, for the corresponding length of time (18 months in human life corresponds certainly to not more than 1 month in a rat's life), it is extremely doubtful if recognizable polyneuritis would develop. With rapidly growing young animals the responses would be different.

Although thiamine (and other B vitamins) is not considered to be "stored" extensively in the usual sense, there is no question but that it is held in the tissues and that a considerable period of depletion is required before the levels become very low.

The experiment was nonetheless instructive, and one could hardly ask human subjects to participate in a more rigorous test. Two facts stand out in addition to what has already been said: (1) Substantial variation was observed among the nine individuals, and (2) this variation may have been due to differences in intestinal flora rather than to more direct differences in need. It should be pointed out, however, that differences in need based upon differences in intestinal flora may be real and just as exacting as if the differences had a different origin. Presumably differences in intestinal flora are due to the different "climates" which are distinctive for each individual (p. 149). If we take the experiments and the authors' interpretation at face value, we are led to conclude that some individuals can get along with practically no thiamine in their diet—a conclusion which certainly points toward high variability of needs.

Most of the other investigations of human thiamine needs[30] are based, like that of Najjar and Holt, upon the assumption that absence of clinical deficiency is equivalent to absence of deficiency—an assumption in which we cannot concur. If our concepts are correct, there are *a great many* tissues, organs, and functions where thiamine deficiency may exist without being easily detected, since it functions in every cell of the body. To rely implicitly on a few acute symptoms—edema, neuritis, anorexia (which, incidentally, cannot be quantitated with any degree of certainty)—is almost sure to be misleading. Although it is not possible to say that a deficiency is present unless there is a recognizable sign, it is an error to conclude that deficiencies are certainly absent because no signs are observed. Because each individual has throughout his body a distinctive pattern of needs, the first deficiency symptoms for one individual would not necessarily be the first symptoms for another, and the minor impairment in the metabolism in a particular tissue would not be expected to cause any violent general or local symptoms. As will be pointed out later in more detail, we need to develop more sensitive signs of deficiencies than we now have before we can know with definiteness how much thiamine any particular individual needs.

One recent study has been made involving attempts to assess thiamine needs on the basis of excretion.[53] Eight normal women were investigated. For six out of eight, 500 µg. of thiamine per 1000 Cal. was judged adequate. A lower level, 300 µg., was judged inadequate for six and borderline for two. There were about 3-fold spreads in the amount of thiamine excreted by different individuals on the same level of intake.

One fact which points toward physiological individuality in thiamine needs is that the thiamine of the blood (mostly in the cells) is usually present either at a low level, 4 to 5 µg. per 100 gm. of blood (about 30 per cent of cases), or at a level about twice as high, 9 to 10 µg. per 100 gm. (about 70 per cent of cases).[54]

Pett,[55] Director of the Division of Nutrition, Department of National Health and Welfare of Canada, has on the basis of the "best data possible, . . . admittedly not entirely satisfactory," arrived at the following figures for the thiamine requirements of 15 individuals:

Mg. Daily	Number of Individuals
0.40–0.59	3
0.60–0.79	4
0.80–0.99	4
1.00–1.19	2
1.20–1.39	1
1.40–1.59	1

If these data are accepted as valid, we find (even in a small group) nearly a 4-fold variation.

Riboflavin needs have been found to vary with different strains of white Leghorn chickens,[56,57] and there appears to be a sex difference in that females require less and thus show greater resistance to riboflavin deficiency.

Najjar and co-workers[58] found on diets furnishing only 60 to 90 µg. of riboflavin per day that the urinary excretion (human) was about twice the intake, and the fecal excretion was about 5 to 6 times the intake. This indicates that for certain individuals on certain diets synthesis of riboflavin by intestinal organisms is sufficient to take care of the entire riboflavin needs. The authors conclude that riboflavin may not be a dietary essential in all cases. If this finding is valid, it certainly points to the probability that human needs vary widely because riboflavin deficiencies in human beings have been observed a great many times on many different types of diets.

Riboflavin deficiency may result in the production of skin lesions, angular stomatitis, and scrotal dermatitis; but, as the Food and Nutrition Board states, "the absence of such lesions does not imply riboflavin adequacy." The Board indicates that clinical signs of deficiency will vary with the individual and his environmental stresses. No record has been found, however, in which the magnitude of the inter-individual differences has been determined.

Niacin requirements are dependent on the tryptophane supply and the ease with which the conversion of tryptophane to niacin can be made. Chickens and rats carry out the conversion readily. Dogs do so less readily. Monkeys and human beings carry out the process relatively ineffectively. Since this conversion involves several enzymatic steps, it is clear on the basis of gene-enzyme relationships why species differences exist. On the same basis inter-individual differences may be presumed to exist also.

That individual monkeys have distinctive niacin needs was shown by recent work of Tappan and co-workers.[59] One animal, for example, required only 11 weeks to show niacin deficiency; weight loss by this animal was halted only when 30 mg. of niacin was given. Another animal required 9 months to show a niacin deficiency and then grew adequately when only 6 mg. of niacin per week was furnished. This seems to show a several-fold range in niacin needs within a small group of fine animals. The tryptophane needs of the different monkeys, as judged by growth responses, were found to vary under comparable conditions from 1 to about 3.5 gm. per week.

That human needs for niacin vary from individual to individual seems obvious from the fact that in populations in which most of the people eat substantially the same diet, only a few contract pellagra. These presumably are the individuals who have higher than average requirements. That one does not have to study large populations in order to find substantial variance is shown by a recent experiment of Goldsmith,[60] "Of three subjects receiving a wheat diet furnishing 200 mg. of tryptophan and .5 mg. of niacin daily for more than 90 days, characteristic signs of niacin deficiency appeared in one subject, evidence suggestive of deficiency in a second, none in the third."

Very little is known about the *pantothenic acid* needs of human beings even though it has been about 14 years since this vitamin in synthetic form became available. The backwardness is due in part to the fact that pantothenic acid deficiency often does not give rise to specific observable symptoms.[61] Dogs on pantothenic acid-deficiency diets, for example, may appear normal up until a day or two before their death from its lack.[62] In young chickens, pantothenic acid deficiency gives rise to chick dermatitis, but this is relatively nonspecific; by the time such symptoms appear[63] every tissue in the chicken's body is deficient in pantothenic acid, deficient in growth, and doubtless deficient in physiological functioning.

It is now well known that pantothenic acid is a part of coenzyme A, a substance of unusual biochemical significance in that it is intimately concerned with the utilization of carbohydrates, and both the utilization and synthesis of fats, sterols, steriod hormones, etc. A partial failure of any of the processes in which it is concerned may not produce a specific lesion, but may nevertheless be a serious detriment to the individual experiencing it.

Many different types of lesions have been observed (very often at autopsy) in animals suffering from severe pantothenic acid deficiency. These may involve the skin, the adrenals, the entire gastrointestinal tract, nerves, and spinal cord. Functionally, in chickens fertility may be reduced by pantothenic acid deficiency to practically zero[64] without any outward signs being shown by the fowls. Recently, pantothenic acid deficiency has been found to produce duodenal ulcers in about 60 per cent of the rats tested.[65] It is required for bone development[66] and is implicated in antibody responses.[67]

About the only direct evidence that there is a range in the need of human beings for pantothenic acid is based upon the observations that its administration relieves the burning feet syndrome,[68] is effective in the treatment of paralytic ileus,[69] improves the reaction of young men to stress,[70] and in isolated cases has been found to aid in restoring memory[71,72] and preventing constipation.[72] In all these cases it may be presumed that the individuals were getting the "normal" amount of pantothenic acid in their food and that it was because of their higher than average needs that they could be helped by an additional supply.

It seems highly probable that, if a diligent search were made, there would be found a large number of individuals who are deficient in pantothenic acid and who manifest the deficiency in a distinctive fashion in some of the ways suggested by the above discussion or in other ways yet to be discovered. A simpler method of testing the validity of the concepts which we have developed would involve the controlled administration of pantothenic acid to a group of perhaps 100 typical children whose growth patterns have been established. If none of these children should give growth responses, this would indicate that pantothenic acid deficiency is at least rare in children. Similar experiments should be done with other B vitamins, for the same reason.

The amount of *vitamin B₆* required by humans is not well estab-lished,[73] and only recently has evidence been obtained that the needs are variable. Hansen and Bessey[74] have found that in some babies 3 or 4 times as much vitamin B₆ is needed to prevent the excretion of xanthurenic acid after a test dose of tryptophane than in others. It is these particular babies who develop clinical vitamin B₆ deficiency when the intake is low. These findings seem to indicate strongly that some babies have vitamin B₆ requirements 3 or 4 times as high as others.

Although we will not discuss further the question of requirements and deficiencies involving vitamin B₆, much of what has been said, both with respect to thiamine and pantothenic acid, applies in princi-ple to vitamin B₆ as well. It, like the other B vitamins, functions in every cell of the body.

An indication that *folic acid* needs may vary from animal to animal is found in the recent investigation of Nelson, *et al.,*[75] in which the young of some animals were affected whereas the young of others were not by an induced deficiency beginning at the 11th, 12th, or 13th day of gestation. Some of the young showed edema, cleft palate, syndactylism, and other abnormalities as a result of the deficiency. It may be noted that the same deficiency affected different animals at different sites.

The fact that certain human adults or infants develop types of anemia which respond to small doses of folic acid can be interpreted to mean that, for reasons which doubtless have some genetic basis, these individuals have unusually high demands for this vitamin. Pre-sumably they develop the disease when consuming diets that do not induce the disease in others. Folic acid needs are (for one reason or another) highly variable from individual to individual among patients as is shown by the fact that many patients will respond to as little as 0.5 mg. folic acid per day, whereas others will not respond at all to 2 to 3 mg. per day. To play safe, Spies and Butt recommend about 10 mg. per day for the average patient.[76] It is probable that there is no sharp dividing line between "normal individuals" who have "normal folic acid demands" and "abnormal individuals" who are susceptible to anemia because of high demands.

The situation with respect to *vitamin B$_{12}$* is of particular interest from the standpoint of our discussion. If there were not individuals who have a hereditary[77] deficiency with respect to producing the intrinsic factor, the antianemia properties of vitamin B$_{12}$ might never have been thought of to date. Such individuals develop pernicious anemia, but the disease can in general be controlled by oral administration of vitamin B$_{12}$ at levels which are actually very low (a small fraction of a milligram a day) but are relatively high compared with what is necessary when the vitamin is administered by injection (about 1 µg. per day). Anemia patients vary greatly in the dosages they require, especially when given by mouth.

That individuals who do not exhibit anemia of any sort also vary in their need for vitamin B$_{12}$ is shown by the fact that its administration induces a growth response in *some children.* This observation, coming from a group who have made an exhaustive study of growth in children, cannot be nullified by negative results which may have been obtained elsewhere because the fact remains that growth responses can be evaluated with certainty and *some* children exhibited them. Furthermore, the findings of Wetzel, *et al.,*[78,79] have in part been confirmed by other investigators.[80]

Further evidence of variability of "normals" with respect to B$_{12}$ is contained in a recent publication of Unglaub, *et al.,*[81] who found basal excretion rates in twelve normals to vary from 13 to 205 µµg. per day. After giving 3000 µg. daily orally to six of the twelve, excretions ranged from 103 µµg. up to 1989 µµg. per day. Intramuscular injections caused variable excretion rates too, but there were only two individuals at each level of dosage, and so ranges for several individuals cannot be given. The 16- and 19-fold variations cited above are weighty evidence in favor of wide variations in vitamin B$_{12}$ needs even among the normal population.

Comparable data are not available with respect to humans, but for rats *choline* requirements vary widely from individual to individual and from strain to strain. These findings have been published in a series of papers from the Laboratory of Animal Nutrition, Alabama Polytechnic Institute.[82,83,84,85]

There is a marked sex difference in that the females have lower requirements and survive on lower levels of choline intake. The F3 generation from two strains HCR and LCR on the average had requirements that differed in the ratio of about 2 to 1. Considering individual animals, however, in the LCR group there were some males and females for which 2 mg. of choline per day was enough (and perhaps more than enough) to keep them normal; at the other extreme there were animals in the HCR strain for which 10 mg. per day was *not* enough.[59] This indicates a probable 10-fold range among individual animals in the two groups.

One item which makes these choline investigations particularly interesting is the relatively recent finding that Sprague-Dawley rats have a *lower* choline requirement for protection against renal hemorrhage than an Alabama Polytechnic Institute strain, but a *higher* requirement for maintenance of normal liver fat.[85] This emphasizes the idea that two animals (or two human beings) may be deficient for the same substance and yet exhibit entirely different deficiency symptoms because of their different patterns of needs.

Why Individual Nutritional Needs?

Before discussing the problem of self-selection of foods and its relationship to individuality in nutrition, we should emphasize at this point that individual differences in nutritional needs may have many basic causes.

We have stressed the direct relationship of specific nutritional needs to enzyme building, but this is only one possibility. In the case of nicotinamide, for example, which in the form of coenzymes I and II functions in oxidation-reduction reactions, an individual's need may be great because of the genetic ineffectiveness of the mechanism for building nicotinamide into enzyme systems, but the difficulty may lie at another site. Possibly there is difficulty in digestion (of the combined forms) or more likely absorption, which precludes the individual from getting a substantial portion of the nicotinamide out of his food to the cells that need it. Even the mechanism for transport may be at fault. We wish to emphasize that the effectiveness or ineffectiveness of the structures and mechanisms which may be concerned at any step are likely to be genetically determined. If one person absorbs and assimilates a nutrient well and another does so poorly, structural differences or enzymatic differences must be involved. Both kinds of differences, however, have a genetic origin. Possibly an individual wastes a particular nutrient because his renal threshold for it is very low, and he continually excretes it in his urine. If so, kidney differences, structural or enzymatic, may be basic, but these too are probably genetically determined.

The augmented need which an individual has for a particular nutrient may involve not only his own internal metabolism, but also that of the intestinal or other bacteria which he harbors. For example, if an individual furnishes a "climate" which is highly favorable to the presence of riboflavin-producing bacteria, he may not need any of the vitamin at all in his diet (p. 173). On the other hand, assuming for the moment that most people get a substantial part of their riboflavin from intestinal bacteria, an individual whose internal climate is highly unfavorable to these organisms may have a need (for this reason alone) which is far above average. The production of a "climate" suitable or unsuitable for specific kinds of microorganisms is doubtless related to natural immunities (p. 150) and to peculiarities in metabolism, both of which are genetic in origin.

In the case of infecting microorganisms, there is always the possibility that they compete successfully with the host organisms for a nutrient, and thereby increase the individual's demand. It is said that in persons with tuberculosis the ascorbic acid and vitamin A needs appear to be increased many-fold. To produce tissue saturation in an active case of tuberculosis may require several grams of ascorbic acid daily.[86] If the augmentation in demand is potentially this great in the case of tuberculosis, there is the possibility that many minor infections can also increase demands in a substantial manner. Since infections are probably never purely environmental phenomena (there is always an *interaction* between the parasite and the distinctive host), we are still concerned in part with genetically determined differences.

In this short discussion we have made no pretense of exhausting all the possibilities, but enough has been said to make it clear that inter-individual differences in needs for specific nutrients can be genetically determined in many different ways. These different factors can, in fact, be superimposed on one another in specific individuals to give them extremely high demands. Such instances as vitamin D-resistant rickets, for example, may be based upon several superimposed genetic factors.

Self-Selection—A Means of Satisfying Individual Needs

We cannot take the space here to review the rather extensive literature dealing with self-selection of food; this subject has been discussed elsewhere.[87,88,89] Instead, we will summarize present-day knowledge of the subject, particularly as it relates to the problem of individual nutritional needs.

One of the fundamental "wisdoms of the body" is the wisdom to eat. Long before any scientist had gained an inkling of *why* we eat and long before the calorie concept was formulated or dreamed about, people knew enough to eat, and often they knew quite as well as moderns when to stop eating. This wisdom of the body is still fundamental, and people in general on a long-range basis still eat because they are *hungry,* select what they *like,* and stop when they feel they have *had enough.*

It is not appreciated, I believe, by nutritionists in general how great this wisdom of the body is, or may be, in individual cases. Take, for instance, a middle-aged man who has little or no tendency to gain weight. During a period of 10 years his weight may be practically stationary; let us say that during this period he gained 5 lb. This means that his intake of food has matched his burning up of food with a remarkably small error. During the 10-year period, if he were moderately active, he would have eaten about 12,000 lb. of moist food. A long-range error in balance of 1 per cent would have made him gain (or lose) 120 lb. An error of 0.1 per cent would have made him gain or lose 12 lb. Actually the wisdom of his body was such as to strike a balance with an error of less than $\frac{1}{20}$ of 1 per cent.

The ability to strike this kind of balance is a wisdom *of the body;* superior knowledge about calories or food values is not at all necessary, since this feat has doubtless been accomplished millions of times quite unconsciously by people who had no basic nutritional knowledge at all or even the ability or machinery to weigh themselves. What is it that makes it possible to perform this feat? We know little about the delicate mechanisms involved; we do know definitely that some people have the necessary wisdom of the body to perform the feat and others do not.

This is but one angle of this wisdom of the body. Long before anything was known about the existence of carbohydrates, fats, proteins, minerals, and vitamins, people were eating them in something like the right proportions, and there were those who did not suffer from nutritional disease. But again we can be sure of one thing, the wisdom of the body possessed by some individuals is deficient; they do not choose wisely. A most extreme example is that of the individual who (regardless of why) chooses alcoholic drinks to the exclusion of food and becomes severely deficient as a result.

While there are doubtless special appetites of several kinds which help people to get the things they need, these wisdoms of the body are not all-inclusive and infallible in all individuals[90]—otherwise everyone would be able to choose what he or she needs at all times, and the study of nutrition would be a waste of time. It will be worthwhile to emphasize the fact that even in a modern industrialized community different individual people do eat differently. It seems probable that the individual needs which we have been discussing are met to a degree by the process of self-selection of foods. To use a simple example, it seems probable that those who for metabolic reasons need more sodium chloride have a greater appetite for salt and are thus able to satisfy this need. People eating from the same table do not choose the same food qualitatively or quantitatively; besides, eating between meals is a factor. How much significance self-selection has in meeting individual requirements we do not know, but we may reasonably suppose that it is considerable.

Experiments have been tried in which small children have been given a free choice of good wholesome foods, with the result that they all chose somewhat differently and all thrived. But babies will get along reasonably well on many different assortments of wholesome foods, and so these experiments do not tell us as much as we would like to know. The question arises as to what would happen if babies were given free choices, not only of approved foods and food mixtures, but also, for example, of candy and sweetened and unsweetened alcoholic beverages. Would their wisdom of the body triumph? The answer is almost certainly that some babies would show vast superiority over others both in their wisdom in shunning the fuels which do not contribute amino acids, minerals, or vitamins and in their resultant growth records.

Self-selection of foods has not been studied from the standpoint of individual differences. We know by observation that some individuals have a "sweet tooth," that "Jack Sprat can eat no fat," etc., but we have no idea except by inference how these characteristics fit in with the metabolic peculiarities of the individuals concerned.

Limitations of Self-Selection—A New Method of Detecting Nutritional Deficiencies

We know something about the factors that enter into making for the wisdom of the body of which we are speaking. Good nutrition itself is an important factor. We have said that one of the wisdoms of the body is the wisdom to eat. But if individuals are fed deficient diets (it is notably true in the case of thiamine-deficient diets), they lose this wisdom of the body. Anorexia develops, and they starve themselves.

Furthermore, with respect to the ability to make wise food choices, it is clear that good nutrition is an important factor. Macy[7] has found in extensive experiments involving giving small children a free choice of sugar in their diets that, when the children are adequately nourished with a diet containing the proteins, minerals, and vitamins that they need, they voluntarily eat less sugar. It is evident that good nutrition promotes this wisdom of the body.

Though our approach was not exactly from this angle, investigations carried out in our laboratories involving self-selection have shown with reasonable certainty that experimental animals such as are used in nutritional investigations have individual differences, quantitatively, with respect to their nutritional needs, and that filling these needs improves their wisdom of the body. Previous to this work, Mardones, et al.,[91] and Brady and Westerfield[92] had shown that rats, when given a choice between water and alcohol, drank less alcohol on adequate diets than on inadequate ones. This, it should be made clear, is a laboratory finding subject to a minimum of interpretation, and its validity does not depend on its possible relationship to the problem of alcoholism in humans. Even if it has no relationship whatever, the laboratory finding has been confirmed dozens of times in different laboratories, and has therefore a substantial basis.

In our work, contrary to the prevailing mode, we paid little or no attention to averages, but watched and recorded the behavior of individual animals when fed ordinary stock diets. There was a high degree of individuality so far as the animals' choice of alcohol was concerned; some drank it heavily from the start; at the other extreme were those which would not touch it. Intermediate were those which drank a little day after day and those in which the consumption rose from low levels to higher levels in the course of perhaps 2 weeks or 2 months.

Most interesting was the fact that in our original colony of rats we could pretty well eliminate individuality in response to alcohol by going to either extreme with respect to diet—a markedly deficient diet or a fortified, abundant diet. When the diet was deficient, all the animals lost their wisdom of the body and consumed alcohol at a high level. Some animals evidently were more easily depleted than others, but all moved in the direction of greater alcohol consumption. When the animals were given well-fortified diets supplemented particularly with vitamins, they all developed wisdom of the body and turned away from alcohol consumption. There were a number of instances in our earlier experiments in which animals consuming alcohol at high levels were caused to cease its consumption practically entirely overnight merely by giving them vitamin supplements. The efficacy of diet supplementation in diminishing alcohol consumption has been demonstrated hundreds of times; and regardless of interpretation, the fact must be accepted.

Further exploration of this line of investigation showed that different colonies of rats and different closely inbred strains are distinctive in their alcohol consumption and in their behavior toward nutritional supplements. The second colony we worked with had a stronger tendency to consume alcohol than the first and was less readily given body wisdom by the administration of available supplements.

The fact that each inbred strain of animals has not only a distinctive tendency to drink alcohol but also a distinctive excretion pattern makes it seem certain that we are here dealing with individual differences (quantitatively speaking) in nutritional needs. It seems evident that when rats are given plenty of everything they need nutritionally they shun alcohol, and that the reason why some shun it less than others is that their requirements for certain items are higher, and they are consequently harder to satisfy. The reason why certain animals on a stock diet refuse alcohol entirely is that they have all their needs satisfied fully by the stock diet, and their wisdom of the body tells them to shun a substance which is very one-sided as a nutrient and can lead them to become deficient.

Recent experiments from our laboratory[93] show that the same general principle holds with respect to sugar consumption. Rats on nutritionally deficient diets, when given a choice, consume more sugar than those which have their nutritional needs better satisfied.

The line of investigation which we have been discussing has brought out strong evidence that (1) individual rats have requirements which are quantitatively distinctive, (2) deficiencies too mild to produce overt lesions are sufficient to reduce materially the wisdom of the body of the individual rats, (3) nutritional substances, not as yet recognized,[94] are needed by rats in order that all individuals exhibit a maximum wisdom of the body with respect to food choices. The lack of these latter substances has only been demonstrated to date by using appetite control as a basic test.

How far the significance of these animal experiments can be translated into human terms is a question we will not discuss here. It is worthy of note, however, that these experiments give strong corroboration of the central ideas of this chapter, namely, (1) each human individual has quantitatively a distinctive pattern of nutritional needs, (2) from individual to individual, specific needs may vary severalfold, and (3) important deficiencies may exist which have not been discoverable clinically by observing acute outward symptoms.

REFERENCES

1. F. William Sunderman and Frederick Boerner, *Normal Values in Clinical Medicine*, W. B. Saunders Co., Philadelphia, Pa. and London, England, 1949.
2. M. P. Hutt, *Am. J. Med. Sci.*, 223, 179 (1952).
3. Irvine McQuarrie, *Potassium Metabolism*, The Sixth M & R Pediatric Research Conference, M & R Laboratories, Columbus, Ohio, 1953.
4. Abraham Cantarow, "Mineral Metabolism," in Garfield G. Duncan,

Diseases of Metabolism, W. B. Saunders Co., Philadelphia, Pa., 3rd ed.,
1953, pp. 237-213.
5. *Borden's Review of Nutritional Research,* 8, 6 (1947).
6. *Nutrition Revs.,* 12, 75–77 (1954).
7. Icie G. Macy, *Nutrition and Chemical Growth in Childhood,* Charles
C. Thomas, Springfield, Ill., and Baltimore, Md., Vol. I, 1942.
8. F. R. Steggerda and H. M. Mitchell, *J. Nutrition,* 31, 407–422 (1946).
9. *Recommended Dietary Allowances,* National Academy of Sciences, National Research Council, Washington, D.C., Publication 302 (rev.),
1953, p. 10.
10. O. J. Malm, *Scand. J. Clin. Lab. Invest.,* 5, 75–84 (1953).
11. Erich Bloch, Ph.D. Thesis, The University of Texas, Austin, 1953.
12. F. E. Lovelace, C. H. Liu, and C. M. McCay, *Arch. Biochem.,* 27,
48–56 (1950).
13. F. G. Harbaugh and Joe Dennis, *Am. J. Vet. Research,* 8, 396–399 (1947).
14. Bert L. Vallee, "The Time Course of Serum Copper Concentrations
of Individuals with Myocardial Infarctions. I," mimeographed paper,
undated, p. 1.
15. G. E. Cartwright, "Copper Metabolism in Human Subjects," in William
D. McElroy and Bentley Glass, eds., *Copper Metabolism,* Johns Hopkins Press, Baltimore, Md., 1950, pp. 274–314.
16. Carl G. Hollberg and C. B. Laurell, *Acta Chem. Scand.* 2, 550–556 (1948).
17. G. E. Cartwright, C. J. Gubler, and M. M. Wintrobe, *J. Clin. Invest.*
33, 685–698 (1954).
18. Hedley R. Marston, *Physiol. Revs.,* 32, 66–121 (1952).
19. Oliver H. Lowry, *Physiol. Revs.,* 32, 431–448 (1952).
20. Bert L. Vallee and John G. Gibson, II, *J. Biol. Chem.,* 176, 445–457
(1948).
21. Bert L. Vallee, Herbert D. Lewis, Mark D. Altschule, and John G.
Gibson, II, *Blood,* 4, 467–478 (1949).
22. Helen M. Tribble and Florence I. Scoular, *J. Nutrition,* 52, 209–216
(1954).
23. Mary Jones Harp and Florence I. Scoular, *J. Nutrition,* 47, 67–72 (1952).
24. Anthony A. Albanese, *Protein and Amino Acid Requirements of Mammals,* Academic Press, New York, N.Y., 1950.
25. William C. Rose, *Federation Proc.* 8, 546–552 (1949) and Personal
Communication.
26. John R. Murlin, Leslie E. Edwards, Estelle E. Hawley, and Leland C.
Clark, *J. Nutrition,* 31, 533–554 (1946).
27. William C. Rose, M. Jane Oesterling, and Madelyn Womack, *J. Biol.
Chem.,* 176, 753–763 (1948).

28. Janet Reed, *Univ. Texas Pub.*, 5109, 139–144 (1951).
29. Advertisement in *J. Am. Med. Assoc.*, Oct., 20, 1945.
30. *Recommended Dietary Allowances*, p. 14 (see ref. 9).
31. Henry C. Sherman and Helen Yarmolinsky Trupp, *J. Nutrition*, 37, 467–474 (1949).
32. H. C. Sherman, H. L. Campbell, M. Udiljak, and H. Yarmolinsky, *Proc. Natl. Acad. Sci. U.S.* 31, 107–109 (1945).
33. H. C. Sherman and H. L. Campbell, *Proc. Natl. Acad. Sci. U.S.*, 31, 164–166 (1945).
34. Harry J. Deuel, Jr., Personal Communication.
35. Henry E. Paul and Mary F. Paul, *J. Nutrition*, 31, 67–78 (1946).
36. Erling F. Week and Frank J. Sevigne, *J. Nutrition*, 40, 563–576 (1950).
37. Hans Popper and Frederick Steigmann, *J. Am. Med. Assoc.*, 123, 1108–1114 (1943).
38. Tom D. Spies and Hugh R. Butt, "Vitamins and Avitaminoses," in Garfield G. Duncan, ed., *Diseases of Metabolism*, p. 473 (see ref. 4).
39. Fuller Albright, Allan M. Butler, and Esther Bloomberg, *Am. J. Diseases Children*, 54, 529–547 (1937).
40. C. I. Reed, H. C. Struck, and I. E. Steck, *Vitamin D*, University of Chicago Press, Chicago, Ill., 1939.
41. R. H. Follis, *et al. Am. J. Diseases Children*, 66, 1–11 (1943).
42. Gilbert Dalldorf, "Vitamin C in Health and Disease," in Michael G. Wohl, ed., *Dietotherapy*, W. B. Saunders Co., Philadelphia, Pa. and London, England, 1945, pp. 293–305.
43. James S. McLester, *Nutrition and Diet in Health and Disease*, W. B. Saunders Co., Philadelphia, Pa. and London, England, 5th ed., 1949.
44. Carl T. Javert, *Texas State J. Med.*, 50, 652–657 (1954).
45. E. A. Park, cited in James S. McLester, *Nutrition and Diet in Health and Disease*, p. 326 (see ref. 43).
46. *Recommended Dietary Allowances*, p. 20 (see ref. 9).
47. Susan B. Merrow, R. F. Krause, J. H. Browe, C. A. Newhall, and H. B. Pierce, *J. Nutrition*, 46, 445–458 (1952).
48. Alice B. Kline and Mary S. Eheart, *J. Nutrition*, 28, 413–419 (1944).
49. Gilbert Dalldorf, "Vitamin C in Health and Disease," in Michael G. Wohl, ed., *Dietotherapy*, p. 293 (see ref. 42).
50. R. F. Light and L. J. Cracas, *Science*, 87, 90 (1938).
51. W. F. Lamoreux and F. B. Hutt, *J. Agr. Research*, 58, 307–316 (1939).
52. Victor A. Najjar and L. Emmett Holt, Jr., *J. Am. Med. Assoc.*, 123, 683–684 (1943).
53. Hellin A. Louhi, Hsi-Hsuan Yü, Betty E. Hawthorne, and Clara A. Storvick, *J. Nutrition*, 48, 297–306 (1952).

54. Otto Bessey, Personal Communication.
55. L. B. Pett, *Can. J. Pub. Health,* 36, 69–73 (1945).
56. W. F. Lamoreux and F. B. Hutt, *Poultry Sci.,* 27, 334–341 (1948).
57. Walter Landauer, *Genetics,* 38, 216–228 (1953).
58. Victor A. Najjar, George A. Johns, George C. Medairy, Gertrude Fleischmann, and L. Emmett Holt, Jr., *J. Am. Med. Assoc.,* 126, 357–358 (1944).
59. D. V. Tappan, U. J. Lewis, U. D. Register, and C. A. Elvehjem, *J. Nutrition,* 46, 75–85 (1952).
60. G. A. Goldsmith, unpublished data, as quoted in *Recommended Dietary Allowances,* p. 18 (see ref. 9).
61. Roger J. Williams, "The Chemistry and Biochemistry of Pantothenic Acid," *Advances in Enzymology,* Interscience Publishers, Inc., New York, N.Y., 1943, Vol. III, pp. 253–287.
62. A. E. Schaefer, J. M. McKibbin, and C. A. Elvehjem, *J. Biol. Chem.,* 143, 321–330 (1942).
63. Esmond E. Snell, Derrol Pennington, and Roger J. Williams, *J. Biol. Chem.,* 133, 559–565 (1940).
64. Roger J. Williams, "The Clinical Possibilities of Pantothenic Acid," in Michael G. Wohl, ed., *Dietotherapy,* pp. 263–267 (see ref. 42).
65. Benjamin N. Berg, Theodore F. Zucker and Lois M. Zucker, *Proc. Soc. Exptl. Biol. Med.,* 71, 374–376 (1949).
66. M. J. Dallemagne, *Ann. Rev. Physiol.,* 12, 101–118 (1950).
67. Peter P. Ludovici, A. E. Axelrod, and Bettina B. Carter, *Proc. Soc. Exptl. Biol. Med.,* 72, 81–83 (1949).
68. Sidney Vernon, *J. Am. Med. Assoc.,* 143, 799–802 (1953).
69. J. E. Jacques, *Lancet,* November 10, 1951, pp. 861–862.
70. E. P. Ralli, "Recent Advances in Nutrition Research with Emphasis on the Newer B Vitamins," *Nutrition Symposium Series,* The National Vitamin Foundation, Inc., New York, N.Y., 1952, Vol. 5, pp. 78–103.
71. Roger J. Williams, *The Human Frontier,* Harcourt, Brace & Co., New York, N.Y., 1946.
72. Edgar S. Gordon, "Pantothenic Acid in Human Nutrition," in E. A. Evans, Jr., ed, *The Biological Action of the Vitamins,* The University of Chicago Press, Chicago, Ill., 1942. pp. 136–143.
73. *Recommended Dietary Allowances,* p. 25 (see ref. 9).
74. A. Hansen and O. Bessey, Personal Communication.
75. Marjorie M. Nelson, C. Willet Asling, and Herbert M. Evans, *J. Nutrition,* 48, 61–80 (1952).
76. Tom D. Spies and Hugh R. Butt, "Vitamins and Avitaminoses," in Garfield G. Duncan, ed., *Diseases of Metabolism,* p. 520 (see ref. 4).

77. Tage Kemp, *Ejnar Munksgaard,* Copenhagen, Denmark, 1951, p. 247.
78. Norman C. Wetzel, Warren C. Fargo, and Isabel H. Smith, *Science,* 110, 651–653 (1949).
79. Norman C. Wetzel, Howard H. Hopwood, Manuel E. Keuchle, and Robert M. Grueninger, *J. Clin. Nutrition,* 1, 17–31 (1952).
80. *Recommended Dietary Allowances,* p. 25 and ref. 184 (see ref. 9).
81. Walter G. Unglaub, Harold L. Rosenthal, and Grace A. Goldsmith, *J. Lab. Clin. Med.,* 43, 143–156 (1954).
82. R. W. Engel, *Proc. Soc. Exptl. Biol. Med.,* 50, 193–196 (1942).
83. R. W. Engel, *Proc Soc. Exptl. Biol. Med.,* 52, 281–282 (1943).
84. D. H. Copeland, *Proc. Soc. Exptl. Biol. Med.* 57, 33–35 (1944).
85. O. M. Hale and A. E. Schaefer, *Proc. Soc. Exptl. Biol. Med.,* 77, 633–636 (1951).
86. E. L. Sevringhaus, Personal Communication.
87. P. T. Young, *Psychological Bulletin,* 38, 129–164 (1941).
88. E. M. Scott and others, series of articles on self-selection of diet in *J. Nutrition* beginning 1946.
89. P. T. Young, *Psychological Bulletin,* 45, 289 (1948).
90. R. J. Williams, *Quart. J. Studies Alc.,* 7, 567–587 (1947).
91. J. Mardones, N. Segovia, and E. Onfray, *Arch. Biochem.,* 9, 401–406 (1946).
92. Roscoe A. Brady and W. W. Westerfeld, *Quart. J. Studies Alc.,* 7, 499–505 (1947).
93. Roger J. Williams, Richard B. Pelton, and Lorene L. Rogers, *Quart. J. Studies Alc.,* 16, 234–244 (1955).
94. J. Mardones, *Quart. J. Studies Alc.,* 12, 563–575 (1951).

XI

The Genetotrophic Approach

In the foregoing pages we have reviewed the cumulative evidence which points to the conclusion that each human being possesses a highly distinctive body chemistry. While the same physical mechanisms and the same metabolic processes are operating in all human bodies, the structures are sufficiently diverse and the genetically determined enzyme efficiencies vary sufficiently from individual to individual so that the sum total of all the reactions taking place in one individual's body may be very different from those taking place in the body of another individual of the same age, sex, and body size.

In the preceding chapter we have assembled evidences that each individual's nutritional needs are also distinctive from the quantitative standpoint. Although every nutritionally important mineral, amino acid, and vitamin is needed by every individual, it follows—if biochemical individuality exists—that the needs are quantitatively distinctive for each individual. Evidence has been presented in the preceding chapter that this is actually the case and that the divergences for many items are wide.

The genic pattern of a fertilized egg cell determines what the developing embryo is going to need during the course of its development. In certain species of mammals (e.g., rats), the over-all nutritional needs are qualitatively different from those of other species (e.g., guinea pigs). In each individual within the human species, the needs are quantitatively different.

Given continuously (1) a suitable ambient temperature, (2) suitable supplies of water and oxygen, and (3) a suitable assortment of food materials, a fertilized human ovum will develop in accordance with the human time scale into an adult human being. Although the genic make-up of an individual ovum may cause it to have needs with respect to temperature, water, and oxygen supply (all of these factors influence enzyme activities) which are slightly distinctive, its needs for particular nutrients—minerals, amino acids, and vitamins—may exhibit highly diverse patterns and thus be highly distinctive.

The genetotrophic principle, as the author conceives it, is a very broad one encompassing the whole of biology. It may be stated as follows: Every individual organism that has a distinctive genetic background has distinctive nutritional needs which must be met for optimal well-being. When stated in this way very few indeed would question its validity. At the human level those who think that individual variations in body chemistry are minimal may well think that the principle, though true, is of little importance. If variations in body chemistry are large, however, the importance seems clear. The importance or nonimportance depends clearly upon how great the individual variability is.

If, during embryonic development, a particular ovum has needs which cannot be satisfied in the environment provided, then it either dies or its organs and functions fail to develop in a well-rounded fashion. If, during childhood, the individual has nutritional needs which are not fully satisfied, his metabolism is altered accordingly; he becomes a prey to infections, and his growth becomes retarded or distorted. If, during adulthood, the individual—through ignorance or for other reasons—fails to meet his particular nutritional needs, he becomes deficient, and this deficiency may contribute to all manner of disease and disease susceptibility. As the individual ages, some of his organs and tissues fail earlier than others because, in accordance with their genetic pattern, they have special characteristics or weaknesses. These weaknesses may involve unusually high nutritional needs for specific substances which are not provided adequately by the environment in which the organ or tissue resides.

This discussion may make it appear that malformation, susceptibility to infection and disease, and degeneration are all foreordained and inevitable consequences of the genic pattern set up in the original fertilized egg cell. Precisely the opposite is true, however, if the genetotrophic principle is operative.

If this principle is valid, we may by a slight extension say that it should be possible, theoretically at least, to meet the needs of almost any developing ovum, even though these needs are unusual, *provided the needs are known.* In case these needs are known and can be consistently met throughout life, then development proceeds in a regular fashion regardless of the presence of untoward structures and partial genetic blocks which augment special needs. No deficiencies develop during childhood, adulthood, or old age, and the individual lives his full span of years and emulates Oliver Wendell Holmes's "Wonderful One-Hoss Shay."

If the genetotrophic principle is valid and variation is as great as our evidence suggests, one of the chief frontiers of medical science in the decades to come will lie in the problem of finding out what specific needs are liable to go unmet, what consequences result from each deficiency, and how these needs can be met practically.

Some of the readers of this volume probably have been tempted to think of the author as a "hereditarian," because without question the importance of heredity has consistently been stressed in chapter after chapter. If, however, the full implications of the genetotrophic principle are grasped, there is ample reason for thinking of the author as an "environmentalist," because of the tremendous potentialities he attributes to nutrition—a strictly environmental factor. Although it is admitted that from a practical standpoint supplying the needed environmental (nutritional) factors may be far from simple, the logical application of the genetotrophic idea emphasizes the theoretical possibility that practically any human weakness, deformity, deficiency, or disease can be combatted with some success by supplying the needed nutrients to the right locality at the right time. In specific cases this may, of course, be difficult or virtually impossible. Conversely, almost any deformity, weakness, or disease could be created or accentuated by a lack of a crucial nutrient from a crucial tissue at a crucial time.

It is pretty difficult to get away from the basic fact which De La Mare has expressed in verse:

It's a very odd thing—
As odd as can be—
That whatever Miss T. eats
Turns into Miss T.

It may be added as a corollary that whatever Miss T. doesn't eat, doesn't turn into Miss T.

The point of view which we have been developing is one with which I believe no sound biologist can quarrel: The importance of heredity cannot be overstressed because without it we are nothing. The importance of environmental influences likewise cannot be overstressed because without them we are nothing.

A basic idea which arises out of the material presented in this volume is a very simple one: *Understanding and appreciating what heredity distinctively does for an individual may make it possible to cope environmentally with his difficulties.* Without the appreciation of what heredity does, it is impossible to make intelligent use of the available environmental influences. Narrowing down the discussion specifically to the genetotrophic principle: *Unless we know about the distinctive nutritional needs imposed by one's heredity, we are in no position to meet these needs.* We cannot know about these needs without studying individual differences in needs. We must be aware of the general facts of biochemical individuality, and in specific cases we must know the needs of the individuals whom we would help.

The science of nutrition, up to the present time, has been concerned largely with basic facts which apply to all mammals and to particular species of mammals (as well as birds). The broader aspects of nutrition apply with considerable uniformity to many species, and there is plenty of room yet for research and discovery in this area. Narrowing down the field somewhat, the study of human nutrition has been concerned with what applies to *all human beings,* and this field of research likewise has by no means been exhausted. Nutrition in future decades will, if the genetotrophic principle is sound and as important as our data indicate, turn its attention more and more to understanding and supplying individual needs—needs that quantitatively do not apply to all humanity but are more or less distinctive and crucial for individuals.

The somewhat phenomenal *success* that nutrition has achieved in

the decades past is unanswerable testimony to the fact that broad
principles do apply in the field of nutrition. Human beings do have
common needs, and it is highly important that these be recognized
and understood. That nutrition has *failed* (as well as succeeded) is
indicated by the fact that the etiologies of a host of human diseases
(idiopathic) remain quite obscure, and yet the probability has not
been explored that nutritional deficiency (incurred because of special
demands genetically imposed) is basic to these diseases.

The application of the genetotrophic principle by medical science
is a *long-range* proposal. Many difficulties and intensive investigations, in addition to natural conservatism, lie in its way, and it may
be decades before it bears the best fruit. The possibilities arising out
of its application hinge upon the prevalence and wideness of the
variations in the body chemistry of human individuals.

From the standpoint of medical history, the genetotrophic principle is an extension and a fulfilling of ideas which have long been
bandied about in the minds of leading medical thinkers. Even Hippocrates strongly hinted at the idea when he thought of man as
"that infinitely variable organism without which human disease is
impossible." He was quite without knowledge of the existence of
disease germs and was led to the conclusion that "the consumptive
is born a consumptive," a statement which we know now to be in
error—and yet it contains an essential truth inasmuch as the evidence
is strong that susceptibility to tuberculosis is an inborn trait. Wright
and Lewis[1] and Lurie,[2, 3] for example, have found that guinea pigs
and rabbits of different strains vary greatly in their susceptibility to
tuberculosis. Gowen[4] has strikingly shown that the course which
another infective disease, typhoid, takes in mice depends equally
upon the virulence of the bacteria and the *susceptibility* of the mice.
This is shown in Figure 17. When Hippocrates said, "the consumptive is born a consumptive," he left out one dimension of the problem—the virulence of the bacteria, organisms he did not know
existed. When one who has had the advantage of twentieth-century
bacteriology says "tuberculosis is caused by the tubercle bacilli," he
is also leaving out one dimension of the problem, the *susceptibility*
of the individual.

We have already quoted Galen the Greek physician, Parry of Bath,
and Sir William Osler, all of whom evidently believed in individual

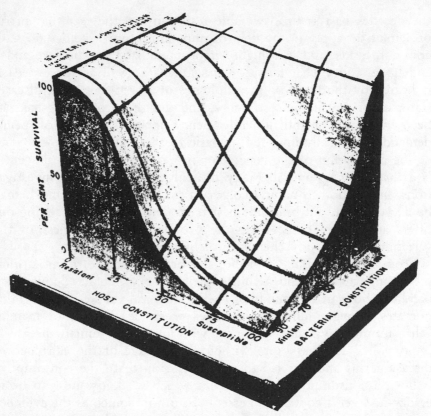

Figure 17. Dependence of survival from typhoid on the constitution of the host and the virulence of the bacteria (Gowen).

disease susceptibility, and we have mentioned George Draper's Consitutional Clinic (p. 2). The policy of this clinic was "to incorporate with its study of sick persons any new method which might further illuminate an individual's constitutional type." Also we have called attention to the idea of Sir A. E. Garrod, expressed over fifty years ago, that probably all individuals differ in their body chemistry (p. 109).

Sheldon's extensive classification of body types constitutes an important contribution to the understanding of the human differences which make for susceptibility to numerous diseases.[5] What he has done with body form is just a beginning; anatomical features such as those mentioned in Chapters III and VI need to be brought into the picture. Classifications need to be worked out at the physiological and biochemical levels. The strategy for making advances in this area will be discussed later.

Another modern exponent of studying constitution in relation to disease susceptibility was Wade H. Brown of the Rockefeller Institute, whose findings in the field of anatomy have already been mentioned (p. 19).[6] A few quotations from his work will serve to illustrate the best medical thinking of his time with relation to the problem under consideration. Regarding constitution he says:

> Still, it is extremely difficult to define the constitutional factor in language which conveys a definite meaning or to say how or why one person differs from another, with respect to the general property of susceptibility to disease. . . .[7]

With respect to "normality," he voices this rather mild, though definite, protest:

> The problem of constitution turns, first of all, upon the determination of what is normal. The usual treatment of this subject is unsatisfactory. The current method of dealing with normality is the method of standardization—the establishment of mean values with limits of variation or of other standards of measurements and the separation of individuals into two classes, the normal and the abnormal. It is apparently assumed that what happens within the limits of normal is either of no consequence or that the methods available for drawing distinctions are inadequate. . . .[8]

He apparently did not consider the possibility which we have expressed, namely, that "normal" individuals are always abnormal with respect to some of their numerous attributes and that to be "normal" in every respect would be most unusual. In summarizing he says:

> Changing conditions of life affect individuals and groups, but as individuals differ in respect of their inherent constitutional equipment, they differ also in their reactions to influences of all kinds. Some are capable of immediate and complete adjustment, others are slow to respond or are incapable of adjustment so that when members of a group

are subjected to a change in the conditions, the response obtained varies according to the capacities of the individual so that, even now, we have some understanding of how and why one person differs from another in respect of the general property of susceptibility to disease and why it is that the susceptibility of individuals and of populations is not fixed but varies from time to time, independent of any immunity that may be acquired through previous exposure to a given disease.[9]

It would appear that Brown recognized inherent "general property of susceptibility to [infectious] disease," but did not give much weight to inborn susceptibility (or resistance) to *specific* infective agents. It is also apparent from his discussion that he could never quite center his attention on the one problem of constitution, that is, "how or why one person differs from another." He had one eye on the problem of why individuals vary from time to time. Each problem, in my opinion, is worthy of attention, but they should not be inextricably mixed. How people differ one from another can best be ascertained by comparing them using *repeated* measurements, under as nearly the same environmental conditions as possible. In this way rhythms[10] and intra-individual differences will be largely eliminated, and the inter-individual differences can be faced squarely.

Of course, Galton and all others who have been convinced of the importance of hereditary influences have taken one step in the general direction of applying the genetotrophic idea. Scholarship in the fields related to medical science, however, has never acted upon the idea that normal human differences per se merit and demand intensive and extensive study. If one needs to become convinced of this, he should look through any book dealing with the sciences basic to medicine—biology, physiology, biochemistry, pharmacology, bacteriology, physiological psychology, etc.—and see how little he finds, if indeed anything, about human variability and human differences.

When we pay attention to differences—anatomical, physiological, and biochemical—we are inevitably led to consider differences in nutritional needs. It is then but a small step to the genetotrophic idea.

It may be argued by those who see the inevitable value in the genetotrophic principle that to supply special nutrients to special individuals because of their peculiar needs constitutes one more way of promoting the survival of the unfit. Admitting that there is truth in this, the fact remains that medical practice has throughout the centuries been dedicated to the saving and prolonging of lives, regardless of the fitness or unfitness of the individuals concerned. To raise the question whether medicine sometimes goes to extremes in this direction would not be appropriate here.

It is interesting to note, however, that the operation of the genetotrophic principle probably constitutes, and has constituted for millions of years, an important means of natural selection. Mutations which impose on an organism extremely high demands for any single nutrient are likely to be lethal because of the impossibility of satisfying the need. Even when demands are moderately high, this imposes on the individual organisms an added difficulty and makes more likely its elimination from the population.

The genetotrophic principle not only offers a basis for understanding many diseases the origin of which is now obscure, but it also clears up the question as to why exceptional individuals exist who in spite of untoward environmental influences live to advanced old age. Fleming[11] cites a case of a man who, in spite of his drinking a quart of Scotch whiskey every day of his life for 60 years, lived to be 93 and managed a successful business almost until his death. Nutritionally, on the basis of what is regarded "normal," this individual should have been deficient with respect to minerals, amino acids, and vitamins. Regardless of how wisely he selected the food that he did eat, he was always "diluting" his diet caloriewise with a large proportion of alcohol; that is, he was substituting alcohol for food. Yet this individual obviously was not suffering (comparatively speaking) from deficiencies, and the only way one can reasonably account for his excellent health is on the basis of a genetic make-up in which the enzyme efficiencies were so high and so well balanced and stable that far less than the usual amounts of crucial nutrients were needed. Possibly, in addition, he had unusual wisdom of the body with respect to selecting the food he did eat. This individual merely represents an extreme case. There are many other individuals (not a large percentage, however) who seemingly have nutritional needs which are readily satisfied under ordinary conditions and live to old age relatively free from infectious and other diseases, even though from the nutritionist's viewpoint their diets may appear to be substandard.

The genetotrophic idea was first conceived in connection with the experimental work on alcohol consumption by rats. When it was found that the alcohol consumption of rats (1) was highly individual[12, 13, 14] (as were also their excretion patterns),[15] and (2) was genetically controlled (as evidenced by the distinctive behavior of each inbred strain and the relatively small variation *within* inbred strains),[13, 14] and (3) could be increased by deficient diets and abolished by fortified ones,[12, 13] the genetotrophic ideas appeared to be the only reasonable interpretation of the facts.[16,17] Since these original observations were made, dozens of other facts, many of which have been and will be presented in the present volume, have become explicable on the basis of the genetotrophic concept. To date there are no observations, so far as I am aware, that appear to go counter to this idea.

Of the several possible attitudes which may develop in relation to our discussion, one is skepticism with respect to the magnitude of the variation of individual nutritional needs. One may admit that there are variations without admitting that they are great or of great importance. To one who has doubt on this point, we would simply say: We have tried to stick to experimentally determined findings; anyone who chooses to think that variations are small should be able to support his point of view with experimental evidence. This, we believe, would be very difficult to do. Our position is that these differences in needs have not been studied intensively. We have presented evidence (admittedly fragmentary at times) to indicate that variations are large; if further study of these needs proves that the variations are indeed smaller than we have indicated, we will retreat from our position and admit that the genetotrophic principle is, to that extent, less important. In other words, our presentation of the possibility of applying the genetotrophic principle may be taken as a challenge to further research in the area of individual nutritional needs. There is nothing impossible about putting the genetotrophic idea to the test and finding out how important it is.

There is one possible obstacle to the application of the genetotrophic concept which should be mentioned at this point. In our discussion of nutritional needs, we have in general made the tacit assumption that they are additive. That is, a person's daily needs include a mg. of calcium + b μg. of iodine + c mg. of threonine + d

units of vitamin A, etc., etc. We have not stressed interrelations, though we have mentioned them several times.

It is well recognized that interrelations exist. How much sodium one needs depends upon his potassium intake; his calcium needs are determined in part by his phosphate intake; his need for a specific amino acid may be determined in part by the amount of the other amino acids that he gets (they can interfere with each other's utilization). Only by further experimentation can we determine how important antagonisms and other interrelations are in human nutrition. If highly important, they will seriously complicate the picture but will not change its basic outlines.

There is reasonable hope that in the vitamin field interrelations and antagonisms may not prove to be unduly disturbing. These substances in general do not interfere with each other seriously; they are usually inert unless built into enzyme systems. The concentrations which have to be administered to be physiologically effective are so low that they are not likely to affect adversely or otherwise any process except the ones which they affect enzymatically.

There was a time when students of nutrition were inclined to think that certain vitamins, e.g., thiamine, vitamin A, and ascorbic acid, were the "important vitamins" and that others brought up the rear of the procession. From the standpoint of ease of discovery on the basis of deficiency disease, there is some justification in this view.

From the standpoint of biochemical genetics and the genetotrophic principle, however, it seems likely that partial genetic blocks (which impose increased demands) may happen anywhere in the entire metabolic scheme in what may be assumed, without further evidence, to be in a random fashion. If this be the case, any and every nutritional need may be represented among those which are observed to be augmented.

Another interesting possibility presents itself in this connection. We have assumed all along, tentatively at least, that all individuals within the same species have qualitatively the same nutritional needs. This, in effect, may not be true, as we have hinted in connection with our discussion of amino acid needs. It is within the realm of possibility and even probability that certain amino acids, e.g., glutamic acid, glutamine, or arginine, may be "essential amino acids" for certain individuals in the sense that they are essential for health and well-being. If this possibility becomes accepted as a fact, it will enlarge the list of nutrients[18] which may be used singly or in combinations as genetotrophic supplements. It seems probable, in other words, that substances which are now regarded as metabolites rather than nutrients may be treated, in the light of highly variable needs, as nutrients, and that their use along with ordinary nutrients may be an effective means of combating genetotrophic diseases.

Summary

On the occasion of celebrating its 200th anniversary, Columbia University organized a large conference on the "Unity of Knowledge." One section of the conference had as its problem "Man's Understanding of His Own Nature," and one question asked was, "Is there any likelihood that a single recognizable picture of man can be discerned among the many detailed and varied arts and sciences?" This represents a current mode of thought which is quite incompatible with the idea of biological individuality.

It is the writer's opinion that in biology and in medicine, as well as in the areas of social sciences and philosophy, we have concentrated too much on "a single recognizable picture of man" and have given too little attention to *men*, the individuals who make up the species, the persons who become patients, and the units who make up society. Of course, we can draw a single recognizable picture of man. He will have a skeleton, muscles, organs, nervous system, hungers, emotions, aspirations, etc., but as long as we hope to solve or understand human problems on the basis of such a generalized being, our operations must be at a very elementary level and many problems will completely elude us.

In medicine we must recognize individuality at the biochemical and physiological level (we shall discuss this further in a later chapter); in social studies we must recognize individuality at all levels. In both fields[19, 20] there are numerous problems which we cannot touch until we disabuse our minds of the idea that what we need above all is "a single recognizable picture of man." What we need is to recognize and understand people and patients for what they are. Knowledge about variability we believe contributes substantially to this understanding.

REFERENCES

1. Sewall Wright and Paul A. Lewis, *Am. Naturalist*, 55, 20–50 (1921).
2. Max B. Lurie, *J. Exptl. Med.*, 58, 305–327 (1933).
3. Max B. Lurie, *Proc. Soc. Exptl. Biol. Med.*, 39, 176–181 (1938).
4. John W. Gowen, *Am. J. Human Gen.*, 4, 285–302 (1952).
5. William Herbert Sheldon, S. S. Stevens, and W. B. Tucker, *The Varieties of Human Physique*, Harper & Bros., New York, N.Y., and London, England, 1940.
6. Wade H. Brown, "Constitutional Variation and Susceptibility to Disease," in *The Harvey Lectures*, Williams and Wilkins Company, Baltimore, Md., 1930, pp. 106–150.
7. *Ibid.*, p. 108.
8. *Ibid.*, p. 109.
9. *Ibid.*, p. 150.
10. N. Kleitman, *Physiol. Revs.*, 29, 1–30 (1949).
11. Robert Fleming, "Medical Treatment of the Inebriate," in *Alcohol, Science and Society*, Journal of Studies on Alcohol, Inc., New Haven, Conn., 1945, p. 391.
12. Roger J. Williams, L. Joe Berry, and Ernest Beerstecher, Jr., *Arch. Biochem.*, 23, 275–290 (1949).
13. Ernest Beerstecher, Jr., Janet G. Reed, William Duane Brown, and L. Joe Berry, *Univ. Texas Publ.*, 5109, 115–138 (1951).
14. Janet G. Reed, *Univ. Texas Publ.*, 5109, 144–150 (1951).
15. Janet G. Reed, *Univ. Texas Publ.*, 5109, 139–143 (1951).
16. Roger J. Williams, Ernest Beerstecher, Jr., and L. Joe Berry, *The Lancet*, February 18, 1950, pp. 287–294.
17. R. J. Williams, *Nutrition Revs.*, 8, 257–260 (1950).
18. Roger J. Williams and Lorene L. Rogers, *Texas Repts. Biol. Med.*, 11, 576 (1953).
19. Roger J. Williams, *Free and Unequal*, University of Texas Press, Austin, Tex., 1953.
20. Roger J. Williams, *J. Public Law*, 3, 328-344 (1955).

XII

Implications for
the Biological Sciences

Now that we have presented pertinent material relating to biochemical individuality and the genetotrophic concept, it will be well to step back and survey various aspects of pure and applied scientific work to see what implications these ideas have. To discuss these implications and what they mean in various areas will be the main purpose of the remaining chapters of this volume.

It is clear to anyone who searches the biological literature that the vast majority of investigators have little or no direct interest in variations and exceptions. When exceptions are encountered in their investigative work, they are perhaps given a nod, such as one would give a passing acquaintance, but the search goes on for the general principles. This is as it should be, and our emphasis on exceptions should not be regarded as an attempt to throw a monkey wrench into the field of biological science. If duly considered, however, the exceptions may be of the utmost importance in connection with applying biological science to the solution of practical problems. It seems to the writer that there are vast areas of biological science for which biochemical individuality has little or nothing in the way of implications, certainly none on the negative side. This can best be made clear by citing a few specific illustrations.

Let us suppose, for example, one is concerned with a physiological or biochemical study of *vision*. This is a fundamental process intimately connected with the life of mammals and many other living things. There is abundant reason for thinking that the process is, in its fundamentals, the same in a mouse, grouse, cat, or rat, and the choice of experimental animals is a matter of convenience. As long as we have much to learn about the fundamentals of vision, it is highly appropriate that those who find the field alluring continue in their intriguing attempts to find out the basic answers. For such the existence of biochemical individuality need be of no concern, certainly not a deterrent influence.

The moment, however, that one becomes interested in *applying* knowledge about vision to the practical end of improving people's vision, then biochemical individuality becomes a *crucial* consideration. The more we know about the fundamental physiology and biochemistry of vision, the more possible avenues develop whereby we can attack any problem of vision. But whatever we may do nutritionally, surgically, optically, or otherwise cannot be done successfully without a regard for the biochemical and physiologic individuality of the person to be helped. Actually I have chosen vision as an illustration because in this field we have become accustomed to the idea of individuality. We would no more think of engaging the services of an ophthalmologist who neglected individuality in eyes than we would buy clothing without regard for size. We are used to buying spectacles that often would be absolutely worthless to anyone except the individual for whom they are made. This is an area where, through necessity, the idea of individuality is well established and relatively well developed.

To consider another area, let us suppose that one is interested in any one of a thousand phases of the general process of metabolism: enzymes, how they are made up, how they are interrelated, how they function; the vitamins, what they are chemically, how they work; the chemistry of the hormones, how they function and interact, how they are related to enzyme systems; biochemical syntheses, how they progress and what catalysts are involved; differentiation, what it consists of and how it is promoted. The problems in this area are legion, and our ignorance is vast. There is room here for investigation on an enormous scale, and all of it is pertinent to life. In recent years we have come to realize how unified nature is and how we may find out much about many fundamental metabolic processes by studying one organism, almost any one that is convenient. All that we know and can learn in this vast area is basic to any applications that may arise later. For those who delve in the area of pure biological science, there should be nothing but commendation and encouragement, and for these the facts of biochemical individuality need be of no great scientific concern so far as their investigations are concerned.

But the moment one becomes interested in *applying* his knowledge of metabolism, enzyme action, or endocrine influences to modifying (ameliorating or the reverse) the life processes of any organism (human or subhuman), biochemical individuality enters as a potent factor which must be reckoned with.

It will be worthwhile, I believe, to consider from this standpoint a field of investigation in which the author has been active, namely, the vitamins. The chemical make-up of the vitamins has been determined by first isolating them in pure form. This has usually involved the use of some test organism which may be a fowl or mammal, a yeast, or a bacteria, but the test organism used is immaterial except for convenience. In order to get test responses as uniform and dependable as possible, it is desirable to have organisms which lack, as far as possible, variation. At this stage of the investigation variation is an enemy.

Another stage in the investigation of any vitamin is finding out about its distribution, its sources, quantitatively speaking. This ideally should be done chemically, if possible; but, if not, assay organisms are used. Again at this stage, variation (in the test organisms) is an enemy. Another important step in vitamin investigation is the determination of how they perform their functions. This usually involves the use of organisms or of tissues derived from them, and certainly much can be learned by using any convenient organism. At this stage again, variation is an enemy, and if an organism in use undergoes a mutation during the course of the investigation the result can be temporarily disastrous.

It is difficult oftentimes to assign motives for research. Pure scientific curiosity is a factor in many cases, but often there is in the researcher's mind the possibility that the desired information may be useful ultimately for human betterment. Certainly the purpose back of the quantitative determination of a vitamin in a series of food materials is based upon the *need* of humans (and animals) for the vitamin and the *use* of the materials for food. The moment we begin to apply this information to the feeding of people (or animals), biochemical individuality becomes a factor. And, although it may make the task more difficult than if individuality did not exist, its recognition becomes an indispensable ally in the pursuit of success.

It is most surprising from this point of view that researchers will often travail and quibble over determining vitamin content with errors of a few percent at most, when the needs of the organisms for which the vitamins are intended are quite unknown and may vary over a several-fold range. Investigators need to be reminded that the *utility* of vitamins does not rest on their ability to make inbred strains of white rats grow and develop. Their utility rests upon their ability to promote health in *heterogeneous* populations of chickens, other fowls and farm animals, pets, and, finally, human beings. Because of biochemical individuality and variation, the vitamin needs of all these—with the possible exception, in some cases, of some pure-line fowls—are highly uncertain from the quantitative standpoint.

There are many areas in biology where fundamental research can and must be done without regard for the biochemical individuality which we have stressed. Let us, for example, consider the area in which both physiologists and psychologists are interested, sensory physiology and psychology. One who is interested, for example, in the sense of smell will utilize certain test materials and certain test organisms. Variation in either test materials or test organisms is an enemy and may stand in the way of the investigators in getting the reproducible, dependable answers they are after. It may be presumed that the fundamental process of smelling is the same in various mammals (at least), and the choice of the experimental organism is based upon convenience rather than upon more fundamental considerations.

The moment one steps over the line into the applied field, viz., *doing anything* about odors—their use or modification, or modifying people with respect to their reactions to odors—biochemical individuality must be taken into account.

Another important and broad area in animal biology relates to the functioning of nerves. Exactly what are nerve impulses? What happens chemically when these impulses travel? Why do nerves have such a distinctive composition and metabolism? These and many more questions require more complete and basic answers than have ever been given. They can be investigated using any one of many different organisms: and, as long as these organisms are relatively uniform, individuality need not be a matter of concern. Variation is an enemy.

The basic information regarding nerve physiology is fundamental to all possible applications, but the moment one becomes interested in applications, that is, doing anything about anyone's nerve action, biochemical individuality becomes a potent factor. If unrecognized, it is an enemy: if recognized and taken into account, it may be a powerful ally.

In the area of bacteriology or microbiology, we have tremendous potentialities for biological research which need not be concerned with biochemical individuality. Many fundamental problems of metabolism as well as those peculiar to lower forms can well be cleared up using microorganisms as test objects. The unsolved problems as to the nature of phages and viruses and how they bring about their effects are alluring ones. Investigations in this wide area constitute basic pure science.

Immediately, however, if one becomes interested in *applications* of microbiology in which human beings (or animals) are directly involved, the factor of biochemical individuality is bound to be concerned. This area of microbiology, including immunity, is certain to be markedly influenced by advancing knowledge about biochemical variation.

In the broad domain of plant biology, the same general principles hold. A tremendous volume of scientific work of a fundamental nature needs to be done and can be done without any more than the usual attention to variability. The moment, however, one becomes interested in applications, biochemical individuality is likely to come into play and needs to be given due attention. We have not used any illustrations of individuality from the botanical field, but this does not mean that they do not exist.

We find here seemingly a differentiation between the "pure science" of biology and the "applied science" of biology. Those who are primarily interested in the pure science of biology, whether chemists, physiologists, anatomists, geneticists, or psychologists, can do their outstanding basic work without regard to the facts of biochemical individuality. They have done and will do the groundwork on which all future applications will be based. Those whose interest is that of applied biology, on the other hand, must, if they are to apply the basic knowledge successfully, take biochemical individuality into account.

Many investigators are not, in the author's opinion, irrevocably classifiable as "pure" or "applied" scientists. Some are very happy to devote themselves exclusively to a highly specialized area. Others like to rove and develop more diversified interests. Some at one stage of their lives may have the viewpoint of a pure scientist, and at a later stage they may think largely in terms of applications. Not infrequently investigators may be both pure and applied scientists at the same time.

The concept of biochemical individuality, as we have tried to make clear, does not throw a monkey wrench into the pure science of biology. There is nothing incompatible between the biochemical individuality concept and the recognition of the basic and fundamental importance of pure biology in all its phases. Investigation in this vast area should and must proceed without significant attention to biochemical individuality.

Certainly the concept of biochemical individuality does not throw a monkey wrench into the field of applied biology either. It furnishes it with an insight which is indispensable. Admittedly applied biology would be simpler if individuality did not exist; but, since it does exist and is a potent factor, its recognition facilitates rather than stands in the way of successful application.

It is perhaps not out of place to remind ourselves that every new insight increases the potentialities of those who gain it. Sometimes those who recognize in an academic way the validity and potential importance of biochemical individuality say, in effect: "So what? What can you do about it?" We will try to answer this question in a more definite manner in a later chapter, but at this point we may say with some assurance that "knowledge is power" and new insights make possible future applications. When Volta evoked a kick out of a frog's leg every time he touched it with two different wires, he did not know how great the future developments of electricity would be. He may not have even realized what we now know, that the new insight was certain to bear fruit.

Before leaving the discussion of applied biology, it will be well to express my conviction that *applied human biology* has unparalleled possibilities in the decades and centuries to come. Regardless of how important pure biology is, and emphatically I think it is *important*, I think it is time for applied human biology to get substantial attention. Individuality is a cornerstone on which it will rest.

In recent years we have been faced by the possibility or perhaps the probability that human civilization as we know it may be shattered if not pretty well destroyed. In view of this it seems not inopportune to remind those who work in ivory towers that the possibilities of *applied* human biology should be looked into. Possibly it holds the key to the solution of more human problems than we dream of. There comes a time when pure scientific curiosity as the sole object of scientists' devotion may be inadequate and even, in effect, destructive.

XIII

Implications for Medical and Dental Research

A few years ago, duly considering many of the facts of individuality, a fundamental strategy seemed clear to the writer. It would be necessary, he thought, in order to develop a science of man, to start inductively and become acquainted *intensively* with individual human specimens, preliminary to attempting any, except very obvious, generalizations. This approach seemed entirely logical and in fact inescapable. During the intervening years, however, the writer has become convinced that because of the tremendous array of items in which human individuality is exhibited, this is not a practical approach.

There is serious doubt in the writer's mind whether it will ever be possible to place individuals in any reasonable number of *general* categories which will have any high degree of significance. If funds were available to make serious attempts, there would be some advantage in trying, but the investment would have to be very large.

The fundamental strategy which now appears to be vastly superior from the practical standpoint is to select specific problems for study and then *investigate how individual human differences enter into these specific problems.* The problems chosen may be of diverse types, but since we are dealing with the areas of medicine and dentistry, let us consider problems which lie within those fields.

The point of view which we wish to outline can best be illustrated by discussing briefly our approach to the problem of alcoholism. Up until the time we began studying the subject, apparently no one had seriously entertained the idea that there might be something bio-chemically distinctive and peculiar about alcoholism-prone individuals. The question which appeared to be considered most pertinent was: Why does *man* become alcoholic?—and man, as referred to, meant the "normal man" whose various attributes are normal.

One of two alternatives is true: Either one's biochemical peculiarities have something to do with alcoholism-proneness, or they have nothing to do with it. If all individuals were equally prone, then there would be no such thing as alcoholism-proneness, and biochemical individuality is in no way pertinent. We, on the basis of all the evidence, arrived at the working hypothesis[1] for which there is much support: One's distinctive metabolism (which is not uninfluenced by psychological factors) is probably crucial in determining whether or not one is afflicted with the disease. Alcohol does things to some individuals which it does not do to others.

If this is so, then the next question to be answered is: *What metabolic peculiarities* are crucial with respect to susceptibility to alcoholism? It is obvious that the answer to this question must be based upon some knowledge of metabolic peculiarities in general. What metabolic peculiarities exist from which one might choose the crucial ones? Because of lack of attention to biochemical individuality, little indeed was known about metabolic peculiarities. When we began the study of alcoholism, the list of known peculiarities was pretty much limited to the relatively rare so-called "inborn errors of metabolism," alcaptonuria, phenyl ketonuria, cystinuria, and the like. The chance that any of these were involved was very minute.

In one study we explored sixty items in a small group of alcoholics and nonalcoholic controls in the hopes of finding some metabolic peculiarities which might be associated with alcoholism-proneness.[2] These sixty items included urinary constituents, salivary constituents, and blood constituents. There were six items which appeared to be significantly different for the two groups. Subsequently, more extensive investigations have indicated that certain of these items are, with even higher probability, distinctively different for alcoholics.[3]

A more fruitful line of experimentation was that described earlier (p. 183), having to do with the factors which promote alcoholic consumption in experimental animals. In this work it became clear that individual metabolic peculiarities were crucially important in determining whether the animals drank alcohol or not, and that supplying them with fortified diets would prevent alcohol consumption by satisfying individual augmented nutritional needs.

It is not our purpose here to discuss the alcoholism problem in detail[4, 5, 6, 7, 8, 9, 10] or to make any premature claims as to having found a practical solution which is universally applicable. We are more concerned here with the basic procedure involved in attacking the problem of alcoholism from the standpoint of biochemical individuality.

It seems obvious that, if a number of other diseases had been investigated previously from the same viewpoint, much more would have been known about metabolic peculiarities in general, and the task of searching out those which are crucial for alcoholism would have been simplified. It seems also clear that in future years, as disease after disease is investigated from this point of view, there will be an accumulation of information and insight with respect to metabolic and other peculiarities so that the investigation of each new disease from this viewpoint will be made much easier.

We are not disposed to try to put anyone's thinking into a straight jacket, because each situation calls for resourcefulness and innovations, but it is our opinion that important progress in medical and dental research can come through applying a general formula such as the following:

1. Select a disease the etiology of which is obscure.

2. Explore the known metabolic peculiarities, and look for new ones, which may be associated with the disease or susceptibility to it.

3. Seek to correct the metabolic failures by applying the genetotrophic principle in whatever manner seems most appropriate for the disease in question.

It will be well to clarify and amplify the meaning of *metabolic peculiarities* since these play a highly important role in our discussion. Briefly, every individual gives evidence of metabolic peculiarities if he has, for example, in his blood, urine, saliva, or tissues, some constituent at a level substantially different from the average, for example, in the 1st or 10th decile of a representative human population. If the level is far removed from the average, the peculiarity is relatively extreme; otherwise, it is mild. On the basis of our previous discussions and the above explanation it is clear, I believe, that every living individual has metabolic peculiarities, probably many of them.

An exaggerated dependence on the idea of normality may lead one to reason in the following fashion: When measurements are made with respect to a well, normal individual, every item is judged to be normal because the individual is well and normal; nothing is wrong with him, and so none of his measurements can be off standard. If any of his measurements appear to be out of line, they are misrepresenting his case, because he is normal. The range of normality will have to be extended to include his case.

This point of view overlooks the fact that every well and normal individual is potentially an ill individual, and the roots of disease may be present in his make-up years before there is any overt disease. A dozen young men used as normal controls may each have metabolic peculiarities that point toward a different metabolic derangement: gout, multiple sclerosis, diabetes, anemia, atherosclerosis, hypertension, nephrosis, hypothyroidism, rheumatoid arthritis, rheumatic heart disease, liver cirrhosis, and myasthenia gravis, for example, and yet at the time of their use as controls these young men may show no symptoms of the disease which is to appear later in life. It seems far from safe to assume that because an individual on clinical examination seems well, all of his blood values, for example, are normal and meaningless so far as disease susceptibilities are concerned.

Metabolic peculiarities in the broader sense may be evidenced in other ways than by blood, urine, saliva, or tissue analysis. Unusual size or activity of any endocrine gland, for example, denotes a significant peculiarity. Unusual responses to any one of a large number of drugs, hormones, etc., would also denote corresponding metabolic peculiarities. Unusual appetites or cravings may be another sign, as may also unusual taste thresholds and unusual nutritional demands as evidenced by mild deficiencies when the individuals are consuming "adequate" diets. All these manifestations as well as those exhibited by mineral, amino acid, vitamin, metabolite, or enzyme determinations on body tissues and fluids make possible the identification of hundreds of metabolic peculiarities which singly or in combination may be indicative with respect to pathology. If one assumes that every individual who appears well is a perfect specimen free from any taint of disease or disease susceptibility, then the number of significant metabolic peculiarities must be small, but this assumption is clearly unwarranted.

Returning to the general formula mentioned earlier, let us consider, first, the selection of a disease of which the etiology is obscure. Many specific diseases which might be selected will, upon careful scrutiny from the point of view of biochemical individuality, turn out to be too complex—they may, in reality, be several diseases rather than one. Whenever what has been thought of as a single disease turns out to be several, each of the several must be studied separately from the standpoint of the metabolic or other peculiarities associated with it.

Consider briefly the disease gout, which is characterized by the precipitation of urates in tissues and by the presence of hyperuricemia. Bauer and Klemperer state,[11] "The etiology of the disease is unknown." As has been pointed out by other writers, the presence of high concentrations of uric acid in the blood may be due to (1) overproduction, (2) lowered excretion, (3) lowered destruction, or, of course, any combination of the three. Let us consider two hypothetical individuals, A and B, 30 years of age who have exactly the same uric acid blood level (4 mg. per cent) and exactly the same amount of blood (8 liters). The total uric acid in their respective bloods is 320 mg. Let us suppose further that the rate of production of uric acid in the two individuals is continuously exactly the same, the rate of destruction in the two is continuously the same, and that they consume exactly the same food. One hypothetical individual, A, however, continuously excretes on the average 0.1 mg. less uric acid per day than the other. This is very little, compared with the usual total excretion of 700 mg. per day. In the course of 10 years, A's uric acid blood level will, however, have more than doubled, due to this increased retention, and he will be in the range of "gouty" as contrasted with "normal" individuals. This could happen by a very gradual increase, in one individual, of the renal threshold for uric acid. Whether excretion, production, or destruction is responsible for the difference between individuals, the total accumulation of uric acid in hyperuricemia is small.

On purine-free diets individuals excrete 300 to 600 mg. of uric acid per day, which excretion incidentally is subject to daily fluctuations, but "remains remarkably constant from month to month in a given individual."[12] We, are, therefore, dealing with an extremely delicately balanced situation. It seems that increased production, decreased excretion, or decreased destruction, even if the increments are infinitesimal, could easily account for the variation in the blood uric acid levels of different individuals. Heightened renal threshold seems particularly important, but none of the other factors has as yet been ruled out. Each one of the three processes may involve genetically distinctive enzymes or anatomical structures, and it is surprising that the blood level is not more variable, from individual to individual than it is.

Gout, of course, is something more than hyperuricemia. There must be precipitation of urates in tissues and many factors, such as distinctive mineral balances, which may make one individual with hyperuricemia suffer·from the disease while another with the same blood uric acid level does not. It is believed that a study of individual metabolic peculiarities, as related to gout, would lead to a relatively satisfactory understanding of its etiology. The enzymes that are involved in the synthesis and destruction of purines are presumably quantitatively distinctive in different individuals; the sodium, potassium, calcium, magnesium balances, etc., are probably likewise distinctive (p. 4). The hormonal relationships are distinctive. Although the subject of gout and uric acid metabolism has been studied extensively in many laboratories, it appears that no one has attacked the disease bearing in mind the facts of biochemical individuality, notably the recognition of the nonexistence of "normal" individuals who are average in all respects.

A recent study in our laboratories[13] involved the determination of the blood levels of 11 items in 11 "normal" young men. In most cases 5 specimens, drawn at about weekly intervals under basal conditions, were analyzed from each individual. The uric acid levels in the two extreme individuals were as follows (mg. per cent):

Subject *B*   6.2, 6.3, 6.3, 6.6, 7.6.   Average, 6.6
Subject *K*   3.8, 5.2, 4.8, 4.3, 4.8.   Average, 4.6

Studies of this sort, involving analyzing repeated samples from the same "normal" individuals, have been relatively rare, and for this reason the role of biochemical individuality in the problem has tended to be overlooked. The study reveals differences between "normal" individuals with respect to blood uric acid levels (as well as all the other items), and it would seem a safe wager that subject B is more likely to be afflicted with gout than is subject K. Since only about one individual in 10 who has hyperuricemia is subject to gout, it is probable that both individuals will escape. As we have indicated, other factors than hyperuricemia are involved.

When, after taking due account of biochemical individuality, the etiology of gout becomes relatively well understood, the measures that should be taken to prevent or cure it will quite possibly be evident. Perhaps an excess supply of one of the vitamins or minerals which is concerned in catalyzing metabolic transformations would counteract accumulation of purine precursors or uric acid itself and thus prevent the very mild kidney damage which may tend to precipitate the disease. Possibly the avoidance of some particular nutrient would restore the delicate balance and avoid hyperuricemia. Possibly it would not be necessary to prevent hyperuricemia (except in extreme cases) and that means based upon individual biochemical differences could be devised for preventing the precipitation of urates in tissues, including the kidneys. Whatever the solutions may be, it seems unlikely that all individuals regardless of the exact seat of the difficulty will respond to the same prophylaxis or treatment. If gout should respond to the addition (or subtraction) of specific nutrients, it belongs in the category of genetotrophic disease.

Arthritis, in its various forms, is related to gout and attacks particular individuals who are susceptible to it. We believe that the background facts of biochemical individuality will be essential to its prevention and successful treatment. It would be out of place to discuss the various related diseased conditions in detail or to comment on clinical failures and successes. We believe that every individual who is attacked by diseases in this group is biochemically predisposed because of biochemical peculiarities. It is unreasonable to suppose that these peculiarities are exactly the same for different individuals.

In view of the facts that pregnancy may cause remission of rheumatoid arthritis and that the hormones cortisone and ACTH have been found effective in treatment, it is desirable to mention a point

of view regarding hormone therapy which is related to the genetotrophic concept. When hormone therapy is found beneficial in individual cases, this suggests that the afflicted individual may be
deficient in the production of the particular hormone in question.
How can this deficiency be corrected? There are two ways: one is
to administer the hormone itself; the other is to furnish the individual
with the limiting nutrients so that the individual's glands can build
the hormone endogenously more effectively. Undoubtedly, each approach may be valuable in its place; the genetotrophic approach,
however, has been largely unexplored.

Although we have discussed briefly the implications of biochemical
individuality for alcoholism, for gout, and for arthritis, these are
merely examples. A host of other diseases need to be attacked with
the same point of view and hold the same promise of success. These
include multiple sclerosis, muscular dystrophy, myasthenia gravis,
atherosclerosis, essential hypertension, ulcers, diabetes, epilepsy,
rheumatic heart disease, nephrosis, liver cirrhosis, congenital heart
disease (as well as a host of other malformations which probably
involve nutritional deficiencies during fetal life) and even infective
diseases such as tuberculosis or poliomyelitis.

It is our opinion that the same general formula may well be applied
to these and many other diseases of obscure origin: Select any one
disease, look for metabolic peculiarities that predispose toward it, and
seek to correct the metabolic weakness by applying the genetotrophic
principle. This does not, it should be emphasized, point to an easy
short cut to success. Following the formula is much easier said than
done, and full fruition cannot be expected immediately. As a storehouse of information about metabolic peculiarities accumulates
through a study of individual differences, the task of initiating the
study of any particular disease will be made easier. As success in
treatment arises out of this approach, its appeal will increase.

So far we have had nothing to say regarding a related approach
which has been relatively highly developed, studying differences in
human physiques. This is the somatotyping of Sheldon.[14] There is no
question whatever but that individuals have innate differences in
body build, just as they have innate differences in their biochemistry.
These body builds have been analyzed exhaustively in the classical
investigations of Sheldon. Although we will not review the subject here,

it is our opinion that the evidence is strong that susceptibility to various diseases, ulcers, gall bladder disease, etc., varies with the somatotypes. This line of study needs to be extended, particularly in the direction of correlating somatotypes with disease susceptibility.[15, 16]

Though somatotyping is probably an important way of studying human differences, it cannot be expected that it will encompass factors which are beyond its scope. Aristotle thought he could read character in people by the shape of the individual's nose (nose shapes are highly distinctive); phrenologists purport to tell character and capabilities by the shape of the individual's head; palmists look at hands. While these procedures are thoroughly discredited, it would be a little extreme and beyond the limits of scientific knowledge to say that size and shape of head or the contours of facial features reveal *absolutely nothing* about the make-up of an individual. If this is so, then a tremendous amount of money is absolutely wasted on facial photography. When a newspaper or magazine goes to the expense and uses the space for the picture of an individual, it evidently thinks it is furnishing something meaningful. If the picture is *absolutely meaningless,* what possible justification is there for its use?

If we really want to know all the ways in which people differ from each other, that is, get a comprehensive view of their differences, we have to look at *all* aspects of their existence. A study of body builds can tell us much; but, of course, there are other more direct approaches which can tell us more, for example, about metabolism. One of the important outcomes of Sheldon's work is the attention it has directed to *human differences.* These we believe to be crucially important, and the plea which is the crux of this book is that all *human differences, including metabolic ones, but not excluding others, be subjected to intensive and extensive study.*

We have in this chapter emphasized the practical advantage of a problem-centered approach in which a problem is selected for study in the light of individuality. An application of this approach would cause one to ask such questions as these: What have somatotypes to do with ulcers? What have they to do with diabetes mellitus? What have they to do with sex functions? The answers to these questions, since somatotyping is on a standardized and systematic basis, should be definite and conclusive. These pointed single questions might well be substituted, in our opinion, for the more general question which must of necessity have a vague and uncertain answer: What have somatotypes to do with clinical diagnosis?

Let us turn next to a problem in the area of dental disease, namely, dental caries. This is a disease the etiology of which is, when one considers all the current evidence, very obscure. The application to this problem of our general formula (p. 211) calls for a search for the metabolic peculiarities which may be concerned in dental caries, but unfortunately metabolic peculiarities in the field which seems most likely to be pertinent—mineral metabolism—are virtually unknown as of the present writing. Are they unknown because they do not exist or because they have not been looked for? The latter seems most probable in view of our previous discussions related to the subject (pp. 4 and 153).

In order to see if there is something to look for, let us analyze a recent study of dental caries in rats made by Julia Outhouse Holmes.[17] Dr. Holmes was kind enough to send me full supplementary information regarding this study not contained in the original paper.

The basic experiment involved placing large groups of Norway rats of three strains, MW, MB, and C, at weaning time on a powdered, synthetic, sugar-rich diet (such as is known to promote caries in rats) and studying the incidence of dental decay in each of the three strains under the same environmental conditions. The forebears of the weanlings had been fed good rations of natural foods, and all the differences between the weanlings at the start of the experiment could be ascribed to differences in genetic make-up. The results of the experiment were clear cut. Regardless of which one of several methods of scoring was used, the C rats had roughly twice as much dental decay as the MW rats and were, therefore, genetically more susceptible. What specific metabolic peculiarities are basic to the differences between these two strains of rats is unknown, but it seems certain that metabolic differences are responsible for their difference in susceptibility.

Even among members of highly inbred strains of rats (brother-sister mated for as long as 50 generations) we have found substantial intrastrain differences in excretion patterns and alcohol-consuming tendencies;[18] therefore, it is not surprising that *within* the strains of animals used in the Holmes experiments, for which no such degree of inbreeding was claimed, there was substantial variation. As a matter of fact, the variation was extreme. This is illustrated by the fact that among the *more* susceptible C rats, for example, there was 1 out of 91 which had no cavities or decay sites whatever. Among the *less* susceptible MW rats, on the other hand, there was 1 which had 27 sites of decay. Evidently even within each of these strains of rats there was marked biochemical individuality.

The simplest interpretation of these results is that a rat which was to exhibit no dental decay had genetically determined nutritional requirements such that, from the time the original egg was fertilized to the end of the experiment, it was supplied with enough of all the elements required to promote growth, development, and maintenance of healthy teeth. On the other hand, the rat that was to show extensive dental decay probably had genetically determined nutritional requirements such that deficiencies did develop, particularly on the caries-inducing diet.

The simplest interpretation is not the only possible one, but it does seem inescapable that the crucial difference between the two rats was a genetically determined difference in metabolism. If bacteria were active in one case and not in the other, it must have been due to differences in the metabolisms of the hosts. It seems very unlikely indeed that one rat had access to an infection that another rat avoided.

It is highly probable that almost any fertilized rat egg cell can be made to develop into a healthy rat with healthy noncarious teeth if its nutrition is adequately cared for during uterine, suckling, and later states. It is likewise highly probable that any fertilized rat egg cell can be made to develop into a rat which will be susceptible to teeth decay if its nutrition is made defective in the appropriate manner. What this "appropriate manner" is, is yet to be discovered. We are again face to face with the problem: What metabolic peculiarities (probably augmented nutritional demands) are basic to susceptibility to tooth decay?

Of course, the basic reason for experiments on dental decay in rats is to throw light on dental decay in humans. One can hardly escape the observation that given access to the same food, different children show tremendous variation in their susceptibility to dental caries. Why? Because of biochemical individuality which probably involves differences in nutritional needs.

How can we find the true etiology of the disease (or diseases if it is multiple)? Only by finding out what metabolic peculiarities make for caries susceptibility. This can be done only by paying careful attention to and giving study to individual differences—a field that has been, up to now, and still is neglected. When we have found out what metabolic peculiarities make for susceptibility to dental caries, for example, we will probably see how to apply the genetotrophic principle to prevent, at least to a substantial degree, the occurrence of this disease. This can only be accomplished by studying individuals and probably by applying remedial measures individually.

Fortunately, for those interested in this particular disease there has recently been published an extremely valuable book which contains a storehouse of information and interpretation on the subject.[19] There is nothing in what we have said in the preceding pages which runs counter to the mass of evidence which has accumulated. Bodecker,[20] for example, states that "the activity of predisposing factors still remains somewhat obscure. Should the predisposing factor be established as one of the causes of dental caries, then the often puzzling immunity to dental caries among certain individuals would be explained." He also cites evidence later in the same article that not only in rats, but in human beings as well, susceptibility to dental caries is inherited.[21]

The importance of nutrition in the dental caries problem is reviewed in 90 pages by Shaw.[22] Although we have indicated that metabolic peculiarities in the area of mineral metabolism seem "most likely to be pertinent" to the dental caries problem (p. 218), it does not follow that interest should be restricted to this field. Because teeth are organic structures produced as the result of metabolic processes, there is not a single vitamin, amino acid, or other nutrient factor which may not be implicated in the disease. Probably many different deficiencies are involved in the production of the sum total of all caries existing in all individuals. Much evidence, of course, has been found to indicate the importance of calcium, phosphorus, and vitamin D, but other items may also be very important.

In his summary material Shaw refers to the subject matter of our discussions as follows:

> Individual variations in the ability to assimilate and utilize the digested nutrients must be considered in an evaluation of the response to a dietary treatment.[23]
> ... Individual variations in ability to utilize calcium and phosphorus have been observed to influence the caries susceptibility.[24]
> The evidence concerning a relation of heredity to dental caries susceptibility in human beings is confused by the overlapping factors associated with the family unit and the locality in which it resides. In experimental animals, definite relationships between heredity and caries incidence have been demonstrated.[25]

We have selected for illustration one of the major problems in the field of dental research—dental caries. In discussing it we have outlined the genetotrophic approach to the problem and have presented evidence indicating strongly that it is a genetotrophic disease. Other dental problems may be approached in a similar manner, and for some, we believe, metabolic peculiarities will be found basic.

In both fields, medical and dental research, we believe the genetotrophic approach abolishes the unfortunate stigma which has become attached to "hereditary diseases"—diseases about which, according to the conceptions of many, nothing can be done. The case of dental caries is a good case in point. Is it an hereditary disease? There is strong evidence that susceptibility to it is hereditary. Is dental caries a nutritional disease? Yes, and in spite of its genetic roots something can be done about it—and is done whenever children are fed superior rather than inferior diets.

The genetotrophic approach also sheds new light on the whole problem of therapeutics. A common mode of thought is that for every specific correctly diagnosed disease, there must be developed, eventually, a treatment which will be *generally* effective for this disease. Unless by "specific disease" one means something much more finely delineated than is usually the case, this idea can lead to serious error.

For example, let us consider *the common cold,* often thought of as a disease entity of great economic importance because so many people are afflicted. Medical science has been searching for decades, and for the most part in vain, for a treatment for this affliction. Many, many measures have been enthusiastically embraced, one after another, and have then been discarded because they do not work, generally speaking.

From the standpoint of biochemical individuality, one suspects that common colds have diverse etiologies, depending upon the susceptibilities of the individual concerned, the distinctive flora which he supports, and the various infective agents which can cause symptoms of about the same type. If this is the case, then the search for a single means of combating common colds will probably always be fruitless, and we will have to be content with a series of measures that will be effective for different groups of people when they have different types of infections.

It seems probable that some of the measures already discovered and discarded are excellent and satisfactory ones, provided they are used for the right cases. And it is entirely possible that we have now at our disposal means for managing *all* kinds of colds, if we were able to classify the colds and apply appropriate measures to each.

We have used the common cold as an example; there are doubtless other examples where the same principle applies and where the recognition of biochemical individuality will make for the avoidance of attempting the impossible and will thus bring improvement to practical therapeutics.

Before concluding this chapter in which we have emphasized the idea of ascertaining how individuality and metabolic peculiarities are pertinent to specific diseases, it may be well to emphasize that acceptance of this concept does not involve the subtraction of one iota from the equipment of those engaged in the fields of medical and dental research or of medical and dental practice. Whatever agents, procedures, or whatnot are already successfully used are no less valuable when the facts of biochemical individuality are known. Actually, their value may be greatly increased.

Although the problems of medical practice lie outside the field with which this book is concerned, it seems worthwhile to say that one potential argument for individualized medicine, and against any system which treats patients as assembly-line products, has its basis in the facts of biochemical individuality. If each individual is as highly individual as the results of our study indicate, then it is clear that the patient-personal physician relationship is an extremely valuable one, and any system which would undermine this relationship should be vigorously shunned. If patients are substantial replicas of one another, the best way to look after their health would be a highly organized scheme whereby they are periodically and systematically put through a government-established "health mill." The facts of biochemical individuality point in quite the opposite direction.

REFERENCES

1. Roger J. Williams, *Quart. J. Studies Alc.,* 7, 567–587 (1947).
2. Ernest Beerstecher, Jr., H. Eldon Sutton, Helen Kirby Berry, William Duane Brown, Janet Reed, Gene B. Rich, L. Joe Berry, and Roger J. Williams, *Arch. Biochem.,* 29, 27–40 (1950).
3. Unpublished findings, Biochemical Institute, The University of Texas.
4. Roger J. Williams, L. Joe Berry, and Ernest Beerstecher, Jr., *Arch. Biochem.,* 23, 275–290 (1949).
5. Roger J. Williams, L. Joe Berry, and Ernest Beerstecher, Jr., *Proc. Natl. Acad. Sci. U.S.,* 35, 265–271 (1949).
6. Roger J. Williams, *J. Clin. Nutrition,* 1, 32–36 (1952).
7. Roger J. Williams, *Nutrition and Alcoholism,* University of Oklahoma Press, Norman, Okla., 1951.
8. Lorene L. Rogers, Richard B. Pelton, and Roger J. Williams, *J. Biol. Chem.,* 214, 503–506 (1955).
9. Roger J. Williams, Richard B. Pelton, and Lorene L. Rogers, *Quart. J. Studies Alc.,* 16, 234–244 (1955).
10. Martha F. Trulson, Robert Fleming, and Frederick J. Stare, *J. Am. Med. Assoc.,* 155, 114–119 (1954).
11. Walter Bauer and Friedrich Klemperer, "Gout," in Garfield G. Duncan, ed., *Diseases of Metabolism,* W. B. Saunders Company, Philadelphia, Pa., and London, England, 1953, 3rd ed., p. 683.
12. *Ibid.,* p. 690.
13. Roger J. Williams, William Duane Brown, and Robert W. Shideler, *Proc. Natl. Acad. Sci. U.S.,* 41, 615–620 (1955).
14. William Herbert Sheldon, S. S. Stevens, and W. B. Tucker, *The Varieties*

of Human Physique, Harper & Brothers, New York, N.Y., and London, England, 1940.

15. George Draper, C. W. Dupertuis, and J. L. Caughey, *Human Constitution in Clinical Medicine,* Paul B. Hoeber, Inc., New York, N.Y., 1944.
16. The Lakeside Laboratories, Inc., 1707 East North Avenue, Milwaukee, Wisconsin, have a brochure on the subject with a bibliography of 42 items.
17. Julia O. Holmes, *J. Nutrition,* 46, 323–333 (1952).
18. Janet G. Reed, *Univ. Texas Publ.,* 5109, 145–149 (1951).
19. *A Survey of the Literature of Dental Caries,* Publication 225, National Academy of Sciences—National Research Council, Washington, D.C., 1952.
20. Charles F. Bodecker, "Pathology of Dental Caries, A Biological Approach," in *ibid.,* p. 177.
21. *Ibid.,* p. 231.
22. James H. Shaw, "Nutrition and Dental Caries," in *ibid.,* pp. 415–507.
23. *Ibid.,* p. 505
24. *Ibid.,* p. 506.
25. *Ibid.,* p. 507.

XIV

Implications for Advance
in Psychiatry

The discussion of psychiatry has been postponed for a special chapter for two reasons: first, because we feel that the implications of biochemical individuality are extraordinarily important in this area; and, second, because psychiatry as it has developed is not well integrated with the rest of medicine, often being treated as something quite apart from basic medicine.

Before proceeding with the discussion we should make clear that our contribution in this area is in the way of additional insight. It is not our purpose to subtract from what is known in this highly important field or to depreciate the attempts of others to fathom the intricacies of deranged minds. We believe that by taking into account all that is already known and adding to it the fundamental concept of biochemical individuality, the position of psychiatry as an advancing field of study will be incomparably improved.

It would be a mistake to think that we can in the space of one chapter encompass the whole field of psychiatry even in the briefest way. What we hope to do is to give some highlights of background material and a discussion of the unique possibilities that reside in the facts of biochemical individuality and in the application of the genetotrophic principle.

It is pretty well agreed, even by those psychiatrists who wish it were otherwise, that psychiatry in America has in years past been dominated largely by Freudian psychology and what has grown out of it. A lay writer has expressed succinctly the Freudian point of view as follows:[1]

> In seeking the answer to the riddle of human behavior, Dr. Freud found (or thought he did) that most character traits or mental attitudes in patients could be explained if only he probed far enough back into the patient's past, back to earliest childhood. He decided that the human psyche at the time of birth was like a blank slate, on which various designs were registered as the growing child adapted himself and his few primitive instincts to his circumstances: to his parents, his relatives and the rules and characteristics of the household and the society.

Some of Freud's followers have carried his fundamental idea still further and have postulated that intrauterine experiences are also important in shaping one's character.

No scientist should be so rash as to deny that the Freudian point of view has some validity. On the basis of the evidence which we have set forth in this book, however, one would not be at all rash to point out emphatically that there are two *additional* places to look for the origin of character traits and mental attitudes which have not yet been explored. One is in brain morphology which probably is, as we have indicated, highly distinctive for each individual (p. 48); the other is in the area of biochemical individuality and distinctiveness in metabolism.

Distinctiveness in brain morphology does not appear to be an "easy hunting ground" because much of the relatively little that we know has been gained post mortem. Nevertheless, human ingenuity is very great and the tools available (electroencephalography, for one) are so versatile that it would be dangerous to say what cannot be done. The probability that differences in brain morphology, if known, would prove meaningful is enhanced when one considers a question discussed by the writer in an earlier writing,[2] "What is the difference between the brain of a newborn infant and the brain of a newborn rat?" Morphologically they are different; metabolically they are different. Although both are blanks, they are very different kinds of blanks; one will become the thinking apparatus of a man, the other the corresponding organ for a rat.

If there are species differences in morphology and physiology between the brains of newborn monkeys, gorillas, chimpanzees, and humans and if these interspecies differences are meaningful with respect to intellectual capacities, how about intraspecies differences in morphology and physiology? Is it not probable that they are also meaningful? It is well recognized in most scientific circles that people are born differing greatly in intellectual capacities. They are also born with vastly different brains, morphologically speaking (p. 48). Could it be that there is no correspondence between morphology and function?

In view of the array of facts relating to biochemical individuality, it can hardly be questioned that, regardless of morphological distinctiveness, the brain shares with the rest of the body with which it is associated a distinctive pattern of metabolism, quantitatively speaking. It is nourished by blood that is distinctive, contributes to the distinctive excretion patterns, is poisoned in its own distinctive manner by a variety of agents including drugs, etc., and is subject to nutritional deficiencies which manifest themselves in a distinctive manner. Here is another place to look (aside from childhood experiences) for the origin of character traits and mental attitudes in adults. It seems likely that metabolic individuality in general, not necessarily that demonstrably related to brain metabolism, will be a fertile field for search because it has already been demonstrated that characteristic urinary excretion patterns are associated with mental deficiency, not only in phenylketonurics, but also in others.[3] Strong indications exist that urinary patterns are also distinctive for those having schizophrenia.[4]

Before we proceed further with this discussion, however, we must call attention to certain outstanding facts relating to brain metabolism. First, the brain is extraordinarily active metabolically. We have already pointed out that the brain of an adult weighs approximately 2 per cent of the body as a whole, but that the metabolism (oxygen consumption) in the brain may be up to 20 to 25 per cent of the total. This means that brain metabolism is at least ten times as active as that of average tissue (including bone). Furthermore, this metabolism is maintained and must be maintained as long as normal mental functioning persists. Whatever happens to other parts of the body (in starvation, for example), the brain maintains its original weight, composition, and presumably its active metabolism. In cases of hyperthyroidism when the metabolism of the body as a whole was up 30 to 88 per cent, the brain metabolism was normal.[5] In schizophrenia the brain metabolism as measured by total oxygen consumption takes place at a normal rate, but this, of course, does not mean lack of derangement. Total metabolism measurements are summations and tell nothing about metabolic details. In senile dementia the total brain metabolism is substantially decreased. In ether and pentothal anesthesia, brain metabolism is reduced 35 to 40 per cent. In diabetic coma the reduction is about the same.[6]

We can hardly escape the realization that brain metabolism is both extremely active and extremely important for the well-being and intellectual activity of the organism, and that unless it proceeds in a normal fashion mental health cannot exist.

Let us consider next some of the factors which are known to influence mental health and how they are related to the problem of the etiology of mental disease and to the subject of brain metabolism. Mental ill health has in general remained a puzzle down through the centuries. To attribute it to demoniacal possession or to psychogenic causes leaves the question shrouded in mystery, and gives an unsatisfactory basis for developing therapeutic or prophylactic measures.

Fortunately, one after another of mental illnesses have been traced to physical and chemical causes. "Mad" hatters in France with their twitches and shakes got that way not through mimicry or mass hysteria or because of any defect in their bringing up, but because they were using mercuric nitrate in the processing of the felt and were being continually poisoned by it. Brain metabolism cannot "take" poisoning any more than can any other living cells; when a poison enters, it renders specific catalysts ineffective, and the normal chemical processes in the brain become deranged.

Many drugs—bromides, morphine, cocaine, hashish, marijuana, mescaline, scopolamine, di-isopropyl fluorophosphate, ACTH, pervitin, sodium amytal, lysergic acid, reserpine and chlorpromazine—are known to have marked effects on the mental processes of the individuals who receive them. These effects are varied and cannot be discussed here. Suffice it to say that some drugs produce symptoms which resemble those observed in mental disease; others work in the opposite direction. There can be no doubt that enzyme systems are affected by many of these agents and that their effects on mental processes result from their alteration of brain metabolism.

Hoch[7] points out the need for more accurate knowledge regarding the action of the drugs which appear to produce derangement and hints strongly at the point of view which we developed in Chapter VIII. He says[8] that "from a psychiatric point of view we do not know whether an individual responds in the same way all the time to these drugs or reacts differently at different times; whether normal or abnormal persons respond in the same manner or differently; whether normal individuals can be made psychotic under the influence of these drugs or if psychotic behavior is induced only in predisposed individuals." Actually the answer to his last question seems reasonably clear in the light of the facts of biochemical individuality. An individual may react distinctively to a drug because of the distinctiveness of his make-up. This, however, does not make him "abnormal." Physiologically active drugs are often active, not always in the same way, on practically all individuals if the dosage is at a proper level, and there seems to be no serious reason for questioning that psychotic behavior of some kind can be induced in almost anyone by a drug which has recognized potency in this regard.

Endogenously produced poisons such as those produced in uremia and eclampsia are also capable of producing severe psychological symptoms.

Paresis involves a type of mental derangement which is caused by another kind of agent, an infection. Up until the time when syphilitic infection was proved to be the cause, this form of insanity was ascribed to such factors as heredity, excesses in drinking and love making, smoking, excessive heat and cold, exhaustive efforts to make a living (insecurity), weak nerves, frustration, and fear. There are several interesting features with respect to this disease which involves a diffuse infection of the brain by *Spirocheta pallida*. It is estimated that one patient in about 200 who contracts syphilis suffers from brain infection. This itself is an evidence of biochemical individuality with respect to the resistance of brain tissue to disease. It is also interesting that the symptoms of paresis are varied, so that almost any type of mental disease is simulated: (1) simple dementia, (2) manic or grandiose states, (3) simple depressive states, (4) agitated depressive states, (5) schizophrenic states, (6) psychopathic personality states, and (7) psychoneurotic states.[9] In speaking of the intellectual deficiency symptoms associated with paresis Kraines says,[10] "These symptoms result from the fact that the cortex is damaged, and not from the kind of etiologic agent."

Other infectious diseases, such as pneumonia, typhoid fever, and erysipelas, may cause delirium, often associated with high fever. The temperature rise (fever) itself alters brain metabolism by affecting different enzyme systems differently. In addition toxic substances produced by infective agents may directly affect metabolic processes.

Senile dementia is another type of mental disease for which physical and chemical causes, aside from aging itself, are known. Cerebral arteriosclerosis is a every common accompaniment, and this is known to decrease the cerebral blood flow and the total metabolism of the brain.[11] This itself is enough to account for the deranged metabolism and the accompanying deranged mental functions.

In an earlier chapter we called attention to the large inborn anatomical differences in the size and pattern of blood vessels which carry blood from the heart to the brain. This could be an important predisposing factor in senile dementia since a mild arteriosclerosis involving small arteries could be more than the equivalent of a severe arteriosclerosis when the arteries are relatively large.

Psychoses may also be brought about by endocrine disorders and imbalances. This subject has recently been reviewed by Cleghorn,[12] and discussions of pertinent material are given by Hoagland,[13] by Liddell,[14] by Selye,[15] by Gildea, Ronzoni and Trufant,[16] and by Malamud.[17] Probably the most striking and well-authenticated fact which has recently been brought to light in this connection is that about two-thirds of schizophrenic patients are quantitatively subnormal in their adrenal stress responses and in their responses to injected ACTH.

In our discussion of endocrine patterns we came to the conclusion that these are distinctively different for each individual and that the spread of specific hormonal activities or potencies for so-called normal individuals is often several-fold. To this fact very little attention has been paid. In the psychiatric field, where individual variation is notoriously great in all patients, this is a very important omission since each individual, because of anatomical and biochemical peculiarities in his endocrine makeup, must be susceptible to quite different causative agents whatever their nature, psychogenic or otherwise. The logical pursuit of this subject demands that we study intensively the *differences* between people and cease putting our trust in normality.

In this connection a consistent observation which dates from the early history of psychiatry is the close association of mental disease with sex and sex phenomena. This is particularly true of the Freudian school. It is highly significant in this connection that there are large differences in normal people (far too little study has been made of the subject) in their sex glands, hormonal output, etc., and correspondingly enormous differences in their sex behavior. Kinsey[18] found that in a typical adult male population the number of "total outlets" per week which occurred most often was 1 (modal number). For at least 2 per cent of the population the value was less than $\frac{1}{10}$ of the mode, and for 3.2 per cent it was at least 10 times the mode. Over 17 per cent exhibited values 5 times the mode, and 66.5 per cent were at least double the mode. Relatively few individuals were close to the mode. In view of the recent extensive studies of Beach,[19] it is increasingly clear that, although hormone-behavior relationships in humans are often complex—and many "psychogenic" factors probably enter—individuality in sex hormone production (using the term sex hormone in the broadest sense) and individuality in sex physiology are basic to all human problems related to sex. If mental disease is closely linked to sex (there is reason to think that this is often the case), then a study of individual differences in sex physiology and biochemistry is basic to an understanding of mental disease. The recent study of Kallman indicates that such complex phenomena as those involved in male homosexuality have a genetic and physiological basis.[20] Inborn differences in sex physiology, which is itself far from simple, probably play a very important role in such problems as impotence, frigidity, and sex aberrations in general. For all we know (because they have not been studied), these differences may be far more significant than childhood experiences so far as shaping later sex life is concerned.

Before we discuss how individuality in nutrition enters into the problem of mental disease, we wish to point out, as has been done by others, that the agents which have been used effectively to combat severe mental disease have been physical and chemical ones; these obviously are capable of bringing about marked changes in brain metabolism. This is true of metrazol therapy, insulin shock and electric shock treatments, and lobotomies. It is a striking fact that a disease such as schizophrenia, which is often thought to be of psychogenic origin, has not in general responded to psychological treatment but has often responded to perhaps the most violent and drastic treatments known.

We now come to perhaps the most important topic of all so far as the relationship between mental disease and biochemical individuality is concerned, namely, the nutritional aspects of the problem.

First, we may say that starvation itself gives rise to psychoneurotic, if not psychotic, behavior, a fact which is based both on observation and direct experiment.[21] If our concepts of individuality are correct, then any specific starvation regime might yield quite different results in different individuals. This is actually the case. In semistarvation experiments some individuals were affected substantially more than others, and different types of psychoneurotic behavior were noted.

Most significant, however, is the well-known fact that niacin deficiency produces pronounced psychoses, and supplying the missing nutrient causes an immediate remission of the psychotic symptoms. There is no question in this case that an enzyme system in the brain has been impaired because of the absence of an essential building material and that brain metabolism has been deranged because of this fact. It is interesting that the psychotic symptoms of pellagra vary greatly from individual to individual; sometimes they precede the typical symptoms of dermatitis and diarrhea, in other cases the psychotic symptoms are a late development. The psychotic symptoms may be very severe and their disappearance on niacin administration highly dramatic. It should be pointed out that, in a population in which the diet is very much alike for all, only certain individuals show pellagra symptoms. This points to variable needs from individual to individual and variable vulnerability of specific tissues in the same individual.

Nicotinic acid, when given at the rate of several hundred milligrams a day, has pharmacological effects of which cerebral vasodilation is one. Nicotinamide does not have this effect, and hence the pharmacological effects of nicotinic acid probably do not involve simple replacement of a deficiency in an enzyme system. The fact that nicotinic acid itself in pharmacological doses appears to be of benefit in some mental cases, through its improvement of cerebral circulation, is not surprising in view of our previous discussion. This, however, is quite distinct from the cure of pellagra by relatively small doses of nicotinamide; in the latter case raw material needed for enzyme building is undoubtedly supplied, and the cure is accomplished by eliminating the deficiency.

Psychoneuroses involving depression, irritability, anxiety, increased sensitivity to noise and painful stimuli, and uncertainty of memory have been induced in human patients as a result of thiamine deficiency.[22] It seems probable that the Wernicke type syndrome, which is more severe, can likewise be caused by thiamine deficiency. In all cases the psychological symptoms are eliminated or prevented by the administration of adequate amounts of thiamine. Here again is a clear-cut case in which mental disease can be caused by a nutritional deficiency and cured by supplying adequate amounts of the missing nutritional factor.

Returning briefly to the subject of alcoholism and the work done on the subject in the author's laboratory, we may call attention to the fact that alcoholism is often classified as a mental disease. It is induced, in certain susceptible individuals, by a chemical agent, alcohol, the consumption of which in the amounts commonly used is conducive to the production of nutritional deficiencies because alcohol crowds out of the diet foods which yield minerals, amino acids, and vitamins.

It appears that the uncontrolled craving for alcohol in certain individuals is a nutritional deficiency disease. I have had intimate contact with several individuals (and less intimate contact with many more) who initially had this craving to an extreme degree, but who, by eating more wisely and taking nutritional supplements, have had their craving completely abolished so that now they behave as individuals who never were alcoholics; they drink little or none as they wish. The fact that we have not yet devised a supplement which will be effective for all individuals is true, but it does not cancel the fact that some have had their difficulty removed.

When one takes into account the facts of biochemical individuality, his ideas as to what is significant or what is not significant must be altered accordingly. If one of the ex-alcoholics mentioned in the previous paragraph were to be told that his cure, even though it lasted several years, was not significant statistically, he would have reason to be amused. It is true that if this sort of remission of symptoms were occurring spontaneously among alcoholics without treatment, or as the result of suggestion, then it might be doubted whether the supplementation had anything to do with the result, but this is not the case. If the genetotrophic principle is valid, it could easily be that the supplement first devised would revolutionize the life of only one alcoholic in ten. This would still be significant and highly worthwhile. A few years from now a supplement may be devised which will be effective for twice as many individuals. The results will still be significant if they are real, regardless of the level of success.

The percentage efficacy of the supplement initially devised is unknown. According to our initial observations, which were *not* the result of controlled experiments, about one-half of the alcoholics treated appeared to be greatly benefited. These were individuals in the upper stratum with respect to social status, who were seriously cooperative and were given sufficient individual attention so that the taking of the medication could be relied upon with reasonable certainty. In a subsequent experiment[23] controlled by the use of placebos, it appears that the percentage efficacy of the supplement is not as high as our observations indicated. Among those under observation for a period of a year or more, there was a striking difference between the groups administered the supplements and those administered the placebos, though the numbers were not sufficiently large to permit statistical analyses. There was reasonable doubt, also, as to whether the supplements were actually taken consistently by all who were supposed to have done so.

From the standpoint of the genetotrophic concept, if *one* alcoholic has really been transformed into an individual who is no longer an alcoholic, this is significant and cannot be canceled out by twenty subsequent failures. There is no law which says that human beings when subjected to the same treatment will yield concordant results and that these results will constitute the "normal" response. What may be normal for one may not be normal for another.

We do not wish to pursue the question of alcoholism further at this time. It is perhaps sufficient to say that we have reason to think (based largely on animal experiments) that the nutritional supplement can be improved for general use and that with high probability more and more alcoholics can be helped as the supplement is improved. Furthermore, it is to be hoped that alcoholics can eventually be studied individually from the metabolic standpoint and that nutritional supplements designed for specific individuals can be formulated.

A sidelight on our alcoholism investigation has tended strongly to support, without our having anticipated it, the genetrophic concept. Our nutritional supplement has helped, in numerous unexpected ways, individuals who have taken it. These reports have in all cases been definite, have been corroborated by medical evidence when possible, and have come completely unexpectedly and without solicitation. From users of this supplement, we have received reports of *striking* benefit in the following conditions: insomnia, one authentic case of hypertension, addiction to barbiturates, excessive sweating of the feet, dizziness and lack of balance, constipation, sinus headaches, hayfever. Since, in the absence of any suggestion, the results were reported independently of each other, the observations are worthy of consideration. They are in line with the idea that many ills may have a genetotrophic origin and that proper nutritional supplements for the appropriate individual may bring unexpected benefits in many diverse conditions.

We have previously mentioned (p. 161) the reported enhancement of intelligence in experimental animals and in mentally retarded children by the administration of glutamic acid. A prominent psychiatrist told me that he had administered glutamic acid to a group of schizophrenic patients, and the results looked very promising for a day or two—the patients seemed to improve markedly—but the trials were stopped because the results did not persist. It seems to me that this result, coupled with the earlier reports, is extremely suggestive that glutamic acid may be *one limiting nutritional factor* for mental health in some human cases, but that there are other limiting factors which need to be spotted. A partial benefit of short duration is exactly what one would expect if this were the case.

One of the important questions with respect to mental disease (particularly schizophrenia) is whether or not it has genetic origins. The twin studies made by Kallmann[20] indicate that it has. Doubtless the inheritance of susceptibility is complicated because there are probably a number of factors involved, each inherited separately and perhaps counteracting each other. The facts of biochemical genetics and biochemical individuality make inescapable the conclusion that each individual must be distinctive in his responses to stresses of all kinds and that vulnerability to mental disease must vary from individual to individual.

If individuals differ at birth in their susceptibility to schizophrenia, for example, of what does their differentness consist? Aside from anatomical differences with respect to brain and endocrine glands especially, there is the possibility that they differ in their nutritional requirements. One may have need, in order to meet the stresses of life and keep his brain metabolism functioning, of a larger amount of certain crucial nutrients than the other. Lacking these nutrients, his brain metabolism gets out of joint and mental disease results.

Certainly the possibility needs to be explored that nutritional supplements [and these may include not only substances known to be necessary for normal nutrition, but others as well (p. 184)] will prevent or cure the various types of mental disease. One cannot hope that a single nutrient factor, such as a vitamin, is going to be *the* answer for a multitude of people, even if their outward symptoms seem to be about the same. As each new vitamin or vitamin-like substance is discovered (and there are probably more to come), there is a great enthusiasm for its possibilities, oftentimes without regard for the fact that it is only one link in a chain and unless all links are present there is no chain. A single vitamin is likely to be *a* limiting factor in some process and not the *only* limiting factor.

Woolley and Shaw[24] have recently put forth an interesting and worthy hypothesis that schizophrenia may be due to interference with the functioning of *serotonin* in the brain. This newly discovered hormone-like substance may be an important key. The evidence on which the hypothesis is based is that various chemically related substances (antagonists), notably lysergic acid diethylamide, produce, when given to well individuals, conditions which in some cases closely resemble schizophrenia.

Following up their hypothesis the authors suggest that serotonin or a long-acting derivative of it may be effective in treatment of schizophrenia conditions. Assuming for the moment that the interesting hypothesis is a valid one, the application of the genetotrophic principle would suggest an alternate procedure. Perhaps the schizophrenia-susceptible individual is deficient in serotonin. This means that he doesn't manufacture it adequately (it is presumed to arise endogenously). Why? Because the enzymatic processes are somewhat partially blocked, and the individual requires an unusually large supply of some particular nutrient to counteract this block. Supplying this nutrient in abundance may allow the adequate production of serotonin endogenously, which is normal, and the individual will then be freed from his disease by nutritional means.

In Chapter XIII we suggested a general formula which might be applied in the fields of medical and dental research. The same formula we believe is applicable in the psychiatric field. (1) Select a disease the etiology of which is unknown, schizophrenia, for example. (2) Explore for metabolic and anatomical peculiarities which may be associated with the disease or susceptibility to it. (3) Seek to correct the condition by applying the genetotrophic principle. This approach to mental disease involves a procedure that has been slighted continuously because of ignorance about biochemical individuality and a lack of *the intensive study of human individual differences—anatomical, physiological, and biochemical.*

What we have been saying is, I believe, not out of line with the best psychiatric thought in America today. The physical and chemical bases for mental ill health have been recognized more fully as time has gone on. It is estimated that three-fifths of all mental disorders are now recognized to have an organic basis. Decades ago the corresponding fraction was small; in the decades to come it will, we believe, become larger and larger.[25]

Stanley Cobb, Psychiatrist in Chief of the Massachusetts General Hospital, says,[26] "As a matter of fact all disease (and every symptom) *is both organic and functional.*" Dean Simmons, of Harvard School of Public Health, has said,[27] "There is a special need for a fresh approach to the investigation of mental diseases. . . . In our current preoccupation with theories of psychic and vague environmental causes, we are dealing with what, at the most, could merely be secondary or immediate causes of mental disturbances. . . . May it not be possible that today we are spending too much time, energy, and money trying to clean up cesspools of the mind, and that we could more profitably try to discover and remove the specific biologic causes of the mental diseases?"

With these statements of opinion I am in hearty agreement.

REFERENCES

1. Robert Coughlan, *Life*, June 25, 1951, p. 66.
2. Roger J. Williams, *Free and Unequal*, University of Texas Press, Austin, Tex., 1953, p. 40.
3. Louise Cain, *Univ. Texas Publ.*, 5109, 198–205 (1951).
4. Kendall M. Young, Jr., Helen Kirby Berry, Ernest Beerstecher, Jr., and Jim S. Berry, *Univ. Texas Publ.*, 5109, 189–197 (1951).
5. Louis Sokoloff, Richard L. Wechsler, Kent Balls, and Seymour Kety, *J. Clin. Invest.*, 29, 847 (1950).
6. For a more extended discussion, see Seymour S. Kety, "Cerebral Circulation and Metabolism," in *Biology of Mental Health and Disease*, Paul B. Hoeber, Inc., New York, N.Y., 1952, pp. 20–31.
7. Paul H. Hoch, "Experimental Induction of Psychoses," in *Biology of Mental Health and Disease*, pp. 539–546 (see ref. 6).
8. *Ibid.*, p. 539.
9. Samuel Henry Kraines, *The Therapy of the Neuroses and Psychoses*, Lea and Febiger, Philadephia, Pa., 2nd ed., 1945, pp. 365–366.
10. *Ibid.*, p. 364.
11. Seymour S. Kety, "Cerebral Circulation and Metabolism," in *Biology of Mental Health and Disease*, pp. 29–30 (see ref. 6).
12. Robert A. Cleghorn, "Endocrine Influence on Personality and Behavior," in *Biology of Mental Health and Diseases*, pp. 265–273 (see ref. 6).
13. Hudson Hoagland, "Metabolic and Physiologic Disturbances in the Psychoses," in *Biology of Mental Health and Disease*, pp. 434–449 (see ref. 6).
14. Howard S. Liddell, "Effect of Corticosteroids in Experimental Psychoneuroses," in *Biology of Mental Health and Disease*, pp. 591–594 (see ref. 6).
15. Hans Selye, "Discussion" of *ibid.*, pp. 595–599.
16. Edwin F. Gildea, Ethel Ronzoni, and Samuel A. Trufant, "Results from the Use of ACTH and Cortisone in Psychoses," in *Biology of Mental Health and Disease*, pp. 600–613 (see ref. 6).
17. William Malamud, "Discussion" of *ibid.*, pp. 613–618.
18. Alfred C. Kinsey, Wardell B. Pomeroy, and Clyde E. Martin, *Sexual Behavior in the Human Male*, W. B. Saunders Company, Philadelphia, Pa. and London, England, 1948.
19. Frank A. Beach, *Hormones and Behavior*, Paul B. Hoeber, Inc., New York, N.Y., and London, England, 1948.
20. Franz J. Kallmann, *J. Nervous Mental Disease*, 115, 283–298 (1952).

21. Ancel Keys, "Experimental Induction of Neuropsychoses by Starvation," in *Biology of Mental Health and Disease,* pp. 515–525 (see ref. 6).
22. Russell M. Wilder, "Experimental Induction of Psychoneuroses through Restriction of Intake of Thiamine," in *Biology of Mental Health and Disease,* pp. 531–538 (see ref. 6).
23. Martha F. Trulson, Robert Fleming, and Frederick J. Stare, *J. Am. Med. Assoc.,* 155, 114–119 (1954).
24. D. W. Woolley and E. Shaw, *Proc. Natl. Acad. Sci. U.S.,* 40, 228–231 (1954).
25. Walter L. Bruetsch, "Mental Disorders Arising from Organic Disease," in *Biology of Mental Health and Disease,* p. 304 (see ref. 6).
26. Stanley Cobb, *J. Aviation Med.,* 13, 249 (1942).
27. James Stevens Simmons, "Medicine of the Future—The Eleventh Annual Charles V. Chapin Oration," p. 6, reprinted from *Rhode Island Med. J.,* 35, 361–67, 370, 404 (1952).

Afterword

Despite much scientific advance since this landmark book appeared over forty years ago, it remains unequaled as a powerful overview and stimulating discussion of what seems among the most interesting and significant facts in biology. Moreover, these basic facts unfortunately still are little known to most students of health, medicine, nutrition, psychiatry and other professions that deal with the physiology of individuals. I hope this new printing will inform and inspire a new generation of students and researchers in these fields.

Of course scientific knowledge about normal human variability is greater and deeper now than when *Biochemical Individuality* appeared. But this new knowledge, it seems to me, merely strengthens the book, without altering its thrust. Williams's insightful discussion and hypotheses seem at least as provocative and important as ever.

When *Biochemical Individuality* appeared in 1956, it was the only broad review of the quantitative aspects of biochemical and anatomical individuality. It remains so, as far as I know. Later reviews are generally far more limited and specialized.[1-11] And few other reviews provide as stimulating a discussion for those inclined to think broadly about improving human welfare.

Why has *Biochemical Individuality* remained unsurpassed? And why are the objective facts in this book, as Williams lamented in 1974,[12] "not treated in supposedly comprehensive works on biochemistry or physiology or medicine"? His answers seem still pertinent.

One reason is the prevailing narrow focus of specialists, who have little time or encouragement for broad studies. Another is our continuing legacy of unwarranted environmentalism. This bias led leading authorities to ignore evidence that genetic factors contribute importantly to alcoholism susceptibility, and to conclude, for example, that girls would be like boys if they were raised like boys, and that autism is caused by emotionally cold mothers.

More fundamental is the persistence in biomedical sciences of the highly limiting ideas of "normal man" and "average person." As Williams noted, these concepts are false and objectionable. Biological scientists nearly always regard individual differences as pesky obstacles to their quest for generalizations, and they often exert great efforts to "average out" or exclude the variations. This approach parallels that of physical scientists who more justifiably seek to "average out" experimental errors. The method serves well in the physical sciences, and for some purposes in biology. But individual differences are far different from experimental errors. "Averaging them out" or ignoring them leads only to dead ends when we attempt to understand, prevent and treat biological problems, such as alcoholism[13-19] and other diseases[3, 5] that have important roots in those very differences.

Genetic influences are far better understood now than in 1956 for major nutrition-related problems such as alcoholism, heart disease, diabetes, hypertension, and cancer. Yet we seem frustratingly slow to integrate this knowledge into clinical practice and common knowledge. Most clinicians still treat and write about these problems as if inborn differences were unimportant. Professional and lay authors still recommend restrictive diets they *assume* are best for nearly everyone. They debate heatedly about which one of the conflicting diets is "right"—high carbohydrate, low carbohydrate, vegetarian, high protein, etc. When will we automatically consider that all these diets likely have merit, but *only for some individuals?*

Perhaps the most hopeful sign of progress is the belated recognition of "paradoxical" reactions to the lipid-lowering diets that have been widely used for decades. For example, researchers at the South-Western Medical Center in Dallas repeatedly find "marked individual variations in response to the diet." In many persons these diets show little benefit, or *increase* LDL cholesterol, serum triglycerides, or body fat. These facts tend to be ignored or downplayed by those who promote oversimplified campaigns such as the National Cholesterol Education Program. As a result the public remains uninformed about crucial realities.

Hypothetical "average" persons—those who are approximately average in all of the myriad aspects of anatomy and biochemistry—presumably do not exist. Even if they did, they would be highly unrepresentative. They would provide little or no insight into real persons and the real biological challenges they face. Real persons have highly distinctive patterns of biochemical abilities, needs, and responses, quite unlike "normal man" or "normal woman." Williams was the first, I think, to emphasize the "truly phenomenal" opportunities that open when we focus on real individuals and their sometimes large deviations from average.

The subtitle of this book, "The Basis for the Genetotrophic Concept," reflects Williams's major interest in disorders that involve interactions between heredity (geneto) and nutrition (trophic). A genetotrophic disease is one caused by a genetic need for unusual amounts of one or more nutrients that are not found in diets which are adequate for most individuals. This broad concept includes genetic needs for an exogenous supply of a metabolite normally produced internally in adequate amounts, such as carnitine or glutamine.

Since Williams and co-workers proposed the genetotrophic concept in 1950,[20, 21] many genetotrophic diseases have been discovered. Stark examples include the so-called nutrient "dependencies" and other nutrition-responsive inborn errors of metabolism.[22, 23] More subtle cases include all the complex diseases now being found to involve both nutrition and genetic predispositions.

Heart disease, for example, shows strong hereditary influences on several risk factors that interact with nutrient intakes. Elevated serum homocysteine[24] usually responds to increased intakes of three B vitamins, B_6, B_{12} and folic acid. High serum triglycerides[25] often drop sharply with increased intakes of omega-3 fatty acids or a decrease in simple carbohydrates. High serum LDL-cholesterol levels[26] may fall with increased intake of nuts, avocados and other food sources of undamaged fats. Genetic variations in lipoprotein(a) levels[27] range about 1000-fold on typical diets, but risky high levels may fall with increased intake of niacin, vitamin C and other nutrients.

Other examples include osteoporosis and vitamin D,[28] and neural tube defects and folic acid.[29] Many cancers involve genetic predispositions; these, too, presumably interact with differing needs for the diverse nutrients and phytochemicals that are protective.

The word "genetotrophic" is rarely used so far, but it deserves new consideration in view of our increasing sophistication about genetics, nutrition and disease. It can include all degrees of nutrition-genetics interactions, from subtle to dramatic, and it seems far preferable to "nutrient dependencies," because we are all dependent on nutrients.

Williams considered his work on biochemical individuality to be his most important scientific contribution. Although he is best known for discovering pantothenic acid and for studying and naming folic acid, he reasoned that these and other major contributions surely would have been made by others if he had not made them. But if he had not collected the data in this book, and contributed important new data, along with highly original discussions and hypotheses, would anyone else have done so? The answers seem mostly no, as suggested by the remarkable 32 years that this book initially remained in print (1956-88), by its continuing uniqueness, and by this new printing.

Williams devoted much of his long career to broad aspects of individual differences, including their social implications. About 100 of his articles from 1947 to 1986 deal partly or wholly with these subjects, representing over half his writings during those 39 years. Nearly 30 articles focus on the prevention and treatment of alcoholism, as do three of his books. Besides his scientific works, Williams wrote interestingly and insightfully about the importance of biological differences in human relations, marriage, politics, international relations, education and religion.[30-33] Some of these writings were widely excerpted or reprinted in publications such as *Reader's Digest,* and they still remain fresh and stimulating.

Most of Williams's books discuss biochemical individuality. Besides this book and *You Are Extraordinary* (1967), which are devoted solely to the subject, the most recent examples are *Nutrition Against Disease: Environmental Prevention* (1971, Keats Publishing reprint planned in 1998), *Physicians' Handbook of Nutritional Science* (1975), *The Wonderful World Within You* (1977, in print, revised edition planned), *The Prevention of Alcoholism Through Nutrition* (1982) and *Rethinking Education* (1986).

A complete list of Williams's books and articles is available on the Internet, and copies of his articles are available (http://www.cm.utex as.edu/faculty/williams/). This site includes tables of contents and prefaces for many of his books, and links to sources for those books in print. Key articles dealing with biochemical individuality are noted here.[34-47]

In 1961 Williams and Siegle[36] described a new medical science of "propetology," named from the Greek *propet* = leaning toward. It "deal(s) with innate susceptibility and resistance primarily to diseases of a non-infective nature," and it now seems ready to flower.

I hope that one day biochemical individuality will be routinely highlighted in all textbooks of health, medicine, physiology, nutrition, and anatomy. And I hope that key aspects of it—about diet, drugs and alcohol, for example—will become part of everyone's education. At least until that day arrives, this classic book has a vital role to play.

Donald R. Davis, Ph.D.
Biochemical Institute
The University of Texas at Austin
August 1997

REFERENCES

1. Calabrese EJ. Biochemical individuality: the next generation. *Regulatory Toxicology & Pharmacology* 1996; 24 (1 Pt. 2):S58–67.
2. Cavalli-Sforza LL, Cavalli-Sforza F. *The great human diasporas: the history of diversity and evolution.* Reading, Mass.: Addison-Wesley, 1995.
3. Simopoulos AP. Genetic variation and nutrition, parts 1 and 2. *Nutrition Today* 1995; 30:157–67 and 194–206.
4. Kadlubar FF. Biochemical individuality and its implications for drug and carcinogen metabolism: recent insights from acetyltransferase and

cytochrome P4501A2 phenotyping and genotyping in humans. *Drug Metabolism Reviews* 1994; 26:37–46.

5. Simopoulos AP, Childs B, eds. *Genetic variation and nutrition,* vol. 63 of *World Review of Nutrition and Dietetics,* 1990.

6. Smith RL. Polymorphism in drug metabolism—implications for drug toxicity. *Archives of Toxicology* Supplement 1986; 9:138–46.

7. Davis DR. Nutritional needs and biochemical diversity. In: Bland J, ed., *Medical Applications of Clinical Nutrition.* New Canaan, Conn.: Keats Publishing, 1983, 41–63.

8. Robertson EA, Van Steirteghem AC, Byrki JE, Young DS. Biochemical individuality and the recognition of personal profiles with a computer. *Clinical Chemistry* 1980; 26:30–6.

9. Kumler WD. Biochemical individuality and the case for supplemental vitamins. *American Pharmacy* 1979; 19(Aug):34–7.

10. Margen S, Ogar RA, eds. *Biological & cultural variability,* vol. 2 of *Progress in human nutrition.* Westport, Conn.: AVI Publishing, 1978.

11. Yablokov AV. *Variability of Mammals,* translation published for the Smithsonian Institution and National Science Foundation, Springfield, VA: National Technical Information Service, U.S. Dept. of Commerce, 1974.

12. Williams RJ. Biochemical individuality: a story of neglect. *Journal of the International Academy of Preventive Medicine* 1974; 1:99–106.

13. Beasley JD. *Food for recovery: the complete nutritional companion for recovering from alcoholism, drug addiction, and eating disorders.* New York: Crown Trade Paperbacks, 1994.

14. Larson JM. *Alcoholism, The Biochemical Connection.* New York: Villard Books, 1992. Also titled *Seven Weeks to Sobriety.*

15. Blum K. *Alcohol and the addictive brain: new hope for alcoholics from biogenetic research.* New York: Free Press, 1991.

16. Beasley JD. *Wrong diagnosis, wrong treatment: The plight of the alcoholic in America.* New York: Creative Informatics, 1987.

17. Ostrovsky YuM, Sadovnik MN, Satanovskaya VI, et al. Metabolic factors and preference for ethanol. *Pharmacology, Biochemistry & Behavior* 1983; 18 Suppl. 1:531–5.

18. Williams RJ. *The prevention of alcoholism through nutrition.* New York: Bantam Books, 1982.

19. von Wartburg JP. Metabolic consequences of alcohol consumption. *Nutrition & Metabolism* 1977; 21:153–62.

20. Williams RJ, Beerstecher E Jr., Berry LJ. The concept of genetotrophic disease. *Lancet* 1950; Feb. 18, 287–90.

21. Williams RJ. Concept of genetotrophic disease. *Nutrition Reviews* 1950; 8:257–60.

22. Elsas LJ II, Acosta PB. Nutrition support of inherited metabolic disease. In Shils ME, Olson JA, Shike M, eds. *Modern Nutrition in Health and Disease*, 8th ed. Philadelphia: Lea & Febiger, 1994, 1147–1206.

23. King JC, Keen CL. Zinc. In Shils ME, Olson JA, Shike M, eds. *Modern Nutrition in Health and Disease*, 8th ed. Philadelphia: Lea & Febiger, 1994, 223.

24. Jacques PF, Bostom AG, Williams RR, et al. Relation between folate status, a common mutation in methylenetetrahydrofolate reductase, and plasma homocysteine concentrations. *Circulation* 1996; 93:7–9.

25. Mitchell RJ, Earl L, Bray P, Fripp YJ, Williams J. DNA polymorphisms at the lipoprotein lipase gene and their association with quantitative variation in plasma high-density lipoproteins and triacylglycerides. *Human Biology* 1994; 66:383–97.

26. Austin MA. Genetic epidemiology of dyslipidaemia and atherosclerosis. *Annals of Medicine* 1996; 28:459–63.

27. Rainwater DK, Kammerer CM, VandeBerg JL, Hixson JE. Characterization of the genetic elements controlling lipoprotein(a) concentrations in Mexican Americans. Evidence for at least three controlling elements linked to LPA, the locus encoding apolipoprotein(a). *Atherosclerosis* 1997; 128:223–33.

28. Sainz J. Van Tornout JM, Loro ML, Sayre J, Roe TF, Gilsanz V. Vitamin D-receptor gene polymorphisms and bone density in prepubertal American girls of Mexican descent. *New England Journal of Medicine* 1997; 337:77–82.

29. Mayo O. Genetic analysis of a complex disease. *Alcohol & Alcoholism.* 1994 Suppl.; 2:9–18.

30. Williams RJ. Individuality and its significance in human life, in *Essays on Individuality*, F Morley, ed., Philadephia: Univ. of Penn. Press, 1958, 125–45. Also in 2nd. ed., Indianapolis: Liberty Press, 1977, 177–204.

31. Williams RJ. *Free and Unequal*. Austin, Texas: Univ. of Texas Press, 1953.

32. Williams RJ. *You Are Extraordinary*. New York: Random House, 1967.

33. Williams RJ. Heredity, human understanding and civilization. *American Scientist* 1969: 57:237–43.

34. Williams RJ. Etiological research in the light of the facts of individuality. *Texas Reports on Biology and Medicine* 1960; 18:168–85.

35. Williams RJ. Biochemical individuality. In Gray P, ed. *Encyclopedia of biological sciences.* New York: Reinhold, 1961. Also in 2nd ed., 1970, 99–100.

36. Williams RJ, Siegel FL. "Propetology," a new branch of medical science? *American Journal of Medicine* 1961; 31:325–7.

37. Williams RJ. Biochemical and physiological variations within groups of supposedly homogeneous experimental animals. In *Symposium on Factors Involved in Host-Agent Relationships.* Ames, Iowa: U.S. Dept. of Agriculture 1966, 1–11; ARS 45–5.

38. Williams RJ, Pelton RB, Siegel FL. Individuality as exhibited by inbred animals; its implications for human behavior. *Proceedings of the National Academy of Sciences* 1962; 48:1461–6.

39. Williams RJ, Pelton RB. Individuality in nutrition: effects of vitamin A-deficient and other deficient diets on experimental animals. *Proceedings of the National Academy of Sciences USA* 1966; 55:126–34.

40. Williams RJ, Deason G. Individuality in vitamin C needs. *Proceedings of the National Academy of Sciences USA* 1967; 57:1638–41.

41. Williams RJ. We abnormal normals. *Nutrition Today,* December 1967, 19–23.

42. Williams RJ. The genetotrophic approach to metabolic disease. In *Exploratory Concepts in Muscular Dystrophy and Related Disorders.* Amsterdam, The Netherlands: Excerpta Medica Foundation, 1967, 103–11.

43. Gutierrez RM, Williams RJ. Excretion of ketosteroids and proneness to breast cancer. *Proceedings of the National Academy of Sciences USA* 1968; 59:938–43.

44. Williams RJ. The individual approach to geriatric nutrition. In *Duke University Council on Aging and Human Development: Proceedings of Seminars 1965–69.* Durham 1969, 138–50.

45. Williams RJ, Heffley JD, Yew M-Li, Bode, CW. A renaissance of nutritional science is imminent. *Perspectives in Biology and Medicine* 1973; 17:1-15.

46. Williams RJ. Nutritional individuality. *Human Nature* 1978; 1(6):46–53.

47. Williams RJ, Davis DR. Differential nutrition—a new orientation from which to approach the problems of human nutrition. *Perspectives in Biology and Medicine* 1986; 29:199–202.

In Memoriam
Roger John Williams, 1893–1988

Roger John Williams' death on 20 February 1988 at the age of 94 brought to a close an extraordinary lifetime of contributions to biochemistry, nutritional science, human health and welfare, and public knowledge. Through his many books and hundreds of scientific articles he eloquently expresses his restless, prolific intellect and his down-to-earth striving for the betterment of humankind. His books powerfully influenced a generation of forward-looking scientists, physicians, students, and laypersons. As probably no other scientist has, he led the way toward a broad view of nutrition and its importance in health and preventive medicine, including the prevention of alcoholism. Almost singlehandedly he recognized and called attention to the biological facts of human diversity and their broad importance in science and human affairs.

Williams' last days came nearly the way that most of us would want ours to come—following a long and fruitful life, filled with the love and admiration of family and friends, and blessed with a mind still creative and focused on the goals and joys of his life. Although physically frail, and dependent on nursing home care for two years, he was comfortable and content. He entertained visitors from his chair, delighting them with his keen memory and wry sense of humor. Through his chair-side radio he followed world events and his favorite University of Texas athletic teams. Sometimes he asked University colleagues to bring his latest book manuscript on their

Photo © by Keith Dannemiller; originally published in *The Texas Humanist*, November-December, 1984, courtesy the Texas Council for the Humanities.

next visit, for he had ideas to improve it. Two days after one such request, he died of pneumonia, the "old man's friend."

More than most of us can hope for, Williams' life was also filled with extraordinary gifts and accomplishments. For over 20 years he and his co-workers worked to discover, isolate, characterize and synthesize the substance he named pantothenic acid, an essential cog in the biochemical machinery of all living things. He also first concentrated and named folic acid, another B vitamin. As founder and director of the Clayton Foundation Biochemical Institute at the University of Texas at Austin from 1940 to 1963, he and his colleagues made many other notable contributions to nutrition and biochemistry.

But beyond these extraordinary scientific accomplishments, Williams was a deep and independent thinker, a visionary, and a gifted writer. For over 40 years following completion of his work on pantothenic acid, he increasingly turned his efforts toward advancing the fields of nutrition, medicine, and human understanding. He took seriously, and in a practical way, the idea that the highest purpose of science and all human striving is to benefit humankind in one way or another. He never quit seeking this goal, even after his retirement at age 92 when he no longer could come to his University office to work. Through his writings he inspired new generations of professionals and laypersons who form the advance guard of a dynamic movement. I and many others well remember the profound impact on our thinking and work of his books such as *Nutrition in a Nutshell, Biochemical Individuality, You Are Extraordinary,* and *Nutrition Against Disease.*

Inevitably, Williams' maverick ideas faced resistance, especially from some physicians, old-line nutritionists and social scientists whose established beliefs conflicted too much with his ideas. He was probably seldom content with the pace his campaigns advanced. Some failed, like his attempts to interest universities and scientific bodies in studying human diversity as a way to help society foster human development and to advance social and international harmony. Nevertheless, his key ideas about the importance of nutrition and variability have gradually gained acceptance. He was pleased by many signs that we are beginning the "renaissance of nutritional science" that he and his coauthors forecast in 1973. Perhaps more than he could know, he helped inspire both the leaders of this renaissance and the various grass-roots movements that are helping to push it along. Transformations such as he envisioned require a generation or more to take hold, and this one is advancing probably as rapidly as can be realistically expected.

Upbringing and Early Experiences

Roger was born on 14 August 1893 to American Baptist missionaries working in Ootacumund, India. Brought to the United States at age two, he grew up in Kansas and California. He was the youngest of four brothers and a sister who were 5 to 10 years older than he. Many years later in 1974 he wrote, "This age gap tended to make me a 'loner,' and more inclined toward self-reliance and independence than I might have been. . . . [It] probably contributed toward making me the kind of scientist I have become." His father was 55 years old when Roger was born, and suffered a crippling hip injury the following year, so Roger never knew his father in his prime. As a youth Roger held interests at various times in the ministry, medicine, literature, and writing, and he enjoyed baseball and other athletics with his brothers. He worked in a nursery where he learned to bud fruit trees, a skill which helped support his college education. His oldest brother, Robert R. Williams, became known for his work on beriberi and the isolation and synthesis of thiamin (vitamin B_1).

Roger received his B.S. from the University of Redlands in 1914 and a high school teacher's certificate in 1915 from the University of California, Berkeley. There he earned his room and board waiting on tables at a fraternity house and cleaning his landlady's house. His studies in organic chemistry left him discouraged about his potential as a chemist. However, after teaching high school chemistry and physics for two years and marrying Hazel E. Wood, a college classmate with whom he would have three children, he decided to resume graduate work in chemistry at the University of Chicago, where his three brothers had graduated. A professor there, Julius Stieglitz, "lifted organic chemistry out of the hopeless state (for me) of being merely something to memorize." He received his M.S. degree in 1918 and his Ph.D. in 1919 (Magna Cum Laude), writing his thesis on *The Vitamin Requirement of Yeast.* The goal of this work and a subsequent year with the Fleischmann (Yeast) Co. was to learn what yeast cells need to grow.

This early work with yeast cells greatly influenced much of Williams' later work and thinking. It led most directly to his discovery of pantothenic acid as a yeast nutrient and to the subsequent studies that spanned two decades at the University of Oregon, Oregon State University, and the University of Texas. Later it led Williams and his colleagues at the University of Texas to use other microorganisms for pioneering research in nutrition and biochemistry. This work helped shift the interest of biochemists toward microbiology, and its rich harvest of knowledge about enzymology, genetics, and molecular biology. These advances fully supported Williams' early and novel intuition that something needed by yeast cells could also be important for plant and animal cells—the now well-recognized biochemical unity of all living things. His experiences with growing yeast cells also contributed to his later idea that nutrition is always improvable,

and to the major theme of his 1971 book, *Nutrition Against Disease.*
In it he proposed and defended his idea *"that the nutritional microen-
vironment of our body cells is crucially important to our health and
that deficiencies in this environment constitute a major cause of disease"* (p. 4).

Eyesight difficulties also had an early and enduring influence on
Williams' career. Although he had keen vision, and enjoyed books,
his two eyes did not work together well. Reading was a chore, like
"walking uphill dragging a log," he recalled in 1954, and he could
not endure it for more than short periods. Eyeglasses, exercises and
an operation failed to help much, and for some years he read with
one eye at a time. Later, special eyeglasses for severe "aniseikonia"
(a disorder not discovered until about 1930) helped some, but still
reading was difficult. Williams came to regard this problem as a bless-
ing, however, and not a curse. Because he could not spend long hours
reading, he had long hours to think, and he was able to do so in a
most productive way. Unlike most scientists who read extensively
about a problem before developing their own ideas, Williams thought
about it first, before his mind became "excessively cluttered up by
what everyone else has thought and written." No doubt his eyesight
problem contributed to his originality and iconoclasm.

It prepared him, too, for his mid-eighties when macular degeneration gradually consumed all ability to read. He had long since developed the practice of thinking and writing in his head at night, so he
merely shifted to dictating his work and having it read to him. Fortunately, he retained enough peripheral vision to continue his long
devotion to walking for exercise (fishing and golfing were passions
in earlier years).

Another significant early experience followed an ulcer operation
in about 1921. Williams was given morphine to relieve pain and induce sleep. It abolished his pain, but rather than inducing sleep, it
caused his mind to race. His doctor's remedy was to administer another, larger dose, for which "There was hell to pay." Williams was
tortured through a long night of excruciating mental frenzy. His
doctor's explanation that Williams had suffered an "idiosyncratic"
reaction to morphine provoked his curiosity and helped inspire his
later major interest in biochemical individuality.

Later Interests and Accomplishments

In 1939 Williams became professor of chemistry at the University of Texas, Austin. The next year, with support from Benjamin Clayton of Houston, Williams founded at the University the Clayton Foundation Biochemical Institute and served as its director until 1963, when he turned 70. During that time more vitamins and their variants were discovered in this laboratory than in any other. Pioneering work was done on pantothenic acid, folic acid, folinic acid, pyridoxal and pyridoxamine (forms of vitamin B_6), inositol, and lipoic acid. Raw egg white was found to contain a protein which tightly binds biotin, a protein which Williams named *avidin*. These studies were facilitated by two important techniques developed or used in early work at the Institute—microbiological assays for vitamins and amino acids, and ascending paper chromatography. Patented processes for the synthesis of pantothenic acid and vitamin B_{12} brought substantial funds to the University as well as to other organizations.

In the mid-1940s, following the synthesis of pantothenic acid and the successful launching of the Clayton Foundation Biochemical Institute, Williams increasingly focused his attention on how science and education could improve human life and help solve common human problems. Significantly, in his first book for a broad audience he wrote, "The ultimate goal of our efforts is social welfare" (*The Human Frontier*, 1946). His chapter titles cite major themes that recur in many of his writings over the next 40 years. These themes include humanics—the science of humankind, the senses and social behavior, metabolism in relation to character traits, education, heredity and environment, employment, marriage, tolerance for others, criminology, psychology and medicine, religion, and international relations.

Williams pointed out that individual differences are deeply entwined in virtually all human problems. "Scientific" efforts to solve health or social problems, for example, are both hampered and fundamentally misleading if they focus on the mythical "average person." In their efforts to discover generalities, scientists tend to ignore and obscure individual differences, and Williams argued repeatedly over the years that we need to study and understand *individuals*, not "man."

Although Williams was not a gifted speaker (he sometimes mentioned this trait), he was extraordinarily able to present his ideas clearly and eloquently in his many books and articles. He devoted much time to thinking, writing and rewriting. He sought comments and criticisms of his work from colleagues and friends, many of them nationally and internationally prominent in diverse fields. For months, or sometimes years, he pondered and revised his important manuscripts. These efforts yielded a legacy of articles and books of remarkably enduring value. The passage of 20 to 40 years has hardly diminished their interest and pertinence. *Biochemical Individuality* remained in print for over 30 years, a most unusual feat in science. It and several other books were also translated into other languages, and two have been reissued in English.

Williams' accomplishments earned him many honors, including the Mead-Johnson Award (American Institute of Nutrition, 1941); the Chandler Medal (Columbia University, 1942, received jointly with his brother, Robert); election to the National Academy of Sciences (1946); presidency of the American Chemical Society (1957, the first biochemist elected to this post); D.Sc. degrees from the University of Redlands (1934), Columbia University (1942), and Oregon State University (1956); and the Nutrition Award of the Arthur M. Sackler Foundation (1983).

Widowed in 1952, Williams married Mabel Phyllis Hobson the following year. A vivacious woman now in her 80s, Phyllis was a beloved confidant and companion on numerous world travels that Williams enjoyed recalling during his last months. He belonged to a Methodist church, but his deeply religious philosophy was nonsectarian. One of his last articles was entitled, "Can We Integrate Moral Principles with Science and Learning?" (*The Texas Humanist*, 1984). In it he stressed the importance of non-material ideas and ideals in both science and life.

In 1986 the International Academy of Preventive Medicine proposed to establish and support a private foundation dedicated to furthering Williams' goals. Named the Roger J. Williams Nutrition Institute for Disease Prevention Research and Education, it was founded in July 1987, with me as Director. The Williams Institute will, to the extent that its resources permit, encourage research and education to advance nutrition and preventive medicine. It also will publish Williams' last book, *Exploring Your Individuality: A Vital Step Toward Human Understanding,* and strive to keep available Williams' other writings. Friends and admirers of Roger J. Williams are invited to join our efforts to advance the work and goals of this most remarkable man.

DONALD R. DAVIS
CLAYTON FOUNDATION BIOCHEMICAL INSTITUTE
UNIVERSITY OF TEXAS
AUSTIN, TEXAS 78712

Editor's note: The Roger J. Williams Nutrition Institute for Disease Prevention Research and Education is inactive, and *Exploring Your Individuality* remains unpublished.

Reprinted from JOURNAL OF APPLIED NUTRITION, VOLUME 40, NUMBER 2, 1988 *Copyright © International Academy of Nutrition and Preventive Medicine*

Index

Codes attached to page numbers refer to figures (f) and tables (t).